SCARED TO LEAVE
AFRAID TO STAY

Paths from Family Violence To Safety

by Barry Goldstein

Robert D. Reed Publishers • *San Francisco, California*

Robert D. Reed Publishers
750 La Playa Street, Suite 647
San Francisco, CA 94121
Phone: 650/994-6570 • Fax: 650/994-6579
E-mail: 4bobreed@msn.com
Web site: www.rdrpublishers.com

Edited, designed and typeset by Katherine Hyde, Hyde Publishing Services
Cover designed by Julia A. Gaskill at Graphics Plus

ISBN 1-931741-08-5

Library of Congress Control Number: 2001098149

Printed in Canada

Author's Note: The cover painting is by the woman I call Melanie Brewster. Melanie had been painting similar scenes with a forest for years until we suddenly realized that she was painting the path out of the violence. I have not used the real names of Melanie or most of the other people mentioned in the book for safety reasons. Anyone interested in Melanie's artwork should contact the author. The painting was photographed by Lauren Spaltro.

To Stephen, Serena, and Brianne
who taught me to be a believer

ACKNOWLEDGMENTS

THIS BOOK IS ABOUT ten remarkable women who demonstrated great courage, strength, and compassion as they struggled to overcome abuse, by loved ones and often by the very courts they came to for protection. These heroines are not famous, and indeed, safety considerations prevent me from using their real names. Many of these women took the time, and more tellingly accepted the emotional ordeal of reliving their most painful experiences in order to speak with me about their lives. They wanted the public to know about their stories so that women and children going through such experiences could be helped by them. Thus we can start to break the cycle of domestic violence. I am grateful for the friendship, appreciation, support, and inspiration these clients have given me.

There was nothing about my life that made me likely to work in this field, but it was inevitable that I would meet Clarice Pollock, who is well known around Westchester for her ceaseless activism for all the right causes on the side of the angels. She persuaded me to join the board of My Sisters' Place, where we served together for over ten years. So much of the wonderful work done by My Sisters' Place was made possible by Clarice, who has never received all the recognition she deserves.

So much of my understanding of domestic violence comes from my work with My Sisters' Place. The staff and board members are some of the finest people I know. Charlotte Watson was the executive director for over twelve years and is an incredible resource in our community; she is responsible for much of my education in this field. Thea Dubow, the assistant director, spent several hours answering my questions and contributing to the second part of the book.

The idea for the book came from many of my clients, who talked about writing their stories, but never did. One client, Barbara Finkelstein, a professional writer, helped me get started with her support, suggestions, and initial editing.

Joyce Sigurdsson-Stellman, a social worker and therapist who has treated many of my clients and testified as an expert witness, has made numerous critical contributions to this book. Her compassion and knowledge of domestic violence help her patients and provide judges with information they often would not get from the less-knowledgeable "experts" frequently appointed by the courts. When I had personal problems, Joyce helped ease my pain. Joyce has read the entire manuscript and significantly improved it with her professional and literary suggestions.

Phyllis Frank, director of the Community Change Project of the Volunteer Counseling Service, answered many questions concerning Part II of this book and was particularly helpful regarding domestic violence prevention classes for men. I have learned so much teaching these classes for the past three years. I particularly appreciate the support and caring provided by Jon Cohen, Kathy Walters, Jim McDowell, Brenda Ross, and the other instructors with the program. Jon Cohen provided many good ideas regarding Part II.

Monica Getz has been a pioneer in this field and made many helpful suggestions. Maryellen Martirano helped explain various criminal issues to me. The National Council of Juvenile and Family Court Judges, and particularly Billie Lee Dunford-Jackson, provided extensive materials to help me compare how different states treat these issues. They were very generous with their time and research and are an excellent source of information.

Several friends I met online have helped me complete this project. Talia Carner read several chapters and made many significant suggestions. I was privileged to read Talia's fiction manuscript regarding issues similar to those treated in this book. She has done a brilliant job, and I hope her book will soon be published. Joan Lloyd gave this novice writer support and suggestions early in the process, which I greatly appreciate. Kim Baker helped me prepare the proposal for this book. Lynn Banducci gave me feedback that helped me clarify one of the chapters. Helen Copley helped me overcome a computer glitch that was holding up the book.

My friend Aaron Pattak has been reading my work from the time I started. He has made many helpful suggestions, and occasionally I have even listened to them. My friend Scott Wasserman twice came to my rescue and helped with computer problems that were interfering with my access to various chapters.

The closest person I have to a brother is my cousin, Stuart

Abramson. He is one of the finest lawyers in Florida. Stu has read many of my chapters and made suggestions. We have also spoken at length about how the courts in Florida handle domestic violence issues. Stu and his wife Barbara have three wonderful children, Stacey, Shelby, and Ryan. I only hope this book will help to ensure that they never experience the kinds of problems discussed here.

When I was growing up, adults sometimes told me how lucky I was to have such a wonderful family. I didn't disagree, but it did not make much of an impression on me. In my mind a loving family was just part of a normal childhood. My work in domestic violence has impressed upon me how lucky I am to have been raised by two loving and supportive parents. One of the important lessons of this book is how very crucial a role the example of a child's parents plays with respect to domestic violence. My dad, Seymour Goldstein, died while I was writing this book, and I miss him. My mom, Judy Goldstein, will enjoy being the mother of an author. This book would not be possible without my parents' support and example.

To Sharon, my bride, your love, support, and frequent logistical assistance have helped make this book ready for publication. The book, like my life, is better because of you.

ABOUT THE AUTHOR

Barry Goldstein has been a practicing attorney in the State of New York since 1978. In 1983 he was asked to serve on the board of directors of My Sisters' Place, which is one of the leading domestic violence agencies in the country. He served on the board for fourteen years, including four years as chairperson. Mr. Goldstein was actively involved during a time when there was a major increase in interest and support for domestic violence issues. He led My Sisters' Place from a small agency with one shelter to an important domestic violence organization with two shelters, a school program, support groups, a legal clinic, and many other services.

As a result of his work with My Sisters' Place, an ever-larger part of his law practice has been devoted to representing victims of domestic violence. Many domestic violence agencies and people working with victims have referred clients to Mr. Goldstein because he is one of the few lawyers with expertise in this area and a willingness to take cases on a pro bono or reduced-fee basis.

The author has worked with the Community Change Project of the Volunteer Counseling Service in Rockland County, New York, since January, 1999, as an instructor teaching domestic violence prevention classes for men. Most of the participants are men who have been convicted of domestic violence crimes. The material presented by Barry Goldstein and his colleagues is the most up-to-date information about domestic violence; it is the same information presented to judges, doctors, therapists, community leaders, and other professionals. The Community Change Project is nationally and internationally recognized, and is often asked to present training programs for other domestic violence advocates. The author has made presentations to Community Change Project participants regarding the legal aspects of domestic violence.

Barry Goldstein graduated from New York Law School in 1977 and from George Washington University with a BA in Political Science in 1974. Mr. Goldstein served as Vice Chairman of the Mayor's Environmental Committee for Action in Yonkers, New York, from 1970–74. He became an expert in returnable bottle legislation and gave many speeches to legislatures and civic organizations. In 1972 he published a report about returnable bottles, "Your Can Is a Waste." Mr. Goldstein was a candidate for Yonkers City Council in 1981. He is also a successful bridge player, having won many tournaments and a listing in the *Encyclopedia of Bridge.*

Barry Goldstein was born in 1952. He is married to Sharon Spaltro and has no children.

CONTENTS

Introduction
FROM SUNDAY TO EVERY DAY   *1*

Part I
THE CASES

Chapter 1
COURAGE
The Brewster Case   9

Chapter 2
THE BELIEVERS
The Wong Case   23

Chapter 3
THE PRICE OF SAFETY
The Thomas Case   49

Chapter 4
ABUSER STRATEGIES
The Delgado Case   61

Chapter 5
RECOVERING FROM SEXUAL ABUSE
The Boyd Case   75

Chapter 6
THE CUSTODY CARD
The Horowitz Case   91

Chapter 7
GENDER BIAS
The Pollack Case 117

Chapter 8
MARITAL RAPE
The Kowalick Case 137

Chapter 9
THE BEST INTERESTS OF THE FATHER
The Morgan/Richardson Case 149

Chapter 10
JUSTICE DENIED
The Jensen Case 161

Part II
COURTING DISASTER
Enlisting the Courts in the Fight Against Abuse

Chapter 11
THE HARM OF DOMESTIC VIOLENCE 175

Chapter 12
THE ISSUES 179

Chapter 13
CHILD SUPPORT
And Other Financial Issues 197

Chapter 14
THE PLAYERS 207

SCARED TO LEAVE
AFRAID TO STAY

FROM SUNDAY TO EVERY DAY

THE FIRST DOMESTIC VIOLENCE LAW was enacted in the early part of the nineteenth century. It said that no husband could beat his wife—on Sunday. This was not viewed as a domestic violence issue at the time, but rather as an issue of Sabbath-breaking. Indeed, the interest and language for dealing with family violence did not develop until the mid-to-late 1970s. While the courts' response to the cases presented in this book is generally unsatisfactory, that response must be considered in some historical context.

The Criminalization of Domestic Violence

When the movement to stop domestic violence developed in the mid-to-late seventies, assaults by husbands against their wives were not treated as crimes unless they resulted in death, or something very close. The first marital rape conviction did not occur until the Rideout case in Oregon in 1978. Marital rape did not become a crime in every state until 1993.

Even after domestic violence was made a crime, many police departments failed to take it seriously. Standard procedure for "domestic dispute" calls was often to let the husband walk around the block to cool off. Women were advised to take the issues to Family Court, where the judge would try to bring the victim and abuser together. Gradually, domestic abuse cases have gone from the sole jurisdiction of Family Court, to a choice of Family or Criminal Court, to the possibility of both Family and Criminal Court being involved.

Initially, when a woman complained about domestic violence, she was treated as if she was the one with the problem and was sent for therapy, where she might learn how to behave so that her abuser would have no reason to attack her. Later, courts and some therapists would treat domestic violence as a couple's problem, in which each spouse had to make changes to stop the abuse. Although some judges and mental health professionals still misunderstand the problem, the law now treats domestic violence as a crime, and the abuser is supposed to be held responsible for his actions.

The policy on arrests has also changed over the years. Even after domestic violence was made a crime, police often had discretion to refuse to make an arrest. Battered women's advocates lobbied for pro-arrest policies. Such policies often were used in harmful ways, when police chose to arrest the battered woman for acts of self-defense, or to arrest both parties. Most states sought to avoid such problems by adopting a "primary aggressor" rule. This requires the police to investigate all the circumstances (not just the last incident) and arrest the primary aggressor. Although this is an improvement, too often the police have mistakenly chosen to arrest the female victim of the violence.

Support for Victims

Throughout this book, I refer to an organization called My Sisters' Place, which runs two shelters for battered women, along with other domestic violence programs, in Westchester County, New York. Originally, in the mid-seventies, they started with a women's center. In the course of running the center, the need for a safe haven from men's violence became clear. There were no shelters or other places where abused women could find safety. Initially, some families invited abused women to stay with them. In the late seventies, My Sisters' Place (then called the Yonkers Women's Task Force) opened a shelter in Yonkers. Today, not only are there many shelters throughout the country, but many other programs are included, such as support groups, legal services, court advocates, second-stage housing, supervised visitation and exchanges, school programs, and political action. Women now have places to go and allies to help them that were unavailable in the seventies.

The formal education of mental health professionals did not regularly include a domestic violence curriculum until at least the late eighties or early nineties. As a result, many of the psychologists and psychiatrists whom the courts frequently consult for custody and other evaluations do not understand domestic violence. This often causes absurd recommendations, such as the one in the Wong case (Chapter 2), where a father was given unsupervised visitation after admitting to kissing his daughters on the vagina. Similarly, many therapists handle domestic violence issues without sufficient training and experience with these problems. Even today, many courts and mental health offices try to treat assault as if it were a mental health problem rather than a conscious choice to control a partner by abuse. This common mistake places the lives of women and children in danger by creating a false belief that the abuser has been "fixed." Since the late seventies, however, there are many more mental health professionals available with the experience and training to help victims of domestic violence. Qualified therapists can easily be found by consulting local domestic violence agencies.

Other parts of the community are now more aware of and involved with domestic violence issues. Educational programs are far more available. Businesses have become involved, by helping their employees cope with abuse and by donating everything from clothing to cell phones to help victims. The news media frequently feature domestic violence stories. (However, they should avoid "equal time" stories about women abusing their partners or making up false allegations; such stories generally fail to place these unusual events in perspective.) The medical profession and the clergy are more willing to intervene to protect victims of abuse. The general public is less likely to consider abuse within a family as a private matter or to tolerate abusive comments or boasts.

Abusers Strike Back

We must be vigilant against the backlash of the abusers. Judges must be aware of the common tactics used to defend abusers and must actively discourage such tactics. Among the common tactics are: perpetuating the myth that women and children frequently make up false allegations of abuse; abusers seeking custody as a bargaining ploy; blaming the victim; stalling criminal cases while in Family or Divorce Court; using economic weapons to continue the abuse; and minimizing the abusive behavior.

Just as during the civil rights movement we heard some white segregationists complain that society had gone too far in protecting blacks, we now hear abusers complain that women have been given too much power. In reality, the laws and enforcement have evolved in a deliberate manner to protect victims of abuse. Each of the lesser measures that abusers would prefer had a fatal flaw. They did not work, and led to large numbers of deaths and serious injuries. If a significant number of men were being falsely accused or imprisoned on domestic violence charges, this would have been discovered and enforcement would have been made more difficult. Instead, we have learned that the stricter laws, enforcement, and support of victims of domestic violence have resulted in a significant decline in deaths and injuries.

Confirmation of the positive effects of stricter domestic violence laws and enforcement comes from statistics released by the U. S. Justice Department. From 1993 to 1998, attacks on women by their intimate partners fell from 1.1 million to 876,340. In 1976, women accounted for just over half of the 3000 people murdered by their intimate partners. In 1998, there were 1320 women and 510 men murdered by their partners. The disparity between the sexes in the reduction of number of murders reflects the fact that men and women kill their partners for different reasons. Men most often kill their partners when they try to leave or end the relationship, while women usually kill their partners out of self-defense and to make the abuse stop. The domestic violence movement has made it easier for women to protect themselves with orders of protection, easier divorces, police intervention, shelters, and other support. These services have given abused women choices for ending the relationships without resorting to violence.

Many men of color in the domestic violence prevention classes complain that domestic violence laws are enforced disproportionately against poor men and men of color. This is a valid complaint that is supported by the Justice Department statistics. From 1976 until 1998, the murder victim rate in intimate partnerships of black men declined 74 percent, that of black women declined 45 percent, that of white men declined 44 percent, but that of white women increased 3 percent. The men in the class say the disparity should be resolved by less enforcement in their communities, but in fact the numbers demonstrate the need to end *discriminatory* enforcement and to stop permitting wealthier white men to avoid the consequences of their abusive behavior. Judges and prosecutors must be vigilant to avoid "cutting slack" to more affluent white men.

Hope for the Hopeless

Most abused women find the decision to leave their partners difficult. They worry about their safety and what their life will be like afterwards. As this book demonstrates, the court proceedings necessary to leave an abuser are often difficult and unfair. Too many women are forced to give up and return to their abusers.

The good news, however, is that there is a better life out there for women who get to the other side. I have had clients who have returned to their partners, but none of my clients ever wanted their old life back after ending the relationship. Many of the women discussed in this book now live good, safe, happy, and fulfilling lives away from the violence.

Although society still has a long journey to go in order to end domestic violence, significant improvements have been made in protecting battered women. I believe this book, and the courageous women described herein, will help other women find the path out of the violence. For centuries we have mistakenly educated men to believe that they had the privilege to abuse and control their partners. All communities must work together in order to end domestic violence.

As I write this introduction, there is a fifteen-year-old girl in Portland, Oregon, suffering terrible abuse at the hands of two female neighbors. She has been threatened with guns and knives, severely beaten, and sexually abused. In one recent incident, the abusers whipped her and cut her with a knife to force her to engage in sexual activities with their six-year-old son. The district attorney's office can't prosecute because they say they don't have enough evidence. The police investigation has included questions such as whether the girl enjoys the abuse. The State Office for Services to Children and Families doesn't intervene when the children are over eleven; presumably they feel the girl should be able to protect herself. (I have not heard why that office supposes it does not need to protect the six-year-old.) The therapist won't help the girl find another therapist she feels she can trust. The *Portland Oregonian* newspaper can't cover the story for fear of legal problems. The parents don't know whether to believe their daughter.

I don't mean to single out Portland, which has many innovative domestic violence programs. The tragedy playing out in Oregon could occur in most communities. The Wong children (Chapter 2) taught us the importance of being believers. When someone complains of abuse, she should be taken seriously and be believed.

We know that social behaviors can be changed. In order for this to happen, society must take such harmful behavior seriously and create serious consequences. This has been done with the issues of drunk driving and cigarette smoking. In each case, laws have been changed and enforcement toughened. As a result of these movements, long-ingrained attitudes have been changed, and the change has resulted in a significant reduction in deaths and serious injuries. The work to eliminate domestic violence has also reduced the number of deaths and serious injuries from this cause, but so much more remains to be done.

The best part of my job is working with the incredible people who are seeking to end domestic violence. The number and quality of the services available to victims of abuse would have been unimaginable just a generation ago. These supportive men and women make an incredible difference in victims' lives. A child protective worker saved the Wong children from unspeakable tortures (Chapter 2). A police officer made sure Charlie Thomas was prosecuted for his constant harassment (Chapter 3). The director of a battered women's shelter helped Maria Delgado escape from her husband (Chapter 4). A prosecutor won a conviction and jail time for Stanley Kowalick after he attempted to rape his wife, Barbara (Chapter 8). A therapist taught Tammy Boyd that the childhood abuse she suffered was not her fault (Chapter 5). Even a lawyer helped a bit.

A Note on Accountable Language

In this society we are accustomed to language that fails to hold perpetrators of domestic violence accountable for their actions. "Every 14 seconds a woman is beaten" is different from "A man beats a woman every 14 seconds." The beating did not just happen. In the first example, the offenders have become invisible, whereas in the second example, the offenders—men—have been named and held accountable in the language. Similarly, we should not use the phrase "an abusive relationship." Speaking accountably requires us to name a person, not a thing (the relationship) as abusive.

At first glance it may appear that I am overly concerned with semantics here, but I believe that unaccountable language—even something as simple as saying "the abuse" rather than "his abuse"—contributes to the tendency to minimize the abuser's responsibility and to place at least a share of the blame on the victim. Yet this type of language is insidious. Even with eighteen years of experience representing victims of domestic violence, I inadvertently included many examples of unaccountable language in the drafts for this book. I hope that most of this language has been removed, but please recognize that some instances may have been overlooked. I hope the reader will be aware of the importance of using accountable language—when reading this book, and in everyday life.

Part I

THE CASES

Chapter 1

COURAGE

The Brewster Case

PEOPLE OFTEN ASK ME how I can continue to work on cases involving domestic violence. There is not much money in taking the side of abuse victims. The stories are unpleasant to hear, and too often the outcomes are less than satisfactory. In short, there is a lot of pain and suffering involved in a practice devoted to domestic violence cases. When I need inspiration or encouragement, I think about Melanie Brewster.

Mankind has always admired the display of courage. Usually, this refers to physical courage. Heroes who exhibit physical courage are rightly honored and respected. Moral courage, such as that described in John F. Kennedy's *Profiles in Courage,* can also be admired, at least when it is demonstrated by someone other than a politician. In contrast, the courage shown by victims of domestic violence is often overlooked or unappreciated.

Those who do not understand will frequently ask why a victim does not leave her abuser. It takes tremendous strength and courage to leave under such circumstances, because a woman is at the greatest risk of death or serious injury when she tries to leave her abuser. She must also overcome the lack of self-esteem and the inadequate resources with which the abuser deliberately left her. Melanie Brewster didn't just leave her husband and save herself; she also repeatedly accepted pain and the risk of further abuse in order to help other victims. If she had done this in war, there would not be enough medals and praise to express our gratitude. There still aren't.

An Abusive Attorney

I first met Melanie Brewster at my office. She was not feeling good about herself or her divorce case. She would have described herself as short, old, out-of-shape, and generally out of it, but in fact, Melanie was a beautiful, fit woman who looked ten years younger than her age of 47. She was soft-spoken, unsure of herself, but very intelligent.

She was dissatisfied with her attorney, Theodore Johnson, and wanted me to replace him. The case was scheduled for trial in a month. The time for discovery (a legal term denoting the process of collecting evidence) was over. Melanie told me she would lose everything if she didn't obtain a different attorney. Ted Johnson had lost her order of protection (a court order requiring an abuser to stay away from his victim) and her joint bank account, and was about to lose her interest in her husband's business and lawsuit. One of my former clients had strongly recommended me to Melanie. I explained the disadvantages of changing attorneys at such a late date.

Our first meeting lasted almost two hours. As I do with most new domestic violence clients, I spent time trying to make Melanie feel better about herself. It is important for battered women to know that they are not alone. They neither caused nor deserved the abuse. Men like Melanie's husband have learned that they can disrespect their intimate partners without penalties. Their abuse is not caused by the woman's behavior, but by the man's need to control. Nothing she could have done, other than leaving, might have prevented the abuse.

Melanie was nervous and self-deprecating during our first meeting. She was fearful of her husband—and of the courts. Over the years since that first meeting, Melanie has revealed much information that she did not discuss initially; she was not even conscious of much of this information at the time. We developed a mutual confidence during this meeting and agreed that I would represent her.

The first problem was for me to replace Ted Johnson. When he learned that Melanie wanted to replace him, Johnson sent her a bill for substantially more than the amount of any previous invoice. She did not have the money to pay him. Furthermore, she disputed the bill and believed Johnson was guilty of malpractice. I tried to work out an arrangement with him so that I could quickly take over the case, suggesting that he maintain a lien (the right to receive payment at a future date) on the proceeds of the lawsuit. Melanie was co-owner of an expensive home; therefore, we knew she would have resources when the case ended. Johnson demanded a mortgage on the property and an agreement about the money owed.

I prepared an order to show cause asking the court to substitute me for Ted Johnson as attorney for Melanie Brewster. (An order to show cause is an emergency motion that is made when there is insufficient time for a normal motion.) Johnson responded by agreeing to the substitution, but seeking as a condition that his fee be paid in full or that he receive a security interest on the property. After a conference with the judge, the court ordered me substituted for Ted Johnson, but permitted him to retain my client's file until he was paid or payment was secured. Melanie refused to give him a security interest in the property. As a result, I was forced to proceed without her file.

There are many complaints about the tactics and ethics of lawyers handling matrimonial cases. As a result of these complaints, new rules were imposed in New York State shortly after this case was tried. Attorneys in divorce actions can no longer withhold files in an attempt to force payment and cannot seek security interests under such circumstances.

The History of Abuse

Melanie was married to Eddie Brewster for twenty-seven years. Her husband was and is an alcoholic. He was verbally, physically, and emotionally abusive throughout the marriage. Eddie frequently punched, kicked, and slapped Melanie. On a few occasions he tried to strangle her, and often threatened to kill her. Eddie frequently beat her about the head, but many of her memories of this abuse were repressed. He deliberately destroyed her property, including family mementos and her artwork. Sometimes he would sneak up on her in the shower or elsewhere to scare her. Eddie liked the movie *The War of the Roses* and often spoke about reenacting some of its goriest scenes. On July 4, 1991, he tried to strangle Melanie and also attacked her mother and sister. After this incident, she abandoned her home and left her husband for good. Melanie and I sometimes joked that his name should be spelled "Bruised-her."

Leaving her husband did not end his abuse. He followed her to meetings, art classes, and her exercise club. Some of her friends refused to associate with her because they were afraid of what Eddie might do. He contacted several of her friends to ask questions and say bad things about her.

After the July 4 incident, Melanie obtained an order of protection from Family Court. Ted Johnson started the divorce action right before the parties returned for the permanent order of protection. (In New York at the time, "permanent" meant for one year, but it can now be given for three years.) The judge used this excuse to dismiss the action on the grounds that a divorce was pending in Supreme Court (this would create a conflict of jurisdiction between the two courts). Johnson, after much prodding, finally sought an order of protection from Supreme Court. Without consulting Melanie, Johnson agreed to mutual orders of protection, which were useless because Eddie could make up false charges against Melanie any time she needed to use her order. (With mutual orders of protection, when a victim of abuse seeks to get the police to arrest her abuser, the abuser inevitably denies his abuse and claims the victim abused him. The police then give the victim the choice of having them arrest both parties or neither.)

Although he had never before been interested in exercise, the day the mutual orders of protection were issued, Eddie joined Melanie's health club. She stopped going to the club because he would spend his time staring at her while she exercised. Ted Johnson sought to treat Eddie's actions as a violation of the order of protection. The judge stated that Eddie was "right on the edge," but refused to hold him in violation or modify the order to prevent such behavior.

The parties had three grown daughters. Melanie told me about earlier incidents in which Eddie had deliberately broken their toys when he was angry. She knew that he was verbally abusive, but was unaware of the extent of the physical abuse he had inflicted on their daughters. I learned about the abuse by speaking to one of them. The daughters were afraid of their father and wanted to avoid involvement in the divorce. Fortunately, there were no issues of custody or child support because the daughters were adults.

Financial Issues

Throughout most of the marriage, Eddie had been the owner of a roofing business. He had obviously done well, because during the marriage they had acquired a $500,000 home, among other property. Melanie had some records, but most of the information was in Ted Johnson's file. The records indicated a big reduction in income in the period right before and during the divorce. Eddie attributed this to an injury from a fall and a bad business climate, but Melanie believed it was an attempt to avoid paying money to her. The value of the business was relevant to the issue of maintenance and equitable distribution.

There was a temporary order of support requiring Eddie to pay $250 per week, but he was regularly several weeks behind on the payments. Ted Johnson hired an expert to evaluate the business. The expert was paid with money obtained from Eddie by a court order. When I sought to speak with the expert, he refused to speak with me and would not return my calls. Accordingly, as we got ready for court, I knew it would be difficult to prove the full value of the business.

The other major financial issue concerned a lawsuit in which the couple had settled for $32,500. The subject of the lawsuit was a fall in which Eddie had suffered a back injury. Normally, personal injury lawsuits are considered separate property and, therefore, not part of equitable distribution. Melanie, however, was a party to the lawsuit on the legal theory of loss of services (meaning that she lost the services Eddie could have provided if he had been healthy). The settlement did not differentiate the portion of the settlement belonging to each party because, at the time, they were husband and wife. The settlement was placed in a joint account, which would suggest that it be treated as marital property.

Negotiating a Settlement

The day the trial was scheduled started poorly when Melanie was served with a summons and complaint (the documents required to begin a lawsuit) on behalf of Ted Johnson. He was seeking $17,000. We went to the trial assignment part, where the judge for our case would be assigned. Before going to trial, we were asked to meet with Aaron Markowitz, the law assistant to the administrative judge. Markowitz had a knack for helping parties reach settlements even in the most difficult cases. He handled the divorce cases at the trial assignment part that no one else wanted. Markowitz met with Eddie's attorney, Mark Foster, and me.

The first issue was the grounds for divorce. Melanie wanted a divorce based on the cruel and inhuman treatment she had suffered. Eddie claimed that he wanted to stay married, but we suspected that this was just a negotiating ploy. The parties had not lived together for over a year. Markowitz said that it was clear that the marriage was dead and there was no point in fighting the divorce. He suggested that we consider doing the divorce based on abandonment or constructive abandonment (the denial of sexual relations). We came to an agreement to do the divorce on abandonment, based on the fact that Eddie's behavior had forced Melanie out of her home. I had no doubt that Melanie could have prevailed on cruel and inhuman treatment, but it would have been unpleasant for her to discuss the incidents of abuse in the courtroom with Eddie present. For this reason, she agreed to the divorce based on abandonment.

The financial issues were harder to arrange. Our position was weakened because Eddie and his attorney knew we were proceeding without the file or the report on Eddie's business. We spent most of the day negotiating a settlement. Markowitz came up with a proposal requiring both sides to compromise. Melanie would continue to receive $250 per week in maintenance for two years. This would give her the chance to get settled and begin earning an income before she would have to be self-supporting. The back support payments would have to be brought up to date. Eddie would keep his business, but Melanie would receive 55% of the proceeds from the house. If the parties netted $400,000 from the house, the extra 5% would be worth $20,000. Markowitz's reasoning was that we could not prove the value of the business, but Eddie was certainly receiving a business that had some value. Accordingly, Melanie should get more of the house to make up for the loss of the business. Markowitz proposed that Melanie receive 10% of the lawsuit settlement. She had to receive some part of the settlement because she was a party, but the bulk of the recovery was for Eddie's back injury. The remaining property was divided roughly equally.

The final financial issue concerned legal fees. Melanie had no money for legal fees. I had agreed to accept a retainer of only $500, but Ted Johnson was claiming legal fees of over $17,000. Eddie had kept control of virtually all of the parties' resources since the separation. This meant that his attorney, Mark Foster, could be paid with marital money, while I had to wait and hope for payment. It is this type of disparity which often puts abused women at a severe disadvantage. Most husbands hate paying money to their wife's divorce attorney. Markowitz made it clear that Eddie would have to pay some legal fees, and we agreed on a payment of $5,000.

We had some concerns about the sale of the parties' home. Other than the support payments, Melanie would not receive any money until the house could be sold. Eddie was living in the house and in no hurry to sell. I proposed that he leave immediately in order to encourage a quick sale. Unsurprisingly, he refused. We agreed, however, that Melanie would be in charge of selling the property. She would select the broker and could agree to a sale provided the price met specified levels. Eddie was required to cooperate in the selling of the house. We hoped these provisions would insure a quick sale.

Melanie wanted to be sure she could resume exercising at her health club. There was no reason that Eddie had to go to her club, but he refused to drop his membership. Finally, we worked out an agreement giving each party certain times when they could use the club. Therefore, Melanie could go to her club at her times without the danger of seeing her ex-husband. This provision would be part of the Judgment of Divorce, but would not be in the form of an order of protection.

I discussed the proposed settlement with Melanie. It was far from what she wanted or deserved, but we were at a disadvantage. This was a workable arrangement for Melanie, an outcome she could live with. As we discussed the terms, she became happier with the proposal. She was particularly relieved to have the whole ordeal over. Melanie had bravely practiced her testimony, but was not looking forward to the trial. Just being in the same room with Eddie was unnerving. Both parties agreed to the compromise, and the terms of the divorce were placed on the record. Melanie was a happy woman when we left the courthouse.

Continued Harassment

Enforcing the settlement proved to be more difficult than reaching it. Eddie was constantly behind in his maintenance payments. I tried working with Mark Foster to obtain the payments. Foster was a decent attorney, but had no control over his client. On at least three occasions, we were forced to start contempt proceedings against Eddie. Each time, he paid at the very last minute. The court refused to punish him for the repeated violations of the court order. On the last proceeding, the court awarded me $500 in legal fees. This was the only penalty Eddie ever paid for his late payments.

Eddie also violated the order concerning the exercise club. Melanie complained to me that she saw him at the club watching her and trying to hide. She also saw him hanging around her car. On one occasion, she came out of the club to find that someone had let the air out of her tire. We tried to get the police to enforce the court order. The police interviewed Eddie, but would not arrest him because there was no order of protection.

We brought a contempt proceeding in Supreme Court based on Eddie's violation of the order. Eddie responded by admitting that he had been at the club, but he claimed to have forgotten which days he was permitted to be there. Naturally, he denied anything having to do with Melanie's car. The court refused to hold him in contempt because there was no order of protection, but issued a permanent order of protection for Melanie. Eddie continued to ignore his obligation to stay away while Melanie was exercising. She called the police a few times, but each time, Eddie left before the police arrived. This is a common problem with orders of protection. The police generally will not arrest someone for violating an order of protection unless he is present at the scene of the violation when they arrive. Eddie succeeded in forcing his ex-wife to give up her exercise club.

The other major problem concerned the sale of the house. Eddie was living in the house and did not want to leave. He told his daughters that he had no intention of leaving. To that end, he refused to cooperate with the broker or provide a key for the house. When appointments were made for potential buyers to see the house, Eddie would leave his large dogs outside untied. This had the desired effect of scaring people away. He also kept the house unrepaired and messy. He did not take care of the grounds; the grass was overgrown and there was all sorts of junk in the yard.

We attempted to resolve the problem by having a conference with the parties and the lawyers. Eddie promised to cooperate, but failed to do so. Again we had to bring a motion to Supreme Court. The court again ordered him to cooperate and gave Melanie permission to go to the house to make it more presentable. After the new court order, Eddie was more cooperative, but still left the place a mess.

Melanie would be without resources until the house could be sold. Eddie's antics served to increase the time she would be indigent. The delay and the poor upkeep of the house forced Melanie to reduce the price. At one point, she had an offer of $441,000 which she wanted to accept, but by the time she could force Eddie to cooperate, the buyers were no longer interested. Finally, almost a year after the divorce, Melanie agreed to accept an offer of $375,000. Just as we were about to enter into contract, there was renewed interest in the property and two more buyers came forward. They bid against each other, and Melanie eventually agreed to sell the property for $425,000.

We were nervous about the closing until it was finished. Eddie kept telling his daughters that he would not leave. He eventually did, but left much of his stuff behind. The buyer had to tell Eddie that any removal costs would come from his share. The actual closing was peaceful. In addition to her 55% share, Melanie received her share of various items which Eddie had kept or failed to account for. She also received the back support and the remainder of all future support. Melanie was pleased that she finally had some resources to work with and would not have to deal with her ex-husband ever again.

Rebuilding a Life

Throughout the time I represented Melanie, we frequently had extensive conversations about Eddie's past abuse of her and her concerns for the future. I spoke with her as an attorney and a friend. Gradually she told me more about his abuse as she learned more herself. It is common for victims of abuse (and other traumas) to be unable to remember all or some of the abuse. While they are trying to survive the abuse, the defense mechanism can be helpful, but afterwards it can cause great harm to their emotional well-being. I helped Melanie understand how these things could happen and that she was not alone. She went to support groups and worked with various organizations fighting domestic violence.

As time went on, Melanie felt better about herself and more confident. She spent much time helping other abused women. It was wonderful to watch this. Sometimes, Melanie worked with some of my newer clients. This interaction was helpful for my new clients and beneficial for Melanie. In helping others, she was empowering herself.

One day, she called to tell me a television reporter wanted to interview her about her experiences. I encouraged Melanie to go on television. We agreed that she did not have to have her face hidden. Melanie appeared on the show and spoke eloquently about her experiences with domestic violence.

On another occasion, she was invited to speak at a party for My Sisters' Place, an organization that runs a shelter for battered women along with other domestic violence programs. I had the pleasure of introducing Melanie's speech and referring to her as "a genuine hero." Her speech was impressive and many people came up to her afterward to thank her. We spoke about the fact that a year or even six months earlier, she never could have considered doing this.

Johnson's Lawsuit

While the post-divorce proceedings were taking place, we had to defend the lawsuit brought by Theodore Johnson. Melanie had many complaints about her former attorney. Before the divorce, she had placed a hold on the joint bank account she had with Eddie. Johnson failed to follow up in a timely manner, thus allowing Eddie to take the money. He lost her order of protection, as we discussed earlier, and failed to get a meaningful new one. She felt that every time she went to court with Johnson, they lost. He failed to prepare her for her deposition or to obtain the records for her husband's business. Johnson repeatedly failed to return phone calls until the very end, when he heard she wanted to change attorneys. Melanie did not receive regular billings; the final bill came as a surprise to her. She was especially offended when Johnson yelled at her, made personal comments (such as an unsolicited suggestion that she start dating), and told her to stop listening to the women at the groups she was working with. These complaints were used in a counterclaim to the lawsuit and in a complaint to the Bar Association.

Johnson chose to represent himself in the lawsuit, despite the ancient bromide about an attorney who represents himself having a fool for a client. He was perfectly pleasant to me, but could not see his mistakes objectively. He fully expected it to be an open-and-shut case in his favor. During his deposition, Johnson was open and often volunteered information against himself. We learned that the expert hired to appraise Eddie's business was a friend of Johnson's. When I had called this expert, he had consulted Johnson before deciding whether to return my call. Johnson did not tell his friend directly what to do, but made it clear that he was hurt by Melanie's change of attorneys and would prefer his friend not to cooperate.

Before the start of the trial, the Grievance Committee of the Bar Association issued its decision. They concluded that Ted Johnson's behavior towards Melanie was inappropriate and issued a caution to him. This is the least severe punishment they could impose, but nevertheless we were pleased with the decision because this type of behavior frequently goes completely unpunished. The finding of the Bar Association would help us in the lawsuit.

The case also went to the trial assignment part and was conferenced by Aaron Markowitz. (*Conferencing* refers to a meeting outside the courtroom between the attorneys and the judge or the judge's assistant.) Johnson was confident of his case and would not agree to anything but a token reduction in his claim. Under the circumstances, the case could not be settled and a judge was assigned.

The plaintiff's entire case consisted of his own testimony. Johnson presented the hours he worked and the bills he sent to Melanie. He expected this to be sufficient to win his case. On cross-examination, he made some damaging admissions. He had done nothing to prevent Eddie from taking the joint account. He had failed to wait for the permanent order of protection before filing the divorce papers, but blamed the judge for the dismissal. He also admitted to his unsolicited remarks about Melanie's private life, but thought nothing of it. Johnson even admitted to discouraging the financial expert from speaking with me. He also brought up the caution and suggested it was of no consequence.

Toward the end of my cross-examination, I asked about the derogatory comments Johnson had made about the women's organizations Melanie was working with. He said that he had told Melanie to stay away from such organizations and not to listen to their propaganda. At this point, the judge interrupted the trial and met with the two attorneys. The judge was scheduled to make a campaign appearance before one of the groups Johnson had disparaged and was friends with their leader. Accordingly, the judge planned to recuse himself (to withdraw from the case). He suggested that we spend some time talking about a settlement before we left.

The judge told Johnson that his case had some crucial difficulties. Johnson had made serious mistakes and could not expect full payment of his claims. The judge met with each side separately and proposed that we settle for $5,000. Melanie did not think Johnson deserved any money, but she had expected him to be awarded much more. Accordingly, she quickly agreed to the settlement. Ted Johnson was unhappy with the turn of events and wanted time to consider the proposal. A week later, we settled for the $5,000.

Aftermath of Abuse

I would like to report that Melanie lived happily ever after, but often life is not like that. Periodically, Melanie and her family have seen Eddie hanging around her neighborhood and her car. One day, she narrowly avoided a serious accident caused by sabotage to her wheel. Initially, the police took the incident very seriously and treated it as attempted murder, suspecting that Eddie had sabotaged the car. After the initial investigation, however, the police became less interested in pursuing the case. They were unable to prove that Eddie was the one who had done the damage. We wanted them at least to interview Eddie and let him know that they were watching him, but the police refused.

Thereafter, Melanie took her first vacation in years. She left her car with a friend in a neighborhood miles from her home. When she returned home, the car was missing. A few days later, the burnt remains of her car were found by the police several miles from where it had been stolen. Melanie discovered that a set of keys for the car had also been stolen from her home. We suspected that Eddie was involved, but could not prove it. Melanie's insurance company, Liberty Mutual, believed that Melanie might be responsible for the loss. They required her to go for a deposition and refused to pay for the car.

Eddie was still not through with his harassment. He followed her in his car while she was driving on a parkway. When Melanie saw Eddie following her, it triggered an unfortunate reaction. After she left the highway, she suffered a blackout. Her car veered onto the wrong side of the road and hit a car that was waiting at a red light, headed in the opposite direction. Melanie was not seriously injured, but the incident marked the onset of a series of blackouts.

Melanie suffered such blackouts for several months and was consequently required to give up her driver's license. After various tests, she was hospitalized to determine the cause of the blackouts. The doctors learned that the seizure disorder was the result of post-traumatic stress syndrome caused by years of abuse, including repeated beatings to her head. This is the same abuse Eddie continues to deny.

Throughout the time I have known her, Melanie has been treated by an outstanding therapist, Joyce Sigurdsson-Stellman. Joyce is experienced in treating victims of domestic violence and has made much progress with Melanie. In therapy, Melanie has discovered that Eddie's abuse was more severe than she originally realized, but she has learned how to live with its effects. Therapy and medication have stopped the blackouts, and Melanie hopes to be able to resume driving and working in the near future.

Liberty Mutual denied no-fault medical coverage for the accident on the grounds that the blackouts constituted a pre-existing illness. In fact, it was the incident that occurred while Melanie was driving that caused the accident and sparked the blackouts. We brought a lawsuit against Liberty Mutual for their failure to honor their contractual obligations. As soon as we brought the litigation, they agreed to pay for the car that had been stolen and destroyed. They have also agreed to reconsider the payment of the medical expenses.

Children, such as Melanie's three daughters, who grow up in a family in which one of the parents is an alcoholic are subject to a wide assortment of problems associated with the effects of alcoholism. The actress Suzanne Somers and others have done much to publicize the problems of Adult Children of Alcoholics (ACOA) and help promote recovery. Such problems go beyond the tendency to excessive drinking and include trust issues, having to guess at what is normal, maintaining harmful secrets, low self-esteem, excessive risk-taking, and other relationship problems. ACOAs often have trouble recognizing their problem because the effects vary with the individual; also, the damage can be caused even when the alcoholic does not drink in front of the children and does not engage in the most extreme forms of abuse.

Melanie is concerned about the effects of Eddie's alcoholism on her daughters. Two of her daughters are married and have children; her youngest daughter is finishing her education. Sometimes ACOAs assume that if they are doing well in some aspects of their life, there is no problem. Melanie's children have been successful, but she has seen signs that their father's alcoholism has taken its toll. Directed therapy with a professional familiar with the problem can often result in significant improvement in a short period of time. None of the daughters has yet sought this help.

Melanie continues to make progress in her recovery from the years of abuse. She continues to help many other women in similar circumstances. Recently, she has experienced the pleasures of being a grandmother. She hopes that the cycle of violence will be broken in this generation.

On the wall in my office, and reproduced on the cover of this book, is one of Melanie's paintings. It shows a path in a forest—a path away from the pain and the violence. Melanie has been a trailblazer in inspiring all of us to follow that wonderful path.

Chapter 2

THE BELIEVERS

The Wong Case

ON DECEMBER 1, 1988, Dr. James Wong, an optometrist, confessed to a law guardian that he had kissed his six- and four-year-old daughters on the vagina. A month later at an open hearing, Judge Albert Pauling of the Yonkers Family Court in Westchester County, New York, awarded Dr. Wong unsupervised visitation. Before the first overnight visitation was over, Dr. Wong had penetrated four-year-old Jennifer for the first time.

Fran Wong, the girls' mother, had filed for custody and an order of protection against her husband because of his egregious behavior. In a petition filed more than a year earlier, she had complained that James had showered with their three children (two of whom were girls), slept in the same bed with them, kissed the girls on the vagina, and administered paddlings, whippings, and spankings four to five times a week to punish them. Based on these allegations, Judge Pauling had barred unsupervised visitation for almost a year. But when Dr. Wong admitted to molesting his daughters, Judge Pauling awarded him unsupervised visitation.

A Simple Divorce

When I first met Fran Wong in August of 1986, I had no reason to expect anything so dramatic. She came to my office seeking a divorce. An attractive Asian woman in her mid-twenties, Fran had black hair that fell on her shoulders. Dressed in slacks and a blouse, she looked neat, but not provocative. Her soft voice matched her shy, hesitant demeanor.

At the time of the interview, her three children—Sammy, age seven, Sheila, age four, and Jennifer, who was almost two—were living with Fran, who had separated from her husband and was living with her parents. My client told me she wanted a divorce because she did not love her husband anymore. I took down the information that was needed and wrote to her husband proposing a divorce settlement.

James Wong refused to hire an attorney. He insisted on negotiating a settlement directly with Fran, demanding that he have sole custody of the children, and she would have visitation two days per week. Fran could have no one else present when she picked up and returned the children.

I advised Fran not to accept this proposal. No determination of custody had been made, and she had at least as good a chance for custody as James. Normal visitation arrangements would include every other weekend plus one day during the week. A noncustodial parent would also receive alternating holidays, school vacation periods, and at least a few weeks in the summer. The provision preventing anyone else from coming with her to pick up and return the children was also unusual. This would be a dangerous arrangement in a case where abuse had occurred, but she denied that he had abused her.

Fran was being asked to give up her right to custody and accept less visitation than a court would likely award, without receiving any benefit for her concessions. She told me she had a private understanding with James that the time with the children would be shared equally, but he would not put this in writing. Anxious to get away from James's abuse, she ultimately accepted a bad deal. I started the divorce action in September of 1986 and, in November, they were divorced.

Discipline or Abuse?

After a few months, Fran called me several times concerning the children. She believed James had been using frequent and excessive physical discipline, hitting each child four or five times a week with hand, paddle, and belt. They were afraid of their father and wanted Fran to protect them.

The distinction between physical discipline and abuse is often difficult to understand, with even some professionals ignorant of the exact boundaries. Often, parents use the same forms of discipline they experienced as children. The courts speak of permitting "reasonable discipline based upon the age, size, and sex of the child." What does that mean when a five-year-old is hit ten times with a paddle?

Generally speaking, the issue is whether the punishment in question could have caused an injury. Therefore, a slap to the face is virtually always abusive because if you miss slightly, the child's eye could be injured. Furthermore, there is the risk of brain damage. Punching or kicking would usually be considered abusive because of the danger of injury. Hitting a child on the bottom would generally not be considered abusive, except in extreme cases, because an injury is unlikely. A second consideration is that a child can be hit only for proper disciplinary purposes.

The law talks about mental or emotional abuse, but in practice, courts rarely take action in such cases. I always remind my clients that there may be a difference between what is legal and what is best for the child. Society is reluctant to interfere with a parent's right to discipline his child. Therefore, many punishments which are harmful to the child are not considered abusive.

The punishments described by the Wong children were not likely to injure them. While we thought the discipline was excessive, the courts were unlikely to interfere with the father's judgment as long as there was little chance of injury. There was some question about whether the hitting was for a proper disciplinary purpose. Later, James would punish the children for mentioning Fran's fiancé. Such punishment is certainly abusive. However, the initial reports, while disturbing, did not legally constitute abuse. Accordingly there were no grounds for changing custody.

Back to Square One

Exactly one year after the divorce and nine days prior to Fran's scheduled remarriage, James filed an order to show cause seeking to revoke the divorce and to stop the marriage. James claimed that the divorce was invalid because he did not have an attorney and that I had used undue influence to force him to sign the stipulation. At the time of the divorce motion, James had attempted to notify the court of his objection to the divorce. The court could not have considered his objection because he had failed to send me a copy. The court, nevertheless, forbade Fran to remarry until the order to show cause could be considered.

The plans for Fran's wedding to Tom Crenshaw had long been completed. They could not cancel or postpone the catering hall reservation without losing the full cost of the affair. We brought our own order to show cause, seeking to revoke the prohibition of the marriage ceremony. We informed the court of the irreparable harm the existing order would cause and that Fran's ex-husband's arguments were unlikely to be successful. The court denied our application, stating that there would have to be a hearing on the disputed facts before it would lift the order. The court did, however, order James to post a bond. The purpose of the bond was that if it turned out that he had no right to the injunction, the money could be used to compensate Fran for the damages caused by the order.

Fran and Tom decided to go ahead with the affair as a celebration of their commitment to each other and their intention to marry when they legally could do so. James sent a spy to the celebration, who pretended to be looking for a caterer for his own wedding. This spy misunderstood the ceremony exchanging promises to marry in the future as the exchange of wedding vows. The next day, James sought to hold Fran in contempt of court based upon this misunderstanding.

I met with Fran to decide what to do next. Of course she wanted the divorce, but this time custody of the children was more important. Since the separation, Fran was no longer subject to her husband's discipline, but the children had become subject to ever more excessive punishments. With the wedding postponed, I advised Fran to consent to revoking the judgment of divorce and the stipulation of settlement. Her ex-husband's contention was that the divorce was invalid because there was undue influence concerning the stipulation. Accordingly, the divorce could not be invalidated without also nullifying the stipulation, which contained the terms concerning custody and visitation. By revoking the divorce and stipulation, Fran would regain equal rights to custody.

The weekend before the court date, Fran had the children for visitation. The children told their mother of an incident that had happened shortly before. James had called Jennifer to him and thought she had taken too long to respond. He yanked her by her arm and gave her a severe spanking and paddling. As a result, the children were afraid to go back to their father and begged their mother to protect them. When James came to pick the children up, they refused to go with him and Fran called the police. After speaking with the children, the police refused to return them to James and ordered him to leave. Instead, James spent most of the night ringing the buzzer and banging on the door. Eventually, Tom had to disconnect the buzzer.

As a result of this incident, Fran sought an order of protection in Family Court for herself and the children. She received a temporary order of protection which prohibited James from threatening or harassing Fran and the children and ordered him to stay away from the children.

Fran decided to follow my advice and consent to cancel the divorce and stipulation. At the next Supreme Court hearing, the attorneys met with the judge. I suggested that since it was too late to go ahead with the wedding as scheduled, we were willing to consent to cancel the judgment of divorce and the stipulation of settlement. The other side was most happy to agree to this arrangement. I do not believe they understood the implications concerning custody; I certainly did not tell them. Judges are always happy to have a settlement, and the divorce and stipulation were quickly revoked.

Investigating the Abuse

The action now moved to the Family Court, where the family offense petition was pending (seeking a permanent order of protection), and both sides quickly filed petitions seeking custody. The preliminary hearing took place on December 21, 1987. A preliminary hearing is the Family Court equivalent of an arraignment. This is when the respondent has his first opportunity to admit or deny the allegations. Motions can be made and a schedule for proceeding is arranged.

The judge appointed to handle the case was Albert Pauling, recently elected to the Family Court, a sixty-year-old man of medium build with white hair and menacing-looking features. Pauling had been a town judge in Eastchester and had long been active in the Republican Party. When he was ready to move up, there was a vacancy in the Family Court. The judge had no experience in family law, but at that time the Republican nomination was tantamount to election in Westchester. The issues of spousal abuse and child abuse were only starting to gain public notice, but Judge Pauling seemed not to see a need to learn about these subjects.

James Wong was a tall, handsome Asian man of thirty-five. Wearing expensive, nicely tailored suits, articulate and acting the part of the professional he was, he made a good appearance. At the preliminary hearing, James vehemently denied the allegations of abuse. Although a general denial was sufficient, James insisted on telling the court that Fran had made everything up and that the children wanted to return to him.

His attorney, John Barker from Rockland County, specialized in fathers' rights. He requested that custody be immediately returned to James. When this was denied, Barker requested extensive visitation. I requested that any visitation be supervised because of allegations of abuse. Judge Pauling decided that the Child Protective Service worker would decide the frequency and manner of visitation. With the agreement of both sides, the judge ordered probation reports, home studies, psychological evaluations, and the appointment of a law guardian.

A probation report is made by a probation officer after interviewing the parties and other people who know the children; it often contains recommendations regarding custody and visitation. The home study is a visit to each parent's home by the Probation Department to check whether the physical surroundings are appropriate for the children. Psychological evaluations are conducted by a court-appointed psychiatrist, usually with the help of psychological testing. The law guardian is an attorney appointed to represent the children. While each parent usually believes she/he is representing the best interests of the children, the children's interests and preferences are usually different from those of one or both parents. Since each parent wants to win the law guardian over to his or her side, a good law guardian can often use this to moderate each parent's behavior, and help them reach a settlement.

The Child Protective Service (CPS) is a state agency that investigates reports of child abuse or neglect. CPS started an investigation after Fran reported Jennifer's beating, the day after she refused to return the children to James. The CPS worker had spoken with the children and was investigating allegations that James regularly showered with the children, slept in the same bed with them, kissed the girls on their vaginas, and used excessive physical discipline. After the court session, the parties and their attorneys met with the CPS worker about visitation. The attorneys made their arguments, and the worker decided that James's visitation would be limited to once a week and would be supervised by CPS.

The History of Abuse

Fran and I started having lengthy meetings and phone calls in preparation for the trial. For the first time, she told me about her life with James and the abuse he had inflicted on her and the children. Pained and embarrassed as she was by much of what had happened, it was obviously very difficult for her to talk about her history. I tried to probe gently, and as time went by, she revealed more details. I suggested several times that we could delay painful discussions, but Fran always continued because she wanted to protect her children. Most of all, she blamed herself for what had happened to them. During her marriage, Fran had never understood that she had the right to stop James's excesses.

Many people do not understand why a woman would remain with an abuser. Often, the husband has convinced his wife that somehow she is responsible for his behavior ("I wouldn't have had to hit you if you hadn't burned the carrots"). The woman is often isolated from family and friends, denied any access to financial resources, and threatened that she won't see the children if she leaves. All of these factors were working against Fran.

During our discussions, I took the time to counsel Fran and let her know she was not to blame, and that James was responsible for his own behavior. I assured her that it had taken a lot of courage to get away from James and then to stand up to him when she refused to return the children. She had reason to feel good about herself. Many other women remain under circumstances that are harmful to themselves and their children. Gradually, Fran's self-esteem improved, which was helpful for our case as well as for Fran.

James had been married to Fran's sister, Sabrina. When Fran was fifteen years old, James and Sabrina lived with Fran's family. James started taking liberties with Fran. He would embrace her, kiss her on the lips, and fondle her. Eventually, James and Sabrina divorced. Fran thought she was the cause of the divorce, but, in fact, James had been physically abusive to Sabrina. James and Fran ran away together when she was sixteen, and they were married after she became pregnant with Sammy.

Naturally, Fran's family disapproved. Even when we discussed this, Fran believed she had been responsible for the breakup of her sister's marriage. Feeling guilty, she thought that any misfortune that happened to her, and especially the abuse by James, was her just punishment for hurting Sabrina. This helps explain her putting up with such terrible treatment. Only later, through therapy and discussion with her sister, did Fran come to understand that her sister's marriage had to end because of James's abuse, not because of Fran. Her family was against her actions not because of the harm to Sabrina, but because of the potential harm to Fran herself. In fact, Fran's family would be very supportive of her throughout the fight for custody and thereafter.

Throughout the marriage, James had been physically and emotionally abusive. Fran described incidents during which James had grabbed and twisted her arm, thrown her around the room, slapped her face and pinched her. On one occasion, without warning, James grabbed Fran by the arm and pulled her over his knee. He pulled up her skirt and gave her a severe spanking on her mostly bare bottom. The assault was so brutal that she had to put cream on her bottom and the pain and redness lasted a full day. Fran was not sure if any of the children had witnessed this abuse, which took place in the living room. Two other times James hit Fran with his paddle and once with his belt.

The children were constantly subject to physical discipline, each child being hit five times per week or more. James started hitting the children with his paddle when they were one year old and with his belt when they reached two years of age. For more serious offenses, the punishments were administered on the bare bottom. If the children cried during the punishment, they received extra licks. James often punished the children in public. At other times, he would grab them, pull them and throw them around the room. Fran objected to the methods of discipline that James used, and particularly disapproved of the public discipline; but when she tried to discuss this with him, he would ignore her or tell her that it was his decision.

During the previous few years, James had become a "born-again Christian." He spent much time studying the Bible and using it to justify his actions. He found biblical passages to justify his severe discipline of the children and his right to punish his wife. He believed that a wife had to be obedient and subservient to her husband, and when she failed to do so, he had the right to chastise her.

Preparing for Trial

The court appointed Sandra Burke to serve as law guardian for the children. Ms. Burke was a soft-spoken woman of thirty. She had a young family to raise and practiced law part-time, mostly as a law guardian. Inexperienced with abuse issues and unduly impressed by the positions taken by the judge, court-appointed psychiatrist, and John Barker, Ms. Burke seemed to favor the father's viewpoint. This did not mean that she wanted him to have custody, but she favored unrestricted visitation. Despite this viewpoint, however, Ms. Burke was always willing to listen to our views and consider them.

Although the trial would not start until almost a year after the preliminary hearing, there were several court appearances in the interim. Three times James brought orders to show cause or other motions seeking a change of custody, or at least more and unsupervised visitation. Each of these motions was denied by Judge Pauling. Dr. Wong also made a motion to have a physical and psychological examination of the children by his doctors. The court refused to order the psychological examinations, but did order the children to undergo physical examinations.

The physical examinations turned out to be traumatic for the children, and they still speak of this experience with horror. The purpose of the examination was to determine whether there was physical evidence of abuse. This required a vaginal exam of the girls. We assumed that James had hired a doctor who was an expert on sexual abuse and who would know what he was doing. Instead, he hired an ordinary pediatrician who did not know the proper way to investigate allegations of sexual abuse. As a result of the doctor's inexperience, the examination took longer and was more painful than it otherwise would have been. The children were traumatized by the experience, which made it harder for them to talk about the abuse they had suffered.

While the custody and family offense matters were pending, we appeared before a hearing examiner to settle the question of child support. The hearing examiner is an attorney appointed by the court system to hear cases involving support and paternity. The trials are conducted by the hearing examiner, but decisions can be reviewed by the Family Court judge.

When the children began living with Fran full-time, James refused to pay any child support. At the time of the first hearing, James was still a student and Fran was awarded only minimal child support. The court also awarded retroactive support to cover the time during which James had refused to pay support. After James finished school and began working full-time as an optometrist, we brought an upward modification petition. The hearing examiner increased the child support to $267 per week for the three children, based on James's income, which was then $60,000 per year.

A month before the trial, the judge conducted a conference with the attorneys and Dr. Felix Schmidt, the court-appointed psychiatrist. The sixty-year-old Dr. Schmidt frequently testified as an expert in the Westchester courts, and the judges listened to him very carefully. He had become a psychiatrist at a time before child abuse and spousal abuse were part of the curriculum, and tried to deal with family violence issues by using general psychiatric principles. This resulted in incorrect evaluations, but after many years he was "experienced" (his mistakes becoming ingrained as experience) in abuse cases. In fairness, Dr. Schmidt had an excellent reputation among judges and court personnel, and frequently was useful in cases unrelated to domestic violence. Some of his colleagues were aware of his shortcomings, but, as is typical among physicians, rarely discussed this on the record. Women who had been abused or whose children were abused hated him with a passion. One client has called Dr. Schmidt "the Dr. Mengele of custody."

Much of the early work on the evaluation was done by Dr. Abdul Gupta, but Dr. Schmidt gave the oral report on the psychological evaluation of the parties and the children. Dr. Schmidt believed that Fran had brainwashed the children and that the accusations against James were exaggerated or false. He thought Fran was using the children to hurt James. Dr. Schmidt acknowledged that Fran had a strong relationship with the children and had done a good job with them aside from the "brainwashing." He also stated that James had a good relationship with the children and was a good father. The psychiatrist said the custody decision was very close and suggested that Fran would have to stop encouraging the children to complain about abuse if she wanted to win custody.

By the end of the conference, Sandra Burke, John Barker, and Judge Pauling all expressed the view that the children's statements should not be believed. I expressed my disagreement with this view, but could not convince anyone of my position. Judge Pauling explored the possibility of settling the case on the basis of physical custody for the mother and liberal, unsupervised visitation for the father. Although neither party was willing to accept such an arrangement, the judge implied that Fran was being unreasonable and uncooperative.

We received another blow to our case when the Child Protective Service ruled Fran's complaint was unfounded. "Unfounded" in CPS lingo means there is not sufficient evidence to substantiate the allegation. It does not establish that the abuse did not occur. In fact, often cases which are at first "unfounded" become "indicated" (meaning evidence shows abuse did occur) after additional evidence becomes available. Five-year-old Sheila told the CPS worker that she had been kissed on her vagina, and this appeared in an earlier report. The implication of the CPS findings was that Sheila was not credible.

The Trial

Several months after the first Family Court petition, the day for the trial on custody and the order of protection finally came. Two days had been set aside for the trial, but it soon became apparent that we had no hope of finishing in only two days. The court's practice was to give us one or two days at a time, and we generally had to wait a month or two between trial dates.

By the time the trial started, Fran was pregnant, and it showed. Fran was living with Tom while they waited for the right to be married. James tried to use her pregnancy to imply that she was immoral. Her marital situation was unusual because her divorce had been rescinded. Her pregnancy really had very little to do with the issues in the case, but I believe it hurt us with Judge Pauling.

We had the burden to present our case first because Fran was the first to file for custody. The family offense petition seeking a permanent order of protection was tried at the same time as custody, because most of the evidence for the two petitions would overlap. Fran was our first witness and was very nervous.

Fran started by testifying about the routine part of family life with James and the children. James was in charge of the discipline and occasionally would bathe the children. Sometimes he would play with them, but beyond this he was not as much involved in raising them as Fran. The daily routine of childcare, the details of running a household and managing small crises are often overlooked in a trial that includes allegations of abuse and other egregious behavior, but custody determinations are often based on such issues. Courts usually do not want to believe that parents are unfit and often will minimize allegations of abuse or assume spouses are exaggerating their charges because they are angry with each other.

Fran testified about the disciplinary methods James had employed during the marriage. After the children resumed living with her, they had many nightmares in which a monster or their father was chasing them. When the doorbell rang, the children would run and hide in case it was their father. They were afraid that if their father took them, they would never see Fran again; they were also afraid their father would resume beating them. The children told Fran about sleeping in the same bed with their father and showering with him, where his genitals were at eye level. The children loved James, but wanted to be protected from him. Fran also testified about how James had abused her. Some of this spousal abuse was committed in front of the children.

A major and continuing disagreement took place during the trial over what subject matter would be considered. Again and again, John Barker sought to object to the inclusion of evidence of alleged abuse by Dr. Wong. He was fond of saying that this wasn't an abuse trial. By this he meant that there was no petition charging the father with child abuse. The fallacy of this argument was that the mother's custody petition included allegations of physical and sexual abuse. Certainly if it was proven that the father had committed acts of abuse against the children, it could not be in the children's best interests to give the father custody. Accordingly, evidence about the father's abuse was very relevant, but Judge Pauling frequently echoed John Barker's view that it was not an abuse trial and that he did not find such evidence helpful or important.

The typical defense strategy in abuse cases, as in rape cases, is to blame the victim. Since the children in this case could not be blamed, all pressure and accusations were focused on Fran. The cross-examination was brutal. The first sexual contact between the parties had occurred when Fran was fifteen or sixteen and James was in his mid-twenties and married to her sister. John Barker sought to ask several questions about Fran's wearing shorts and other supposedly sexy outfits around the apartment.

I strongly objected to these questions. At one point I told the court, "If she had run around the apartment stark naked and begged James for sex, it would not have justified an adult having sex with a minor." What he had done was a criminal act. Given the allegations of sexual abuse, this previous history was relevant. Fran's alleged come-ons as a teenager (all untrue) did not justify James's behavior and had no relevance to her behavior as an adult and mother. Despite this, Judge Pauling repeatedly overruled my objections and required Fran to answer questions about what she had worn ten years earlier. Even more shockingly, the judge commented about this testimony as if it were an important issue.

John Barker questioned Fran extensively concerning her relationship with Tom Crenshaw. Barker always referred to him as "your paramour, Tom Crenshaw." Fran and I joked that Paramour must be Tom's first name. James made up several quotations from the children to the effect that they wanted to live with their father, that Fran was telling them to make up stories about James, and that the children were forced to call Tom "Daddy." John Barker asked Fran many questions about these make-believe quotations. Fran denied all of this. I thought she handled the intense pressure from Barker and the judge quite well under the circumstances. She stuck to her story and placed the essential evidence in the record. Despite this, James had succeeded in making Fran the issue, and the judge and other lawyers had cast aspersions on her honesty and fitness as a parent.

The law guardian typically asks questions designed to elicit information that has not been addressed or about which she has concerns. He or she usually does not act in an adversarial manner. Ms. Burke followed this custom, and her questioning of Fran was fair, but skeptical.

Our next witness was Charlotte Watson. Charlotte was the executive director of My Sisters' Place and one of the foremost experts in the area of child abuse, spousal abuse, incest, and other subjects related to domestic violence. A very compassionate person, she always finds time to help others, whether friends or strangers. Charlotte is adept at counseling women in desperate circumstances and at obtaining support from political and business leaders. She makes each person feel that he or she has her full attention.

It was obvious to me that Judge Pauling was clueless when it came to abuse issues. Dr. Schmidt did not have the training or understanding to help the court. The discussions during the many conferences were based on a complete lack of understanding concerning domestic violence. I hoped to use Charlotte's expertise to rectify this mass ignorance.

Charlotte was prepared to testify that it is extremely rare for women or children to make up allegations of physical or sexual abuse. It is embarrassing and painful to discuss such things. Children are forced to discuss subjects they normally would know nothing about until they were much older. Even when victims do come forward, their allegations usually minimize the full extent of the man's abuse. Like Fran, victims usually blame themselves for incidents the abuser is solely responsible for. Abusers virtually always deny or minimize their responsibility, and they almost never stop the abuse or change their behavior except in the face of serious consequences. Therefore, someone like James, who had sexually abused Fran when she was fifteen or sixteen, was unlikely to cease such behavior.

Common sense might suggest that someone who is abused would complain to someone, but in fact, victims usually suffer in silence. Similarly, victims of abuse frequently choose to remain with the abuser long after common sense would suggest that they leave. The fact that a victim stays is not an indication the abuse did not occur.

It is very difficult for children to come forward and seek help against an abusive parent. If they have the courage to tell an authority figure, whether that person is a parent, teacher, police officer, or judge, it is important that they be believed. The failure of an authority figure to believe and protect them puts children at great risk of being abused in future relationships, as well as of drug abuse, suicide, alcoholism, prostitution, and other dysfunctional behavior.

I sought to have Charlotte Watson qualified as an expert witness. An expert witness is permitted to give opinions, which other witnesses cannot do. In order to qualify as an expert, one must have specialized education, training, or experience in a subject that gives one knowledge the general public would not have. Charlotte testified about her credentials. At the time of the trial, she had worked as executive director of My Sisters' Place for about four years. For several years before that, she had worked on a volunteer basis at battered women's shelters in Texas. She had read extensively on the subject and studied with recognized authorities. Since coming to My Sisters' Place, Charlotte was frequently a speaker or panelist at seminars, educational forums, and conferences concerning various aspects of domestic violence. Nurses, doctors, police, teachers, social workers, and other professionals often came to her for training in this area. She had been interviewed frequently for television, radio, newspapers, and magazines because of her expertise on abuse issues. It is hard to imagine how we could have found a better or more knowledgeable expert witness.

After the presentation of Charlotte's credentials, I moved to qualify her as an expert in domestic violence issues. Incredibly, John Barker objected to her credentials and, even more incredibly, Judge Pauling refused to treat her as an expert. They claimed that she could not be considered an expert because she did not have a college degree. Nothing in the law requires a college degree or other particular education. In cases involving auto repairs, for example, mechanics without college degrees or even high school diplomas testify as experts. The mechanic is not asked if he has a college degree.

Psychiatrists, psychologists, and social workers all testify as expert witnesses, but because of the additional educational requirements, in general, psychiatrists' testimony is given more weight than that of psychologists, which in turn is given more weight than that of social workers. Accordingly, the fact that Charlotte did not graduate from college might reasonably affect the weight given to her testimony, but it was not a proper reason to bar her as an expert witness. Since this trial, Charlotte has been qualified as an expert witness in other cases in which I have called her. No other judge has refused to hear her valuable testimony.

It is ironic that Charlotte had more knowledge and understanding of domestic violence issues than any of the "expert" witnesses who were permitted to testify. Her analysis of the circumstances proved to be more accurate than those of the more educated, but less knowledgeable experts who did testify, but Charlotte was never given the opportunity to educate the judge.

If there was any question of Judge Pauling's strong feelings against Fran, his decision against qualifying Charlotte as an expert witness confirmed that he was firmly on James's side. I submitted a memorandum of law (a legal document citing statutes and cases supporting our position) demonstrating that Charlotte should have been allowed to testify, but the judge refused to correct his ruling.

At the end of the first two days of the trial, John Barker made a motion to give James unsupervised visitation. The law guardian supported this motion; I vigorously opposed it. I pointed out to the judge that if there was any doubt, he must err on the side of protecting the children. The court ruled that there was nothing in the evidence thus far that would justify supervised visitation and ordered unsupervised (but not overnight) visitation to start in a week. Fran was, of course, upset at the way the trial was going, and certainly had reason to be discouraged. She blamed herself, but, in fact, she had done everything she could. I did my best to lift her spirits.

In the Twilight Zone

A few days later, I received a call from Sandy Burke. She had spoken with James and the children's babysitter by conference call. The babysitter was a middle-aged woman who had worked for the Wongs before they separated, and continued to take care of the children occasionally after the separation. During the phone call, the babysitter confronted James with the fact that he had admitted to her that he had kissed his daughters on the vagina. In response, James admitted to the law guardian that he had kissed both Jennifer and Sheila on the vagina.

The fact that James had done this was not a surprise, as Sheila had told this to CPS, and both girls had told this to Fran. I was surprised that James admitted such a serious offense. I hoped it meant that he would get professional counseling and would drop all ideas of anything but supervised visitation. Surely no judge would permit unsupervised visitation after this admission. Ms. Burke told me that despite the admission, James wanted to go forward with the unsupervised visitation and still wanted custody. This was totally unrealistic, and both Ms. Burke and I fully expected that his admission would end the custody issue, guaranteeing nothing more than supervised visitation for the father.

Ms. Burke told me that I had been right all along about who should be believed. She was very gracious and professional in acknowledging her mistake and proceeded to fight very hard to protect the children throughout the remainder of the proceedings.

The immediate problem was that James was scheduled to have his first unsupervised visitation in less than a week. We were not scheduled to be in court before then, and needed emergency relief to protect the children. We decided to work together to submit an order to show cause asking that any visitation be supervised. Ms. Burke took the lead in presenting the papers, as the court was more likely to listen to her request.

The court promptly signed the order to show cause (which is routine), and scheduled a hearing before the first unsupervised visit. The hearing consisted solely of the testimony of Dr. Wong. By the time of the hearing, he had altered his story. He now claimed that on some occasions after a shower, he would dry off the girls and kiss them all over their bodies. While he was doing this, he kissed them *near their vaginas*. This contradicted the statements to the court by the law guardian, both orally and in her written affidavit, that James told her he had kissed the girls *on their vaginas*. James also claimed that he had stopped doing this, on his own, about two years earlier (he had had no unsupervised visitation in over a year). In fact, the girls told Fran that this had continued until the unsupervised visits stopped. James also testified that he had not done this for sexual pleasure.

If Judge A. Pauling had heard Charlotte's testimony, he would have learned that it was highly unlikely that James would have voluntarily stopped the abuse two years before. Instead, the judge announced he had consulted with Dr. Schmidt prior to the hearing. According to Dr. Schmidt, Dr. Wong's behavior was inappropriate and raised questions. Incredibly, though, this "expert" recommended that the unsupervised visitation proceed as planned. The judge used this recommendation to provide cover for his decision allowing unsupervised visitation.

How was such a decision possible? It seemed to come from the Twilight Zone. Fran was devastated. She had promised to protect the children. We had a frank discussion of what to do. An appeal was out of the question because we did not have the time or money to pursue it. The issue was whether or not to obey the court order.

For me, this was an impossible situation. How could I recommend that she leave the children with someone who had acknowledged abusing them in the past? Yet as an attorney, I am an officer of the court, and therefore ethically bound to support compliance with all legal court orders. This is true even when the judge is as badly mistaken as Pauling. I explained to Fran that I was ethically obligated to advise compliance, and anyway, there was no practical alternative. Fran had little money and no place to go. If she failed to comply with the court order, not only was she likely to be found, but this judge would give the children to their abuser. I hated the idea of giving the children to James—even aside from the sexual abuse, I was concerned that he would use physical discipline to frighten them about telling what he was doing. But there simply was no good alternative. Fran consulted with her family and friends and came to the same conclusion.

Fran's predicament was similar to that of Dr. Elizabeth Morgan, the Washington M.D. who elected to spend two years in jail rather than give unsupervised visitation to a father who she believed was molesting their daughter. I believe that the abuse did take place and I have no criticism of Dr. Morgan's actions. She was fortunate to have the resources to have some hope of protecting her daughter by hiding her. The real culprit is courts that put mothers and children in impossible situations.

While I was forced to counsel compliance with the court's order, we continued to search for ways to reverse the decision. To that end, I spoke with many individuals who were active in the fight against domestic violence. Many letters expressing outrage over the decision were sent to Judge Pauling and the administrative judges above him. Another idea was to contact CPS with the new information. The original charges had been designated "unfounded," and the case closed, but this was before the father admitted kissing his daughters on the vagina. In the Twilight Zone of Judge Pauling's courtroom, such behavior might be tolerated, but presumably CPS would know that it is unacceptable.

I made the report to CPS and informed them of the past history and the new developments. They took the report seriously and quickly interviewed Fran and the children. CPS arranged for the girls to have a physical examination by a doctor. An experienced evaluator met with the girls to determine who was responsible for the abuse. Unfortunately, it would take a few weeks before this information would be available.

The children tried to hide to avoid the first unsupervised visitation and begged not to go; finally they had to be forced to go. The children did not report anything improper about the visitation, but they had nightmares following it.

About a week later, we returned to the court to continue the trial. Before the trial resumed, a conference was held among the three attorneys and Judge Pauling. I told the judge and the other attorneys about my report to CPS. The judge was furious with me and started yelling at me. He said that CPS had already investigated the charges and did not find any abuse. He complained that I was trying to reopen issues that had already been settled. In fact, I had provided CPS with vital information. Sheila's statement that her father had kissed her on the vagina (which CPS, Dr. Schmidt, and Judge Pauling had disbelieved) was confirmed by James himself. It is totally appropriate to contact CPS when you have reason to believe that a child might have been abused. Judge Pauling never gave me the opportunity to explain this during the conference.

When the trial resumed, we called Elise Gibbs as our next witness. Ms. Gibbs was a social worker who was treating Fran and had some contact with the children. She did not have a lot of credentials or experience, but because she was the treating caregiver, the court had to permit her testimony. Elise proved to be a good witness. She had had discussions with Fran about James's abuse of her before it became a court issue, which buttressed our claim of abuse. Fran had also discussed her concerns about the children and had received training in parenting skills from the therapist. Unlike Dr. Wong, Fran was willing to work on her parenting skills and to accept instruction from a professional. Fran's flexibility was in marked contrast to James's rigidity and belief that he never made a mistake. This should have benefited Fran with respect to custody. Ms. Gibbs also explained the harm that could be caused to the children if the court failed to provide the protection the children requested, or if the court sent the message that abuse was acceptable by giving James liberal visitation, or worse, custody.

We completed our case by calling some of Fran's family. They testified that she was a good mother and had a close relationship with her children. The children displayed tremendous fear and apprehension about being alone with their father.

James was the first witness for the opposition. He was well prepared and spoke with confidence. He said he could never do the kind of things he was accused of. He testified that he had never hit Fran, and complained that Fran had brainwashed the children to say things against him. James made up quotations from the children saying how much they loved him and that "Mommy says you hurt us." He said that the children kept asking when they could come live with him. James spoke of his religious views and the effect of his Christian beliefs on his life. He made a point of involving the children in his religious activities and implied he was more moral than Fran.

After watching James's performance, I was anxious to begin the cross-examination. I started by trying to show James to be a controlling individual. It is well known that control is an important part of abuse. James not only admitted to making most of the family decisions and controlling the finances, but also expressed the view that this was the only moral way for a family to function.

I tried to ask questions concerning his religious views. Judge Pauling angrily refused to allow questions about religion on the ground that everyone has a right to his own beliefs. I told the court, "You have permitted him to repeatedly use his religion to pretend to be virtuous and moral, and now you won't let me show how he misuses his religion to justify control and abuse. He has told my client that the Bible requires harsh physical discipline of children and subservient wives. His beliefs affect his behavior towards the children, which is most relevant." Nevertheless, I was not permitted to ask any questions about his religious beliefs.

James cast many aspersions against Fran's relationship with Tom and was particularly upset by the relationship between Tom and the children. While he denied punishing the children when they said anything positive about Tom, James volunteered a story in which he searched eight-year-old Sammy's wallet while he was sleeping and found a library card on which Sammy had written the name Crenshaw. James told the story to support his contention that the children were being brainwashed. He had no clue that it instead demonstrated his controlling nature and his failure to respect boundaries. Even the judge disapproved of this invasion of privacy. Dr. Wong saw nothing wrong with kissing the girls "near the vagina," showering with the children, and sleeping in the same bed with them. He said these acts were proper because they were not done for sexual purposes.

Towards the end of my cross-examination, James finally admitted to spanking Fran once. I asked for no justification and none was given, because one of the basic rules of cross-examination is that you never ask a "why" question—it gives the witness the opportunity to say something to help himself. John Barker never asked for an explanation, during his next turn questioning James, because it was a damaging admission and he wanted as little said about it as possible.

I thought the cross-examination had been successful. The admission of the spanking demonstrated that his inappropriate behavior with the children was not isolated, but part of a pattern. Since the admission came after James denied ever hitting his wife, it should have devastated his credibility and put into question his other denials. His violation of Sammy's privacy was clearly improper and supported our view of him. None of this seemed to get through to Judge Pauling, however. At the end of the day, on a motion by John Barker, James was given unsupervised, overnight visitation.

The next day, Barker called Dr. Schmidt as a witness for James. In order for Dr. Schmidt to testify, he had to be qualified as an expert witness. With a witness of Dr. Schmidt's experience, this would normally be routine. Through questioning by John Barker, he gave his educational background, experience as a psychiatrist, and lengthy history of being qualified as an expert witness. There was no way I could prevent him from being qualified as an expert, but after the court's failure to qualify Charlotte Watson, and Dr. Schmidt's recommendation of unsupervised visitation for a father who admitted kissing his daughters on the vagina, I resolved to challenge his qualifications. Dr. Schmidt acknowledged that he had received little training about domestic violence when he was in school. He also had limited exposure to conferences or seminars about abuse issues. He testified to interviewing many women and children who had been victims of abuse.

"In your experience, is it common for women and children to make up false allegations of sexual abuse?" I asked.

Such false accusations are rare, but Schmidt stated, "I have encountered some allegations I do not believe, but I don't know how common they are."

"If a child comes to an authority figure, such as a judge, seeking protection from abuse, and the court refuses to protect the child, how is that likely to affect the child?" I asked. The research demonstrates that such children are at great risk for substance abuse, prostitution, suicide, and other harmful behaviors.

Dr. Schmidt responded, "I'm not aware of anything specific."

Judge Pauling severely limited my questions on the repeated ground that "this is not an abuse trial." He qualified Dr. Schmidt as an expert.

By the time of his testimony, Dr. Schmidt had met with both parties and the children. He testified that he believed Fran had brainwashed the children into making false allegations of abuse. He disbelieved the children. Dr. Schmidt stated that James had acted inappropriately with respect to where he kissed the girls. He believed all James's explanations—that the kissing occurred near rather than on the vagina, that James had voluntarily stopped this behavior two years earlier, and that he had voluntarily come forward with this information. Dr. Schmidt's opinion was not affected by James's admission of spanking Fran. He said that the children loved both parents. He stated that, while each parent had some drawbacks, either parent would be an appropriate custodian. According to Schmidt, there was no need for visitation to be supervised.

The next witness was Dr. Lawrence Parker, a fiftyish psychiatrist hired by James as his expert. He had experience and education as a psychiatrist, but no training or background in abuse issues. I objected to his credentials, but got no further than I had with Dr. Schmidt. Dr. Parker had met with James five times and saw the children during visitation periods. He testified that James had a good and loving relationship with the children. The psychiatrist made the point that the children showed no fear of their father when he saw them together. He believed this was an important indication that no abuse had occurred. He said that James dealt with the children in an appropriate manner. Like Dr. Schmidt, he accepted James's version of kissing Sheila and Jennifer. Furthermore, he saw nothing wrong with such a "loving gesture." Although he had never met Fran, Dr. Parker was critical of her and expressed the belief that James was the only appropriate parent for custody. On cross-examination, he acknowledged that his ability to judge Fran was limited by his lack of contact with her. He also demonstrated a lack of understanding of fundamental abuse issues. Dr. Parker did not see a need for James to have therapy and repeatedly expressed an uncritical view of him.

The next witness on James's behalf was Bertha Makarian, a social worker who had treated the children and James. The treatment started after the unsupervised visitation began, and was initiated by James in hopes of helping his position in the litigation. Since she had been the children's therapist, she could not be prevented from testifying. She also totally accepted James's story. She testified that he was a good father and that the children were comfortable being with him. The children demonstrated no fear of their father when she saw them together. Furthermore, she was convinced that Fran's allegations were untrue because James could never do such things. Ms. Makarian stated that Fran had kissed the children under their arms and suggested this was the equivalent of the allegations that James kissed his daughters near the vagina. Although she had never met Fran, she strongly recommended that James be given custody. In one of the most bizarre parts of the trial, Ms. Makarian stated that there was respectable professional opinion that there is nothing wrong with a father kissing his daughters on the vagina. While she did not think this was a good idea, she believed it did not suggest any concerns about a father who would do such a thing.

The next few witnesses were friends of James whom he had met in the course of his religious activities. They all spoke highly of James and did not believe he could have done anything like what he was being accused of. They emphasized his strong religious beliefs and honesty. They believed he had good character and would not do anything immoral. These witnesses had also observed James interacting with the children. They testified that the children were not afraid of their father and there was a close relationship between them.

James returned to the witness stand to make new allegations against Fran. He claimed that Fran had fraudulently obtained welfare payments from Orange County for herself and the children at a time when she was living in Westchester and James had custody. This was during the period after the divorce and before the first order to show cause. In practice, the children were spending equal time with both parents, and Fran was living with her grandparents in Orange County. She had moved there in order to take care of her grandparents and to be further away from James, whom she feared. She had explained the circumstances to the Social Services worker and followed their instructions. While this issue had nothing to do with custody, it was considered because it could affect Fran's credibility. The day ended before James could finish his testimony.

As we left the court, Fran had some startling new information. She had just learned that James had also molested her cousin. The cousin was now eleven years old. I suggested we provide this information to CPS and the district attorney, but the girl and her family were not willing to come forward. The information could not be used without their help.

James's charges of welfare fraud resulted in a hearing concerning child support. We tried to explain the circumstances. The hearing examiner decided that she did not have enough information and suspended James's payments until a determination could be made. It would be over a year before James was again required to pay child support.

Reason Prevails

While the trial continued, CPS was working on its investigation of my complaint. This time they did a thorough job. They arranged for the children to see a validator and a physician. The doctor determined that there was a tear in each of the girls' vaginas. This created the likelihood that there had been sexual abuse, but did not prove who had done it. James repeatedly suggested that if there was any abuse, it probably had occurred while the children were with Fran. It is very difficult to get statements from young children, and the validator needed to be careful not to suggest to the girls what they should say.

Finally, CPS completed their investigation and determined what had taken place. James had penetrated Sheila for the first time when she was four, during the period when he had custody. He penetrated Jennifer, also when she was four, for the first time during the first unsupervised overnight visitation, which Judge Pauling had ordered. James had penetrated his daughters with his fingers. CPS brought charges of abuse and neglect against James.

I spoke with the assistant county attorney who would handle the case. He told me the custody hearing would be suspended while they proceeded with the abuse and neglect charges against James. If the county's petition were successful, there would be no need to complete the custody trial, as Fran would have to be given custody. While the charges were pending, James would have nothing but limited, supervised visitation. The visitation was supervised by Janet Robinson, who proved to be very protective of the children.

The trial of the neglect and abuse petition would be heard by Judge Pauling in the Family Court. This was a civil proceeding, so that James could not be jailed if found to have committed the abuse. However, he could lose his right to custody and have visitation rights severely limited. As the mother of the children, Fran had the right to participate in the trial and be represented by an attorney, but the county attorney and the law guardian advised us to limit her participation. They said that my involvement was unwise because of the dislike Judge Pauling had for Fran. Although they did not say it, the judge also had a low opinion of me, ironically because of my complaint to CPS. We concurred in their view of the judge's opinion, and Fran's participation was limited to a brief appearance as a witness.

The case was also referred to the district attorney's office for possible criminal prosecution. The Westchester district attorney's office has a special office for domestic violence cases. It was the first such office established in this country and maintains an excellent reputation. While there was no question that the crime of sexual abuse had been committed, proving it beyond a reasonable doubt in a court of law when the only witnesses are extremely young is problematic. It is difficult for a young child to speak of sexual abuse, and there are many obstacles that an experienced defense attorney can put in the way of a conviction. The children had trouble remembering the dates of the abuse and other details necessary for a conviction. For this reason the district attorney decided not to prosecute. We were sorry that James would get away with the sexual abuse, but pleased the children would be spared the ordeal of testifying against their father.

The Family Court trial on the neglect and abuse charges took several months. The court would schedule a day or two at a time and then adjourn the trial for a month or two. James continued to deny that he had done anything wrong and to blame Fran for the accusations against him. The evidence, however, was overwhelming. In addition to Fran's prior testimony about the excessive discipline and the fear the children had of their father, the county brought in the doctor and validator who had examined the children. These were genuine experts who understood abuse issues and were impartial.

Near the end of the trial, James was finally persuaded to accept the Family Court equivalent of a plea bargain. He agreed to admit that he had abused the children by kissing his daughters on the vagina, in exchange for the other charges being dropped. The agreement further stated that he would give up any right to custody and that any future visitation would be supervised. The act of abuse he had admitted was the one Dr. Schmidt and Judge Pauling had accepted as too insignificant to warrant any restriction on visitation!

Fran and the children were pleased that the long ordeal was over. The children preferred that there be no visitation, but were willing to live with the supervised visits. The visitation was being supervised by Janet Robinson, and she was sensitive to the children's needs. The purpose of the supervisor is not just to prevent any inappropriate physical contact, but to stop any improper or suggestive statements. When James did anything like this, Ms. Robinson was quick to stop him; the children came to feel close to her.

Fran and Tom held a special dinner with the children to celebrate the award of custody. Janet Robinson and I were invited to share the occasion. The children now were glowing with happiness. Their long ordeal, the danger to their bodies and souls, was over. They were well behaved even with all the excitement. Sammy, Sheila, and Jennifer made gifts for Ms. Robinson and me. They had a name for us: they called us "believers," because we believed them when the judge, psychiatrist, and others did not.

On days when I get discouraged in my fight against domestic violence, it helps to remember their name for me. Judges who don't protect children, and lawyers who serve as apologists for abusers, have a fatal flaw. They are not "believers."

Free at Last

With the custody decided, it was time to get Fran divorced. Support had been determined in Family Court. Equitable distribution was irrelevant because there was no property to divide. Accordingly, the only issue left was the grounds for divorce. In other states, no-fault grounds such as irreconcilable differences can be used, but New York has no such procedure. There is a ground of living apart according to a separation agreement, but it requires more than a year to complete. Commonly, when both parties want a divorce, they use the grounds of constructive abandonment, which is the denial of sexual relations. Since no one knows what happens in the privacy of a couple's bedroom, if they both agree, the divorce can go through easily. Often, this is used when the real grounds are cruel and inhuman treatment, but the abuser will not agree to cruelty as the grounds. James, on the contrary, objected to the grounds of constructive abandonment and insisted that Fran obtain the divorce based upon the true grounds, which were his cruel and inhuman treatment of her. The divorce was completed within a few months, and Fran was finally able to marry Tom.

Every six months, we had to return to Family Court for the order of supervised visitation to be renewed. James repeatedly stated that he had done nothing wrong and that there was no need for the visitation to be supervised. He refused to get any treatment for his problem and was never mandated to do so. Child abusers such as James cannot hope to get better without directed therapy. Some therapists will not treat patients unless they admit what they did and cooperate with the therapy; this is usually a prerequisite for successful treatment. Abusers who go through mandated therapy but deny the problem will not get better. Although supervised visitation was always ordered, Judge Pauling implied that at some point he would consider unsupervised visitation.

Several years later, a serious incident occurred during the visitation. Sammy, age fourteen, got into an argument with his father and James jumped at Sammy and punched him. The visitation was stopped and we sought an order of protection for the children. At this point, James approached us with an offer to consent to have the children adopted by Tom. James claimed to be doing this in the interest of freeing the children from the disagreeable supervised visitation. In reality, letting Tom adopt the children had an economic advantage for James: he would no longer have to pay child support. Six years after he had fought for the right to raise them, he saw his kids only as a financial burden.

Judge Aaron Markowitz presided over the adoption. Adoptions are generally happy occasions, and this one was particularly so. The judge remarked about how enthusiastic the children were. I told Judge Markowitz the story of the "believers" and expressed my pleasure that the adoption was taking place with a judge I knew to be a "believer." I also spoke about Fran's courage in fighting for the children and about Tom's love and generosity in undertaking such a responsibility. Most of all, we celebrated three children who insisted on a life free of abuse.

Today Sammy, Sheila, and Jennifer are thriving with their mother, father, and two younger sisters. Fran made sure they had the therapy and support needed to overcome the trauma of abuse and the legal ordeal. The children are doing well in school and have many friends. They are very supportive of each other and their younger sisters. Sammy is looking at colleges and considering the most competitive schools. There is every reason to expect these children to have happy and successful lives. They could do this only because they got away from the judge, the court-appointed psychiatrist, and the father who were supposed to protect them.

Chapter 3

THE PRICE OF SAFETY

The Thomas Case

T HE SHADOW OF HIS SHOE suddenly appeared. I was sitting in a waiting room of the Family Court while my client's abusive husband was stalking the halls outside. At the time, I joked that this line would make a great beginning for a book, but this man's actions were deadly serious. The ultimate outcome regarding custody would be determined not by the law or the court, but by his extralegal activities.

I first met Karen Thomas while she was living at a shelter for battered women run by My Sisters' Place. She went to the shelter after her husband had beaten her up and threatened to do worse. Karen was a slim and very attractive woman in her mid-thirties, with long black hair. Her soft voice was made even softer by her overwhelming fear of her husband.

Alcohol and Abuse

Karen had heard about me because of my work with My Sisters' Place. During our first meeting on a Friday afternoon in my office, I learned most of her history. She was raised in an upper-middle-class family and had many material advantages. Her father was a doctor from whom she was estranged, mostly because he had been unfaithful to her late mother.

Alcoholism permeated Karen's life from the time she was 16 or 17. Despite her talent and intelligence, she barely completed high school and never finished college because of her drinking problem. Karen had a rather promiscuous sexual history, which she attributed largely to the alcohol and to poor self-esteem.

Karen met her husband, Charles Thomas, on a night when she was drinking heavily, and went to bed with him that first night. He cheated on her during the courtship, but they were married in Las Vegas a few months after they met.

A few years before they met, Charlie Thomas had been involved in illegal manipulation of securities and was caught by the SEC. He managed to avoid the brunt of the prosecution, but did have to agree to a plea bargain. As a result, Charlie pleaded guilty to a felony and served a brief jail term. The fine was far less than the money he had made on the scheme, and he managed to keep his assets hidden. He would brag afterwards that he had gotten away with his activities.

Although the couple had little or no reported income, they managed to enjoy a wealthy lifestyle. At the beginning of their marriage, they lived in an expensive apartment in Manhattan and bought an art gallery. They later moved to Westchester County, to a suite at a country club where he had lived as a child.

Karen and Charlie had been married for about eight years at the time I met her, and they had a little girl, Vanessa, who was six years old. Although Karen was an active alcoholic most of her adult life, she managed not to drink during her pregnancy.

Karen had only recently recognized and accepted the fact that she was an alcoholic. She had been to several psychiatrists since her teen years, but they did not help her. She and Charlie had a lawsuit in progress against a prominent psychiatrist who had treated her for a few years, but failed to diagnose her alcohol problem. Finally, she was admitted to the Smithers Institute (several years before Dwight Gooden went there) and received the help she needed.

Since Karen had been released from Smithers, several months earlier, she had not had another drink. She went faithfully to Alcoholics Anonymous meetings, where she obtained a sponsor and made some friends. My client referred to herself as a recovering alcoholic and had a good attitude. She told me that she had to take it one day at a time, and would always be in danger of a relapse. Karen took her efforts to stay off alcohol very seriously and took full personal responsibility for her problem.

Charlie was physically and emotionally abusive to her throughout the marriage. There had been many incidents in which he would slap her in the face, punch her, throw her around the room, or kick her. Most of this occurred when she had been drinking. He often yelled at her. His behavior isolated Karen from friends and family. She had accepted the brutal treatment because she thought she deserved it, and because of the alcohol.

The last beating had occurred while she was cold sober. My client realized she could no longer tolerate such treatment. Karen was still afraid of Charlie, and waited until he left their apartment before seeking help at a shelter. She did not try to take Vanessa with her because she was afraid of what Charlie might do. Once before she had run away, and he had tracked her down, dragged her home, and administered a severe beating. She had hoped that if she left Vanessa with Charlie, he would leave her alone.

Some people are afraid to go to a shelter for battered women because they think it will be unsafe, like some homeless shelters. In fact, the shelter operated by My Sisters' Place is located in a residential neighborhood and from the outside looks similar to the other houses nearby. Each resident has her own room and they share kitchen duty and other chores. Drugs and alcohol are not permitted; any woman who violates this policy is asked to leave. The shelter provides counselors to help the women with the numerous problems involved in leaving their abusers. Often, the women help each other in a variety of ways. Karen lived at the shelter during most of her case.

Despite her fears, Karen hoped to obtain custody of Vanessa, and she wanted a divorce. She warned me of Charlie's ability to hide assets, but believed that if Vanessa were to live with her, Charlie would voluntarily agree to provide some money to benefit their daughter. Karen did not have any money to pay me. I hoped the court would award me legal fees, but under all the circumstances, I was not going to allow Karen to be unrepresented.

Telephone Harassment

Charlie Thomas called me just a few minutes after Karen left my office. He must have been spying on her, because he had no other way of knowing that I would be representing her. It is unethical for an attorney to speak to an opposing party if he or she has an attorney. Accordingly, I asked Charlie whether he was represented by counsel, and he said he was not. He told me not to represent his wife, saying that she was a "nut case" who could not be believed. He said that I would never find any assets or income and would never receive one penny. "You will rue the day you met Karen, if you take the case," the bully threatened. I told him that I believed his wife's story and that I would not be intimidated from doing my job. He then called me a few obscene names and ended the conversation.

At that time, my office was in my home, where I lived with my parents. As soon as I hung up with Charlie, I started receiving one hang-up call after another on both of my phone lines. Karen had warned me that this was a tactic he liked to use. Some of the calls involved some talking or sounds, but most were pure hang-up calls. I received a few hundred calls that night and several hundred during the weekend.

The shelter for battered women where Karen was staying has a hotline for victims of domestic violence that is used for emergencies and is covered by staff at the shelter. During this same weekend, Charlie obtained this emergency number and flooded the phone with hang-up calls. During some of the calls, he made rude statements, but mostly he just hung up. The shelter contacted the police, with whom they work regularly, but the police were unable to trace or stop these calls.

The annoyance calls let up a little at my office on Monday, but continued on and off for the next few months. Whenever something happened in the court case that Charlie did not like, the calls became more frequent. I contacted the police, but the officer who came did not take the problem seriously. I then contacted the annoyance call bureau of the phone company, who advised me to keep a record of the calls. The phone company was reluctant to use the equipment necessary to catch Charlie despite the records I provided to them. Evidently it was costly to do this, and they hoped the problem would go away. Just when they seemed close to installing the equipment, the calls subsided for a while and nothing was done. I do not know whether Charlie learned about the potential taps or whether the reduction in annoyance calls was a coincidence.

Preliminaries

Karen and I discussed in which court to proceed. In New York State, only the Supreme Court has jurisdiction over divorce and equitable distribution, but the Family Court has concurrent jurisdiction over the issues of custody and support. The Family Court has more resources available for custody hearings. There is the added advantage that filing fees are not charged in Family Court as they are in Supreme Court. Karen was hoping that if she won custody, her husband would agree to a financial settlement that would be in Vanessa's best interests. For all of these reasons, we decided to file a custody petition in Family Court. Charlie quickly responded with his own custody petition.

The first appearance in Family Court was for a preliminary hearing.

The judge was Jane Parker, who at the time was fairly new to her office, but knew what she was doing. Charlie Thomas was a big man, about 6 feet tall, 240 pounds, 45 years old, with graying hair that he was starting to lose. His attorney was Frederick Chatsworth, who appeared to be an old-line WASP from a large and expensive New York City law firm. He was in his late thirties and looked a lot like the character Arnold Becker on the television show *L.A. Law*.

Each party denied the allegations in the other's petition. Chatsworth requested that my client be tested for alcohol, to which we consented. We requested visitation while the proceeding was pending, and this was granted.

Charlie had a tendency to make rambling statements that were attacks on his wife. This did not help his standing with Judge Parker, who seemed to understand the kind of man she was dealing with. The judge even stated that women usually do not go to battered women's shelters without a good reason. The trial was scheduled to start in about two months.

In the meantime, I received a letter from the Grievance Committee of the Westchester Bar Association, based upon a complaint made against me by Charlie Thomas. He thought that I had some financial interest in My Sisters' Place and that my representation of his wife created a conflict of interest. He also did not like the advice I was giving her, which he claimed was not in her best interest.

The normal procedure is for the attorney to submit a written response, and when the complaint is obviously baseless, as this one was, the complaint is quickly dismissed. I explained to the committee what the facts were and how Charlie was using them to continue his harassment of his wife. I told them about all his improper actions in the case. Despite this, I was shocked to receive a notice from the committee that they were scheduling an evidentiary hearing on these frivolous charges. When I called to find out what was going on, they told me that Charlie had been calling their office constantly, and that they were giving him the hearing to appease him (although they weren't so direct in saying it). As it turned out, though, the hearing had to be postponed a few times because of scheduling conflicts, and eventually Charlie decided to withdraw his complaint.

My Sisters' Place conducted a fundraising affair at the Hudson River Museum in Yonkers and asked Karen to give a speech about her situation. She was very nervous about speaking in public, but gave a good speech that was inspiring to the audience.

Karen and I met a few times to work on the trial. Most of her friends would not testify because they were afraid of Charlie. He called all of her friends and told them terrible stories about her. He also suggested that if they helped her, he would investigate them, harass them, or otherwise cause them grief. With his track record, these threats were effective. Some of her friends from Alcoholics Anonymous did agree to help, but, as a result, they were subjected to annoyance calls and learned that they were being investigated.

The Shelter

For Karen, one of the best parts of this time period was her visitations with her daughter, Vanessa, who seemed to be a happy child. Although 70 percent of men who abuse their wives also abuse their children, Charlie had never abused Vanessa, and she was comfortable with both parents. During the visitation periods, Karen took Vanessa on outings such as to the zoo or the beach. Sometimes they would go with other families who were staying at the shelter.

Most of the women at the shelter are supported by public assistance. Many of them were not in need of public assistance before they left their abusers, but without their husbands' income, they are without funds. This was true of Karen, who was used to a rather lavish lifestyle but now was without resources.

The shelter is intended to be a temporary refuge for women as they struggle for a new life free from abuse. Under the Social Service regulations, a woman could stay at the shelter for a maximum of 90 days. As we were getting closer to the trial, it was also close to the end of this 90-day period. Karen's circumstances were unusual because Charlie continued to harass her even while she was at the shelter. In addition to all the phone calls, he had threatened to come to the shelter (its location is supposed to be secret in order to protect the residents). His intimidation of friends and relatives further complicated Karen's ability to make arrangements for life on her own. Under the circumstances, we were able to obtain a waiver so that she could remain at the shelter a while longer. This got us past the initial trial date, but only postponed the problem.

Further Harassment

The harassing phone calls continued on and off at my home and office. I spoke with someone in the district attorney's office, who suggested that I start taping Charlie's calls. Late one afternoon, I caught him on tape. It was one of the calls in which he wanted to speak with me. I had told him many times not to call me, but he did as he pleased. At the beginning of this call, I again asked him to terminate the call and not to call again. He said that he could do whatever he wanted and refused to hang up. Charlie said that as long as I insisted on helping Karen, the unwanted calls would continue. He also said, as he had many times before, that he knew what he was doing and could never be caught. There were no threats of physical violence, but he certainly threatened to continue harassing me.

After checking to make sure the tape was complete and audible, I called the police. This time Officer Barbara Rogowsky came in response to the call. I told her the story of what had been going on and played the tape for her. While the harassment had been occurring much longer by now than it had the first time the police had responded, and while I now had strong evidence, the difference in the police response was primarily due to Officer Rogowsky. She was younger, better trained, and much more sympathetic than the first officer. In my experience, there is often a marked difference in the way different police officers handle cases related to domestic violence.

Officer Rogowsky promised to follow up with the district attorney's office, and her word was good. I was called in to file a complaint, and misdemeanor charges of aggravated harassment were brought against Charlie Thomas. While the case would take four to five months to complete, the judge issued an order of protection preventing Charlie from calling or otherwise harassing me. This proved to be effective, and I received no further annoyance calls from him.

Charlie reacted to the charges as the wise guy he is. He threatened to sue the district attorney and denied that he had done anything improper. As a result of his response, he was required to appear in court several times. The Yonkers Criminal Court is not a pleasant place to be for someone who is used to country club living. The time spent in court and the legal fees were considered part of his punishment. Ultimately, Charlie plea-bargained to a violation, which did not require any jail time. By the time of the plea, the custody case was long over and we could not use it against him. As part of the plea bargain, I received a permanent order of protection.

The Custody Trial

It was finally time for the custody trial to begin. Although a trial is scheduled well before the appearance, there are still many emergency petitions the judge must hear before the trial can start. Whenever we had to spend time waiting outside the Family Court, Charlie would walk back and forth, stalking Karen. We finally enlisted the help of the guards on the floor. They were extremely cooperative once they heard the story, especially because they could see how he was acting. They not only ordered Charlie to stay away from Karen, but walked with us to the parking garage when it was time to leave.

The trial was a typical "he said, she said" affair. Karen had been the primary parent, and we took the time to describe the many routine activities she did with Vanessa. Karen told of her problems with alcohol and was honest about the mistakes she had made because of it. She had worked hard to prevent the drinking from affecting Vanessa; most of it occurred after the girl was asleep. Karen took full responsibility for her past and explained the activities designed to keep her sober. The blood tests confirmed that she was not currently drinking.

Some of the abuse Karen had suffered at Charlie's hands was discussed, but this was limited because, for the most part, it did not occur in front of Vanessa. Under New York State law at the time, spousal abuse that was not observed by the children was not considered relevant to custody and visitation issues. However, research demonstrates that such abuse has a harmful effect on the children even when they do not observe it directly. At the very least, the children will notice the effects of the abuse on their mothers. Domestic violence now must be considered in all custody and visitation cases.

Karen acknowledged that Charlie loved Vanessa and treated her well when they were together. Since Charlie worked during the day (albeit not "on the books"), and Karen was not working, she was in a better position to take care of Vanessa.

Through cross-examination and then his testimony, Charlie provided a very different view of family life. He testified that Vanessa loved her mother, but thought she was pathetic because of the drinking. He claimed to have a close relationship with Vanessa, although he acknowledged that he spent less time with her than Karen did. Charlie claimed that the drinking totally dominated Karen's life and caused her to do many self-destructive things. He argued that the drinking had caused her to make up the false allegations of physical abuse. Charlie acknowledged that he was very aggressive verbally, but claimed that he was never physically abusive.

He also claimed that only he could support Vanessa properly, and that giving custody to Karen would force the two of them to live on welfare or some menial existence. The father can and should be required to pay child support (and possibly maintenance), but Charlie assumed Karen would get little or nothing. Vanessa was attending a very good private school, and Charlie claimed that this could continue only if he won custody. He also claimed that Vanessa had expressed her desire to live with him. Arrangements had been made to have Vanessa cared for when he was working. Charlie acknowledged his criminal conviction, but claimed it was a technical violation. He minimized or denied all of his own faults, while presenting Karen in the worst possible light.

The only other witnesses were friends of Karen's from Alcoholics Anonymous. They testified that she was diligent about attending the meetings and staying away from alcohol. They explained the AA program and reported that Karen had abided by its rules. No one had ever seen Karen drink since she had been at Smithers. Even Charlie did not claim to have seen her drinking, although he did speculate that she might have done some drinking. Karen's friends also told about some of the harassment (mostly phone calls) that they themselves had been subjected to at Charlie's hands.

I was in the middle of cross-examining Charlie when the day ended. The next available trial date was two months later. This is common in Family Court, where the judges have other matters scheduled for the next day.

It was hard to tell how the trial was going. The past alcohol history was a problem, but we hoped the judge was impressed by Karen's serious attitude about her recovery. We were concerned about the support issue, however. Everyone realized that Charlie could successfully avoid paying proper support because his assets and income were well hidden. This was, of course, unfair, but it also meant that materially, Vanessa would have a much better life with her father. The other big consideration was Charlie's criminal and harassing actions. We could not prove much of his improper actions, but some evidence of his aggression was before the judge. Judge Parker was an intelligent woman, and she bent over backwards to help us during the trial. At times, she even signaled to me when to make an objection. This was encouraging, but did not mean Karen would necessarily receive custody.

The delay worked against Karen, because even with the exemption, her time to remain at the shelter would expire before the trial resumed. With complaints to workers' supervisors and threats of lawsuits, Charlie had managed to pressure Social Services to remove his wife from the shelter. You would think that Social Services might be more interested in making Charlie pay his wife's expenses, but his constant calls made them more concerned about protecting themselves.

Upon leaving the shelter, Karen arranged to move in with a distant relative whom she barely knew. It was understood from the start that this was a temporary arrangement. Charlie quickly learned where she was staying and bombarded the home with phone calls. This created still more pressure for her to leave after a few weeks.

Her next home was a welfare motel in northern Westchester. This was a scary place to begin with, and much more so because there was no way to protect her from Charlie. Furthermore, neither Karen nor her husband was willing for Vanessa to visit Karen while she lived there.

I met with Karen and discussed her situation. She decided that the only way to buy Charlie off was to give him custody. She hoped and even believed that if she gave him custody, Charlie would leave her alone and provide some support. Accordingly, we entered into negotiations over custody. We had to fight hard to obtain some reasonable visitation. The agreement was put on the record in front of Judge Parker. The judge tried hard to make sure it was a voluntary agreement, but when Karen repeatedly said that it was, there was nothing Judge Parker could do but accept the settlement.

Unhappily Ever After

The custody agreement did not persuade Charlie to leave Karen alone. He continued to monitor her living arrangements, and her friends continued to receive unwanted calls. Charlie denied Karen any visitation with Vanessa and refused to provide any support. He started a divorce action. Karen had no objection to the divorce, but it was obvious from the papers filed that he would deny any income or assets and make sure she never received any support or property. Karen realized that Charlie's vendetta against her would not end voluntarily, and he would continue to punish her as long as he could find her.

Karen decided that she would have to run away in order to have any life. Already, Karen sorely missed her daughter and hated the thought that she would not see Vanessa grow up. I discussed this with her, but could offer no other solution to her problems. She expressed deep appreciation for the work I had done for her and promised to contact me periodically. In order to help protect her, I never knew her new address or phone number. She moved to another state far away.

Karen had found the help she needed to overcome her drinking problem. She was assigned a decent judge and was able to obtain a pro bono attorney. Many other women are not as fortunate, but still the outcome was so unsatisfactory.

Periodically, I would receive a call from Karen. She started a job working with substance abusers and liked the work she was doing. She continued that job as long as she kept in contact with me. Karen used what she learned from her drinking problem to help others. I think this was therapeutic for her, but she greatly missed her daughter. After a while, she met somebody and was considering marriage.

About a year or two after Karen left, I received a call from Charlie. The lawsuit against her psychiatrist was coming to trial and he wanted her to testify. Karen, Charlie and Vanessa were all plaintiffs, and Charlie hoped to use this to get money for himself and Vanessa. When Karen called me, we discussed the lawsuit. I conducted some negotiations with Charlie concerning a share of any proceeds from the lawsuit for Karen and Vanessa. We also discussed some possible visitation arrangements while Karen was in town to testify. Charlie agreed to provide some expense money for the trip to New York. He claimed that he knew where Karen was living, correctly revealed the state and area in the state, but did not know the address or city. In the end, Karen decided that she could not risk returning to New York because Charlie might hire someone to follow her.

I never heard from Karen again after this. As far as I know, she has not seen her daughter again.

Chapter 4

ABUSER STRATEGIES

The Delgado Case

On New Year's Eve, 1994, Anne Scripps Douglas was brutally murdered by her husband. The homicide took place at her home in Bronxville, New York. The court system in Westchester County was severely criticized because it had failed to protect Mrs. Douglas. She had an order of protection with the standard language prohibiting her husband from assaulting, threatening, or harassing her and had twice unsuccessfully sought to expand the order to keep him out of her house. This request was turned down by Judge Sophie Hirsch, the Family Court Judge in New Rochelle. Other judges responded to this tragedy by reducing the burden of proof for women to obtain protection from abusive partners. Judge Hirsch responded by hiring a public relations firm.

Two months later, Maria Delgado went before Judge Hirsch to seek an order of protection against her husband. Her petition included allegations that her husband had sexually abused her and had physically abused their daughter. Maria asked the court to remove her husband from the marital home. Judge Hirsch could have granted the order of protection; she could have asked for more specific information about the abuse. Instead, Judge Hirsch listened to Maria for less than five minutes, denied the order of protection, and sent Maria back to live with her abuser.

In April of 1995, I received a call from Charlotte Watson, Executive Director of My Sisters' Place. I had been working with Charlotte to seek changes in the court system in response to the Douglas murder. Charlotte told me about Maria Delgado and asked if I could help.

The History of Abuse

I made an appointment to meet with Maria the next day. She was a short woman in her mid-twenties, with shoulder-length blond hair and a slim figure. My client was friendly, but nervous. Maria was outraged at the treatment she had received in court, but, at the same time, wondered if there was some justification for it. She hated the way her husband treated her, but worried that somehow she shared the blame.

Maria and Michael Delgado had been married for five years and had a four-year-old daughter, Christina. Michael worked for the phone company. Maria did not work outside the home, but occasionally gave manicures. The marital home was a rented apartment.

It is common for everyone, and particularly for insecure, battered victims of domestic violence, to be nervous when going to court. Sometimes they forget to tell the judge about critical events. Often they do not remember or understand what the judge says. I wondered if this could have happened to Maria, but she gave me a transcript of her appearance before Judge Hirsch. The transcript clearly demonstrated that Maria had told the court about an incident in which her husband grabbed their daughter and threw her across the room, leaving marks on the little girl's arm. Maria also told the judge that her husband had sexually abused her. Judge Hirsch never asked for the specifics of the sexual abuse or sought to understand what Maria was referring to.

Maria had followed the normal procedure to obtain an order of protection. She went to the court and met with someone from the Probation Department. Maria filled out the petition, which is a two-page form. She provided information about her husband's abuse and requested an order of protection that would include a provision requiring him to stay away from the marital home. Maria then appeared before the judge. She was sworn in and stated under oath that the allegations contained in the petition were true.

When a petition contains allegations of a family offense (usually harassment, assault, disorderly conduct, or other criminal conduct within the family), and there is no reason to disbelieve the allegations, a temporary order of protection is routinely granted. In my judgment, Maria satisfied the prerequisites for the order; it was unusual and improper for the order to be denied. The judge did not dismiss the petition, but Maria did not understand that she could still obtain an order of protection if she prevailed at a trial. She therefore failed to serve her husband with the papers, and the petition was dismissed.

We decided to file a new petition with the court, but this time I would prepare it. We needed to include as many examples and as much detail as possible so the judge would have to grant the order of protection. At first, Maria could not tell me of other instances of abuse. This is a common problem, caused by the victim's belief that some types of abuse are acceptable and legal.

"You don't have to have marks, bruises, or broken bones in order for there to be abuse," I explained. "There is a big difference between spousal abuse and child abuse. A parent is permitted to hit a child. Therefore it is sometimes hard to determine the line where discipline ends and abuse begins. With spousal abuse, there is no such problem. Any nonconsensual touching is improper."

Maria thought that she had certain wifely obligations that required her to accept abusive behavior from her husband. Even before they were married, during intercourse he would sometimes spank her. She did not like it, but did not object. After they were married, the spankings gradually became harder and more unpleasant. She told him that it hurt and she wanted him to stop. Repeatedly, she told him not to spank her any more. Michael responded by saying that it didn't hurt and that she really liked it. The spankings became so severe that her bottom became numb and there was redness and soreness for a day after the abuse.

Maria also complained that while she was working in the kitchen or elsewhere in the apartment, Michael would slap her bottom hard and rub up against her in a sexual way. She felt demeaned by his actions. Maria told Michael that this hurt and she did not want him to do it, but he continued to do it whenever he wished. On several occasions, Michael rubbed his penis against her bottom and ejaculated on her without permission. On another occasion, he kept squeezing her arms and legs while trying to persuade her to have sex. Maria started sleeping on the couch to get away from him, and he insisted that if she entered the bedroom, he was entitled to have sex with her.

I spent time during our meetings trying to make Maria feel better about herself. The fact that she had remained with her husband all that time did not mean she wanted the abuse or that she deserved it. It may not seem logical to stay with an abuser under such circumstances, but it is common. Maria needed to know that she was not alone. The average abused spouse makes seven attempts to leave her husband before she is successful. Each time she tries, the woman learns a little more about the services available and how to make it on her own. Maria was dependent on her husband financially and emotionally, and Michael had told her that if she ever left, he would receive custody of their daughter. Under the circumstances, Maria displayed great courage in seeking protection.

Maria had started a divorce action and obtained permission to proceed as a "poor person," a designation that waives court costs and results in the appointment of a no-fee attorney. In Westchester, attorneys are generally assigned one or two "poor person" divorce cases per year. They are required to represent the client without charge, but can seek compensation from the client's spouse in appropriate cases. Maria was unhappy with her appointed attorney because he did not return her calls and was unfamiliar with abuse issues. She wanted me to represent her in the divorce. I agreed to take her case, and her original attorney was happy to cooperate in the substitution.

Maria's major concern was custody. Shortly after the birth of Christina, Maria had been hospitalized for depression. She was still in therapy and taking medication. Michael was threatening to use this condition to obtain custody. Throughout the marriage, he had made fun of her condition and put her down. Accordingly, she had low self-esteem. The pressure of a contested divorce would not be good for her, but she needed sole custody.

Maria was also afraid her husband would make allegations concerning drug use. Prior to and early in the marriage, they had both used cocaine. The early spanking incidents occurred when they were both high. Michael had been the one to obtain the drugs and used them more than Maria; nevertheless, he threatened to reveal the drug use in any custody battle. Throughout the marriage, Michael had made false accusations that Maria was sleeping with other men, and she thought this would come up in a trial. In my experience, it is common for abusers to make such false accusations as part of their effort to control their partners.

The Order of Protection

I prepared a detailed petition for an order of protection that included all the recent instances of abuse. We specifically mentioned that Michael had relatives he could stay with. This was included so that the judge would have no excuse to keep Michael in the marital home. Normally, a woman could easily obtain a temporary order of protection with these allegations, and there would be no need for an attorney until the preliminary hearing. I made arrangements to go to court with Maria the next day, because of the prior denial by Judge Hirsch.

We waited most of the morning to appear before Judge Hirsch. She questioned Maria closely about the allegations and finally agreed to issue the order of protection. I explained the need to remove Michael from the home. We were afraid he would react violently to the order of protection. Maria told the judge that if her husband was not removed from the home, she would have to leave in order to be safe. Courts are reluctant to remove someone from his home, especially when the person is not in court and able to state his side of the dispute. However, a judge can and should remove someone when there is good reason to believe the petitioner would not be safe otherwise. In my judgment, this protection should have been provided to Anne Scripps Douglas. But Judge Hirsch had not learned anything from the Douglas case. Our request to remove Michael Delgado was denied, forcing Maria and Christina to leave their home.

Maria moved to her parents' apartment with Christina. Michael was served with the order of protection and the petition when he came home from work at about 10:30 P.M. He immediately called Maria and started yelling at her. She tried to calm him down and explain why her actions were necessary, but he continued his harassment. Maria hung up and called the police. They tried to discourage her from enforcing the order of protection, but she insisted. Within an hour of being served, Michael was arrested for violating the order of protection.

I learned of the arrest early the next morning when I was awakened at home by a phone call. I met Maria at the courthouse. She had to file a violation petition in connection with the harassment for which her husband had been arrested. Maria was nervous and upset, but she was also proud that she had had the courage to stand up for her rights. She would not have been able to do this even a month earlier. Maria's father was with her to provide support.

Edward Larson was Michael's attorney. He immediately claimed that the arrest of his client was outrageous and that the order of protection should be dismissed because it had been misused. He made it sound like it was Maria's fault that Michael was arrested so soon after service of the order of protection.

Judge Sophie Hirsch met in conference with the two attorneys. Judge Hirsch had been elected to the bench two years earlier. When she ran for office, Hirsch knew enough about abuse to say all the right things, but she had been a disappointment since taking office. She still knew what to say about abuse and was capable of doing a good job on some cases. Unfortunately, there were too many cases, like the one involving Mrs. Douglas, in which Judge Hirsch's actions were inexcusable.

After a brief discussion of the circumstances, the judge told us that the likely outcome was that Michael would be released from jail, the order of protection would remain, and a trial would be scheduled. I argued that the violation of the order demonstrated that Michael should be removed from the home. The court's failure to remove Michael had forced the victims of the abuse to move out of their home, which was unfair. The judge refused to modify the order of protection. She asked the parties to try to settle the matter. If this was not done, an arrangement regarding visitation with the child was needed.

The order of protection was on behalf of Maria and Christina. The petition included the incident when Michael threw Christina across the room, leaving marks on her body. He would be ordered to stay away from Christina except for scheduled visitation. Therefore some visitation arrangement was needed, although custody and visitation were not pending in Family Court. Maria had no objection to reasonable visitation, because aside from the one incident discussed above, Michael had not physically abused his daughter. He did not spend much time caring for Christina, but he loved her and tried to be a good father.

With no custody or visitation petition pending, we were in a good position to bargain on visitation. For the present, Michael could only obtain the visitation we agreed on. Furthermore, by putting the agreement in writing, we would obtain protection against the father taking the child for visitation and failing to return her. I advised my client to be reasonable. If we agreed to reasonable visitation, it was unlikely to be changed if a petition was later filed.

The Abuser Fights Back

I met with Edward Larson to negotiate a visitation arrangement. He told me that his client had unlimited resources for legal fees and would do whatever was necessary to fight the abuse allegations and obtain custody. I suggested that if he had so much money for legal fees, Michael could pay my fees as well. Larson said the money was coming from Michael's brother and that Michael himself had little income and no assets. He suggested I go easy on this case because I could never collect any legal fees.

Larson implied that he had attended a meeting that was called to support people accused of abuse. They were planning to attack women who made accusations of abuse and to target the professionals helping them. The complaint Woody Allen filed against the prosecutor in Connecticut came as a result of this meeting. (When the prosecutor announced that Allen would not be charged in the sexual abuse of his daughter, the prosecutor expressed his opinion that Allen had in fact committed the abuse. Allen responded by filing a grievance against the prosecutor for this statement.)

I did not know if Larson's claims were true, but the implication was that they would use frivolous lawsuits and baseless complaints to the Bar Association in order to discourage women from protecting themselves against abuse. Although such actions would be unlikely to prevail on their merits, the time and expense necessary to defend them would bankrupt the victims of abuse and make it too expensive for lawyers or other professionals to help them. These threats were disturbing, because advocates for abusers had already succeeded in slowing the progress against domestic violence by using false and exaggerated claims—such as that women often make false accusations of abuse to gain an advantage in custody or divorce disputes, that children who don't want to see their father have been brainwashed by their mother (Parental Alienation Syndrome), and that women have an unfair advantage in the courts.

An attorney is required to defend his client zealously within the confines of the law. A client's right to counsel would be impaired if an attorney had to worry about false and frivolous charges and lawsuits in response to an allegation of abuse. Abusers often have more money and resources for lawyers and litigation than their victims, who frequently must rely on attorneys who will take cases pro bono or for greatly reduced fees. This threat of reprisals could make it even more difficult for victims to obtain competent representation. The uneven battle could tilt further in favor of the abusers. I sent a letter to Mr. Larson in which I repeated his threats (so there would be a record of them) and let him know I would not be intimidated.

I was also concerned about the larger problem of the backlash in the courts against victims of domestic violence and their advocates. Abusers and their apologists have enjoyed significant success in discrediting the valid complaints of domestic violence victims. Although women and children rarely invent false allegations of sexual abuse, in more and more courts you will hear attorneys for abusers, and even some judges, talk about mothers playing the "sex abuse card," instead of recognizing a deeply hidden problem coming to the surface. Some courts have taken to discounting the testimony of qualified mental health professionals because "they always find abuse." *They find abuse because it exists.* Some journalists think that fairness requires them to produce stories about false accusations of abuse and about men who are abused. The reporting often fails to make clear the infrequency of such events in comparison with the domestic violence the reporters are trying to balance.

I used to believe that gradually, as society and the courts became more aware of domestic violence and more victims stepped forward, courts would improve, and there would be fewer tragedies caused by the courts. In fact, over time, there have been some improvements. Recently, however, this backlash has stopped the progress and in some ways moved things backwards.

Visitation Negotiations

In the Delgado case, "normal" visitation would be every other weekend from Friday to Sunday, and possibly an additional weekday for a few hours. Maria was willing to permit this amount of visitation. Larson suggested that the time with the child be shared equally, as in a joint custody arrangement. I made it clear that this was out of the question. Furthermore, Michael worked full time (sometimes at night) and was not available for so much visitation.

Ultimately, we reached a compromise whereby Michael had visitation every other weekend from Friday night until Sunday evening. On the weeks that the father had weekend visitation, he received one extra day for four hours, and on the other weeks he received two extra days for four hours each. The agreement also provided for regular telephone calls. The father was required to provide 24-hour notice of any change in visitation. Both parties were forbidden to make any derogatory remarks about the other parent in front of Christina.

Larson promised that if I persuaded Maria to accept this proposal, he would use his influence to make Michael more cooperative. Maria preferred less visitation, but agreed to the proposal in the interests of harmony and to establish the precedent of the child residing with her.

The parties and the attorneys were called into the court. We advised Judge Hirsch of the agreement, and it was read into the record. Michael denied the charges in the petitions regarding the family offense and violation (the threatening phone call). The judge stated that she would release him from jail (where he had spent the night). As a result of the alleged violation of the order, I moved that the order of protection be amended to remove Michael from the marital home so that Maria and Christina could return. The judge denied my motion, but agreed to amend the order to require Michael to stay away from Maria and Christina except for scheduled visitation.

Larson moved to have the petitions dismissed. He referred to the subject of the petitioner's allegations as the parties "merely engaging in rough sex." The motion was denied. Larson then asked to have joint orders of protection. Such orders are useless, as explained in Chapter 1. It has become common practice for abusers to seek orders of protection to nullify their victim's order. Too many judges have permitted this tactic to succeed on the idea that it treats both parties equally.

The law prohibits mutual orders of protection if only one party has filed a petition. Michael had no petition pending; therefore, the motion had to be rejected. Larson started to reargue the same motions as the judge grew impatient. It was obvious that Larson was unfamiliar with Family Court procedure. Judge Hirsch finally ordered him to stop.

The trial was scheduled for August. We were particularly pleased with the date of the trial. Judge Hirsch was scheduled to be transferred to the Yonkers Court before that time, so the case would be heard by a more favorable judge.

The Divorce Action

Maria and I started work on the divorce action. The complaint prepared by her prior attorney was incomplete and faulty. We were permitted to amend the complaint because her husband had not yet served an answer. The complaint was amended to reflect most of the incidents of abuse. We also prepared a *pendente lite* motion (a motion which seeks temporary relief while the divorce action is pending). The motion sought custody, child support, maintenance, personal property left in the marital residence, and legal fees.

The new Family Court judge in New Rochelle was Patricia Moakley. Judge Moakley had been elected to the bench two years earlier. She was experienced in domestic relations in general and domestic violence in particular. This judge was widely respected because of her willingness and ability to listen. She had been moved to New Rochelle to clean up the problems left by Judge Hirsch; it was rumored that this was in response to the Douglas murder.

Judge Moakley met with the attorneys before trial to seek a settlement. She told me that even if we proved everything in our case, Michael would not be punished beyond the time he had already spent in jail. She told Larson that if Maria testified at all credibly to the allegations in the petition, she would receive the permanent order of protection. Accordingly, there was no reason to try the case. We quickly reached an agreement whereby Michael did not admit or deny the allegations, but Maria received a permanent order of protection. The violation petition was withdrawn.

The parties and their attorneys met in the courthouse in an attempt to settle the Supreme Court action. For the first time, Michael indicated that he might be willing to forgo his request for joint custody. This had been a major roadblock to settlement. Courts like the idea of joint custody because it saves them from having to decide a difficult issue. Some judges mistakenly view this arrangement as beneficial to the children; it may also make the collection of child support easier.

The problem is that joint custody does not work unless the parents are on good terms and can cooperate with each other. This, of course, applies to few couples getting divorced. Joint custody is never appropriate where there has been abuse, as in the Delgados' case. Abusers have made the request for custody or joint custody a standard tactic in divorce actions. They do this to better their bargaining position (some mothers will give up all financial rights in exchange for their children) and as a way to control their wives. I have seen many cases where mothers were pressured to accept joint custody and were sorry afterwards.

Most of the discussion centered around the visitation schedule. Each party wanted more time with their daughter then the existing schedule permitted. Michael complained that Maria had much more time with Christina than he did and thought this should be evened out. Maria pointed out that if you considered the time Christina was unavailable because she was sleeping or at school, Maria actually had relatively little time with her. Furthermore, Michael could do all the fun things with Christina, while Maria had to do the responsible things required of a custodial parent. Under the existing arrangement, Michael had his daughter six of every fourteen days, and Maria had to handle all the obligations during her eight days. When holidays and vacations with Michael were included, Maria would have very limited quality time with her daughter.

Michael's attitude was that the more visitation he had, the better it would be for Christina. He did not want to understand that it was beneficial to Christina to have fun times with her mother as well. The parties were able to agree on holiday, summer, and every-other-weekend visitation, but they could not agree on whether the father should have one or two extra weekdays every week. At one point Michael was willing to agree to one weekday per week, but Larson quickly sabotaged the agreement by threatening to quit as Michael's attorney if he made the deal.

We ended the meeting close to a deal on custody and visitation. No serious discussions on the financial issues had begun. Michael wanted Maria to waive maintenance in return for his agreement not to seek custody, but we did not agree to this proposal.

Edward Larson delayed the Supreme Court motion with three adjournments. The court scheduled a preliminary conference while waiting for the answering papers to the motion. The case was assigned to Judge Harold Schwartz. Judge Schwartz had been elected to the Supreme Court two years earlier, but I had not met him before this case. He turned out to be reasonable and accommodating. In conference, we quickly agreed that there was no reason to try the case. We told him of the progress we had made on custody and visitation. He made suggestions regarding child support and maintenance which became the basis of settlement.

Michael was planning to file for bankruptcy to obtain relief from some credit card and other debts. Larson suggested that if Michael and Maria both went bankrupt, this would take care of her debts and they both could start fresh. Michael agreed to pay the cost of the joint bankruptcy. The judge said I was probably entitled to some legal fees, but Michael would not agree to pay them. Instead, we agreed that if the other issues could be settled, Judge Schwartz would determine the issue of legal fees based upon affidavits to be submitted by each party.

I spoke with Larson a few times between court appearances. We worked out a visitation arrangement. The every-other-weekend visitation would be extended to Monday morning. This would give Michael more time with Christina, but require him to take responsibility for getting her ready for school on Monday. He would have only one other day per week for four hours. Michael also agreed to pay me $500 in legal fees, which Larson promised would be paid.

We returned to court to place the agreement on the record. Larson arrived an hour late and then stated that we did not have an agreement because there were new issues they wished to discuss. Michael refused to file a joint bankruptcy on the grounds that Maria had failed to declare income for her manicures. He was afraid this would result in the bankruptcy petition being denied. Michael now wanted two extra days per week in visitation in addition to the Friday-to-Monday weekend visitation. He also demanded new language restricting Maria's right to move out of the immediate area. We had previously agreed that she could not move more than 35 miles from the marital residence. Now they demanded that she also could not move outside New York State.

I was angry that they were raising new issues after we had compromised on the other issues and reached a complete agreement. I told Larson that this was not an honorable way to conduct business. Judge Schwartz suggested that they drop the request on the residency and the second extra visitation day and that we drop the joint bankruptcy. Michael and Maria agreed to this compromise, and it looked as if the divorce would go forward. But Larson talked to Michael again, and thereafter Michael refused to compromise. Maria felt pressured to finish the divorce and agreed, against my advice, to Michael's demand that she remain in New York State. Again, Michael wanted to settle and again Larson talked him out of it. When an agreement could not be reached, a trial was scheduled.

On the day of the trial, Judge Schwartz met with the parties and the attorneys in an attempt to settle the case. Larson raised new issues. He wanted a provision that, if Maria was unavailable to take care of Christina (for instance, if she was hospitalized), Michael would have visitation. He also wanted notice if Maria had to take the child out of state, even in an emergency. The proposals were not so terrible, but it was unfair to raise such issues at the last minute. We spent almost the entire day negotiating. I warned Larson that if we had to spend more time negotiating new issues, I would demand additional legal fees.

Larson threatened to try the whole case, including custody, if he did not get what he wanted. Judge Schwartz told him it would be improper to seek custody in order to win a little extra visitation. The judge said that this would not be in the best interests of the child and implied he would hold it against Michael. This statement helped break the logjam. The parties agreed that Michael would receive one extra day on weeks he had weekend visitation and two extra days when there was no weekend visitation. Michael would take Christina if Maria was unavailable for more than 72 hours. If Maria had to take Christina out of state in an emergency, she would provide notice if practicable. Michael was required to pay $1000 in legal fees. The agreement was placed on the record and the parties were divorced.

Less than a year after the divorce, Maria remarried, and a few months later she gave birth to a son. Ten months after the marriage, a terrified Maria called to tell me that her new husband was abusing her. This was discouraging news after we had worked so hard to free her from an abusive husband, but the work was not wasted. This time, Maria quickly recognized the problem, pressed criminal charges, and left the marriage. She is now attending college and trying to make a safe life for herself and her children.

Chapter 5

RECOVERING FROM SEXUAL ABUSE

The Boyd Case

OVER THE YEARS, My Sisters' Place has helped thousands of women and children overcome the harmful effects of abuse. The organization runs two shelters for battered women, several support groups, educational programs, and many other activities. The school program has always been my favorite. Staff members and volunteers go to several schools each year to teach children about the different forms of abuse, provide a forum for the students to discuss their concerns about domestic violence, and provide counseling for anyone requesting help.

The other programs are designed to help people overcome the effects of abuse, but the school classes can prevent abuse from ever happening, which is what makes the Domestic Violence Education Program so exciting. The classes are held in high schools and junior high schools, and a pilot project has been started for sixth-graders. Some parents and school officials have been reluctant, however, to expose younger students to the program. They say the children are too young to hear about such issues and should not be exposed to these problems. Tammy Boyd knows better.

A Tragic Childhood

Tammy Boyd's father was an alcoholic and a binge drinker. He grew up in an alcoholic family, and as a boy he was frequently beaten. His father made his own wine and made it strong. Tammy's mother also was a binge drinker. Tammy's parents had frequent arguments, which often ended with her father beating her mother. The mother was unwilling or unable to protect herself or her children. Tammy had three brothers and two sisters, ranging in age from eleven years older to six years younger than Tammy. Tammy's father regularly beat his sons and verbally abused his daughters. The family was a disaster waiting to happen.

The family lived in Duchess County, about 100 miles north of New York City. Tammy's father worked as a driver for the State Transportation Department and later as a chef. He lost the transportation job because of his drinking. He continued drinking until he had a heart attack, when he was 65 and Tammy was 18. He died 15 years later. Tammy's mother is still living.

Tammy was born in 1956. As a child, she never knew what to expect. There were days when her father was happy and the home was relaxed. At other times, her father would be sad and depressed. Tammy did not know the changes were caused by his drinking. The worst of the drinking generally took place on the weekends. Tammy learned to accept whatever treatment she might suffer and to keep the family's secrets. These are common attributes of children of alcoholics, which make them especially vulnerable.

Richard was the third child born to this family. He was eight years older than Tammy and ran with a bad crowd from an early age. His friends were several years older and often in trouble. They introduced him to drugs when he was only eleven or twelve. Richard was sent to a boys' school when he was 16 after getting into trouble. He became an active alcoholic like his father and spent much of his adult life in jail for crimes involving drugs and robbery. The worst robbery was what he did to his sister.

It started when Tammy was only three years old and Richard was eleven. While their parents were drinking and fighting, Richard was supposed to watch Tammy as they played in a cornfield. This is when the sexual abuse started. Richard would pull down her shorts and fondle her crotch and bottom. He would take sticks and insert them into Tammy's anus. He may have started the spankings then, but Tammy is not sure. The "play" continued in the cornfield for several months until the family moved. Then the location changed, but Richard's abuse continued for five years. Tammy recently discovered that another brother had watched this abuse and done nothing to help her.

In the new home, the abuse generally occurred after Tammy had gone to sleep. Richard would wake her up and take her to his room. The abuse would last a few hours. During these sessions, Richard removed whatever clothes Tammy was wearing, spanked her bare bottom, fondled her crotch and bottom, stuck sticks and other objects up her rectum, and made her perform oral sex on him. There was no set order to the various types of abuse; frequently some of the activities were repeated. The abuse sessions took place once per week and sometimes more.

The spankings were lengthy and grew harder and more painful over time. The severity of the spankings increased as Richard increased his drug use. Tammy remembers the glassy look in her brother's eyes when he abused her, but at the time did not understand the connection with drug use. Tammy had to endure the spankings without yelling because her brother threatened to kill her if she made noise. Richard's room was in the attic, which helped him to abuse his sister without their parents hearing what was happening. The parents, absorbed with their drinking and fighting, provided little supervision for their children.

As Richard sank deeper into drugs, the spankings became ever more severe, and Tammy had more difficulty enduring the abuse. After some particularly severe spankings she had to ask permission to stand in school because it was too painful to sit. She made up excuses for why she needed to stand. The discomfort of sitting was caused by the objects inserted in her anus as well as by the spankings.

Finally, Tammy decided to seek help in ending the abuse. She told her mother what had been happening, but her mother refused to believe her. Tammy next told her guidance counselor. Her schoolwork had deteriorated because she was up late being abused, and at times she had fallen asleep in class. When the guidance counselor called her in to find out what the problem was, Tammy asked the counselor to "tell my mom and dad to make him stop." Tammy says today that she would not have been able to tell if the counselor had been a man.

As Tammy left the office, the counselor was making a call to help her. When Tammy returned home from school, she learned her brother had been sent to a boys' school. Tammy does not know how this came about, but Richard was also in trouble for stealing, and the two problems seem to have contributed to the decision to send Richard away.

After Richard was sent away, Tammy was one happy girl. There is a marked difference between her school pictures in first and second grade, when she was downcast and did not look at the camera, and third grade, when she had the biggest smile ever. Tammy was glad the physical abuse was over, but nothing was done to help her recover emotionally. Her parents refused to discuss the abuse. Her father did not believe in therapy, and this eight-year-old little girl was left to cope with the aftermath of her brother's abuse on her own.

Despite their son's abuse of their daughter, Tammy's parents always regretted signing the papers to send Richard to the boys' school. They believe Richard learned to be a criminal at this school. He spent most of his life in prison for drug and robbery offenses. In the last few years, Richard has been out of jail and on SSI for his alcoholism. He has stayed out of trouble, but remains a danger. Tammy sees him occasionally at family functions, but they have never discussed his abuse.

The Aftermath of Abuse

The sexual abuse of Tammy occurred well before such issues were a common subject for media attention and public awareness. Much valuable work has been done concerning the treatment of incest survivors. Books by Laura Davis, Ellen Bass, Suzanne Sgroi, and others have helped victims of such abuse and their supporters. It is important to understand that help is available and can make a big difference in people's lives. Tammy was denied this help until a few years ago.

People have to have ways to cope with life's problems. We all use defense mechanisms, which can be a healthy way of helping us get through difficult situations. When the problem subsides, however, the defense mechanisms can be detrimental to a person's health and well-being. This is why therapy is so important in overcoming the effects of incest. Surprisingly, the chances of recovery without treatment for someone subjected to "minor abuse," such as a single incident of fondling, are not much better than for those subjected to serious sexual abuse, such as Tammy or the Wong daughters (described in Chapter 2). In each case the sense of trust and safety has been violated. How do you develop an ability to trust if your father or brother could do such a thing to you?

On the other hand, the prognosis for victims of either "minor" or serious sexual abuse is excellent with early treatment by a therapist who understands abuse issues. Often victims of more serious abuse are more likely to recover because they are more likely to receive treatment. The need for treatment is more likely to be understood for a victim who was brutally raped than for one who was "just fondled."

It is important for the victim to understand that she is not to blame for what happened and did not deserve the mistreatment. It is common for victims to blame themselves. Tammy felt guilty because part of the abuse was pleasurable. She received pleasure from the fondling and thought there was something wrong with her. These feelings are particularly hard for a young child to understand.

Although Tammy was happy that the abuse stopped, she had no opportunity to heal. She had no one she could talk with about what had happened. Her defense mechanisms helped her to forget. After several years Tammy could no longer remember the abuse, but it continued to harm her in many ways.

Throughout her life, Tammy has had problems with trust, particularly of men. She did not date until she was eighteen, then married at nineteen. She was uncomfortable performing oral sex, and indeed often wanted nothing to do with sex at all. Like many abused women, Tammy is uncomfortable having people touch her. Even an innocent hug or hand on her shoulder by someone she likes and trusts can be uncomfortable. The man she married was controlling and abusive, but she stayed long after she realized she did not want to be married to him. Eventually she learned that ignoring or hiding the problem did not make it go away.

When Tammy started dating, she was aware of the problems in her family and anxious to avoid such problems, particularly the alcoholism. When she was 19, Tammy started dating Norman Boyd. He was a serious man studying to be an engineer. Tammy particularly noticed that he did not use drugs or alcohol. She thought she was breaking the cycle when she married him.

One day after they were married, Norm was giving her a massage as part of foreplay. He started to spank her, not hard, but for sexual gratification. The sound of the slaps on her bottom reminded her of the previous abuse, and sent shivers down her spine. Tammy told Norm she did not like what he was doing, and he stopped. At the time, she remembered vaguely that there had been some abuse involving her brother, but did not recall most of the details. Tammy did not discuss it further with Norm. She also had flashbacks triggered by movies, television programs, or other events. Over time, she became more aware of her childhood abuse.

Norman Boyd became an engineer and the couple prospered. Over the seventeen years they were married, they came to own three houses and lived a middle-class lifestyle. They had two daughters, who are now eight and twelve. The older girl is moderately retarded and has cerebral palsy. Taking care of her has been expensive and time-consuming.

There were problems in the marriage almost from the start. Norm pressured Tammy into having an abortion at the beginning of their relationship. Two years later she suffered a miscarriage. Norm has a rigid and controlling personality. He kept control of the family finances and made most family decisions. Tammy was unable to stand up to Norm or insist on her rights. There were also abusive incidents in which Norm forced Tammy to have sex against her will, and some physical abuse, such as pushing her.

Disputes over sex and other issues led to marriage counseling. Norm found a therapist to do joint therapy. It is inappropriate to conduct therapy with both parties in the room when one of the parties is abusive. A therapist familiar with abuse issues would know this, but the therapist Norm selected was quite ignorant about domestic violence. His idea to solve the problem was for Tammy to wear sexy negligees. Tammy quickly ended the counseling sessions.

She started her own therapy with Dr. Jan Woolsey, a psychologist. This was the first time Tammy received treatment related to the abuse by her brother. She gradually recovered much of her memory of the incest. It was painful to remember, but helped her feel better. In one session, Dr. Woolsey pointed to an empty chair, pretended it was the three-year-old Tammy, and asked Tammy to tell her child self what she had done wrong. In that instant, Tammy came to understand, in her heart as well as her head, that she was not to blame. She continued to make progress with Dr. Woolsey until Norm stopped paying for the therapy when the couple were about to start divorce proceedings.

The Custody Issue

As the marriage deteriorated, each party sought custody in Putnam County Family Court. Tammy hired a local attorney to represent her. He was a good attorney, but became involved in running for office. As a result he did not have the time to represent her. Tammy consulted with the Putnam County Women's Center, who recommended me because of my work with victims of domestic violence.

I met with Tammy at my office prior to a scheduled court conference. She wanted sole custody of her children, but had no objection to giving her husband normal visitation. The parties were still living in the same home. Tammy wanted to win custody before separating from her husband. Her daughters were then four and eight, and Tammy stayed home to take care of them. Norm was involved with his daughters' care—especially that of Jill, the older, disabled child—but my client was the primary parent. We hoped this would help her win custody.

Tammy described Norm as controlling, but stated there were only minor incidents of abuse. She did not tell me about the sexual abuse she had suffered from her husband, nor did she mention the childhood sexual abuse; at the time she had only started to become aware of it. Later in my representation, Tammy confided in me about this abuse and we had several frank discussions. The subject was always painful, but as Tammy felt better about herself, she was more willing to speak openly with those she could trust.

The Family Court proceeding had been pending for three months when I made my first appearance. I had to catch up quickly. The law guardian was Mary Healy. She was an experienced lawyer in her late thirties, approachable and professional. Norm's attorney was Randi Herman, an experienced attorney in her mid-forties. She told me she had a reputation for being an attorney you could work with, and this proved to be accurate. Ms. Herman worked hard for her client, but did so without being rude or obnoxious. The judge was Francis McLaughlin, young, knowledgeable, but sometimes with a closed mind (Chapter 7).

When I arrived at the court, I met Ms. Healy and Ms. Herman. They suggested that I read the psychological report before we explored a possible settlement. The report stated that both parents loved their children and made positive contributions to their care. The strengths and weaknesses of the parents complemented each other. Norm was firm, but rigid. He was good at setting limits, but had difficulty showing flexibility or emotions. Tammy was good at providing the love and emotional support the girls needed, but had trouble setting limits. The report recommended joint custody, but stated that if this was not possible, Tammy should have custody.

The court had appointed a psychologist, Dr. Peter Wigoda, to work with the parties and help resolve their disputes. Tammy told me that Dr. Wigoda was helpful and that she had great confidence in him. Ms. Herman also spoke highly of Dr. Wigoda. Ms. Healy gave an oral report of Dr. Wigoda's recommendation. He had similar findings to those of the psychological report. His recommendation, however, was unusual. Dr. Wigoda suggested joint custody, with Jill living with her father and Molly living with her mother. Dr. Wigoda explained that Norm was better at working with Jill's therapy. It was particularly important that someone set limits for Jill. Molly could benefit more from her mother's warmth and flexibility. It is rare for a court to separate siblings, but Dr. Wigoda thought the girls would benefit from such an arrangement and still be able to spend time together.

The three attorneys met in an attempt to settle the case. Ms. Herman and I advocated for our clients, but it was done in a nonconfrontational manner. Ms. Healy did not take sides, but rather tried to promote an agreement. I believe if she had to pick one, Ms. Healy would have preferred Tammy for custody, but I was afraid this would change if she thought we were not cooperating.

We each initially recoiled at the idea of separating the children, but after a while, the idea seemed to have some merit. We discussed alternating the weekend visitation so that the girls would be together three of every four weekends and each girl could be alone with one parent the other weekend. We met briefly with Judge McLaughlin, but needed more time to consider the various possibilities. We agreed to take one more shot at settling the case before scheduling a trial.

I met with Tammy to prepare for the next conference. Aside from the issues concerning the children, Tammy needed to consider where she would be living and how to support herself and the girls. Tammy had made inquiries about a job and expected to be hired by the Post Office. This would require her to start work before the children left for school, but would allow her to take care of them after school. We worked out a proposal for joint custody whereby the girls would be with Tammy each weekday from after school until after dinner and alternate weekends. This would allow Norm to do his work and still have the girls in the evenings and mornings. It would satisfy his demand that the girls sleep in his home. The parties would alternate weekends. In order to make the plan work, Tammy had to have an apartment nearby. The parties owned three houses on the same block, two of which were being used as rental property. Norm had to provide an apartment for Tammy as part of the agreement.

Our other concern was about decision making. Joint custody means that the parents are supposed to share decisions. We anticipated that this would be a problem because Norm was so controlling and had so little regard for Tammy's opinions. We proposed that Dr. Wigoda continue working with the parties and that he could make decisions if the parties could not agree.

When I arrived at court, I presented the proposal to Ms. Healy and Ms. Herman. They each reacted positively to the proposal and it became the basis for the negotiations. With some modifications, the agreement was made and quickly approved by the judge.

Unfortunately, the agreement did not work as we had hoped. Tammy did not get the Post Office job and was available to spend time with her children that was not allowed under the agreement. Norm frequently made unilateral decisions and sometimes deprived her of scheduled visitation. We attempted to involve Dr. Wigoda, but Norm refused to go to sessions or listen to him. We filed complaints as part of the divorce, but beyond stopping the interference with visitation, little was accomplished. At first Tammy regretted allowing the girls to live with Norm, but now believes the arrangement has worked well for the children. Jill would be uncontrollable without the limits placed on her by Norm.

Financial Issues

With custody and visitation settled, the divorce should have been easy. Tammy wanted some maintenance for a year or two while she established herself on her own. She would have agreed to no child support. The marital property that had to be divided consisted of three houses and Norm's business. Two houses were in both names and not subject to dispute. Norm had owned half of the third house prior to the marriage, but bought the other half and paid the mortgage during the marriage. Tammy should have received part of the value of this house, and we were willing to settle for 25%. The value of the business would be hard to establish; Tammy would have accepted any reasonable offer. She was not looking to fight. The grounds for divorce in the complaint were cruel and inhuman treatment, but she would have accepted constructive abandonment as part of a complete settlement.

I discussed settlement with Ms. Herman at the beginning of the divorce. She agreed that the case should be easily settled, but could not obtain her client's cooperation. I decided to make a *pendente lite* motion, which tends to accelerate settlement of divorce cases. The temporary support award is usually a good indication of the final award and therefore becomes the basis for settlement of support issues. The legal expenses associated with the motion also encourage settlement, especially when the husband is required to pay his wife's legal fees.

Tammy did not have records of her husband's income. Based on a bank statement, we calculated his income at approximately $100,000 per year. We asked for maintenance and child support based upon this figure. The issue of child support was somewhat unusual in that the parties had joint custody and the children resided with Norm. Normally child support goes to the residential parent. In this case, however, Tammy spent most days with the children and gave them dinner most nights. We argued that the provision of the apartment and the residence of the children should reduce but not eliminate child support. We asked for medical and dental insurance. The medical insurance was particularly important because Tammy needed a hysterectomy and wanted to resume therapy with Dr. Woolsey. We asked that Norm pay for the operation and outstanding medical bills. One of the houses was in foreclosure, and we requested that Norm pay enough to avoid the foreclosure. I also sought legal fees.

In his reply, Norm claimed that his annual income was only $17,000. It was hard to believe that a professional engineer who had acquired three houses in fifteen years was earning so little. His failure to support his claim with tax returns or other financial documents ruined any chance of his convincing the judge. Tammy was pleased with the court's decision. She was awarded $150 per week in maintenance and $100 per week in child support. The judge ordered Norm to pay the mortgage and provide medical insurance, and said legal fees would be decided at the time of the trial.

The judge assigned to the case was Harold Chatsworth. I had some misgivings about him because of the report of another client (see Chapter 6), but he turned out to be a decent and courteous jurist with whom I have enjoyed working. My only criticism is that he sometimes gives too much benefit of the doubt to recalcitrant litigants.

The parties and attorneys were ordered to appear in court for a conference regarding discovery and settlement. Ms. Herman and I met together and with Judge Chatsworth in an effort to settle the case. We reached the parameters of a settlement which was worth about $100,000. Ms. Herman promised to explain the facts of life to Norm. It appeared that we had a settlement, but Norm wanted to discuss the logistics with his parents before agreeing. We scheduled depositions (sessions in which one party or other witness answers questions put by the other party's attorney) and other discovery in case the settlement fell through.

Norm rejected the settlement, so we went to Ms. Herman's office for the depositions. When we arrived, she told me there was a problem. Norm did not have the tax returns he was supposed to provide. Furthermore, he had not filed tax returns for the last several years. Under the circumstances, Ms. Herman quite properly refused to permit him to answer questions concerning his income or business.

Before starting the depositions, she and I had a conference call with the judge's law secretary. We agreed to complete Tammy's deposition and the other parts of Norm's deposition. Norm would attempt to prepare and file the tax returns as soon as possible. The law secretary implied that Norm would have to pay for the extra deposition made necessary by his refusal to answer questions, and that other sanctions would be considered. The depositions completed that day were uneventful.

Over the next several months, we had frequent problems with the payment of support and the completion of discovery. Norm was upset with the support order and did not pay any part of the support for several weeks. He made some payments when we had a conference scheduled, but the payments continued to be sporadic. Three times I had to make contempt motions in an attempt to collect the support. Each time the judge forced Norm to bring the payments up to date. After the third motion, Judge Chatsworth imposed sanctions of $500 in legal fees.

The law would permit deadbeat parents to be jailed under such circumstances, but in practice they are permitted to avoid contempt by making the payment at the last minute. This gives the offender the opportunity to delay payment, make his wife and children suffer, and take a shot at persuading the court to reduce the payments. Norm claimed that he had no money to pay support, but each time he was threatened with jail, the money magically appeared. Sometimes judges agree to reduce support in the hope of coaxing parents to pay. This obnoxious tactic is therefore frequently rewarded and rarely punished.

Ms. Herman made several promises about when discovery would be completed. Each time the deadline passed, there were more excuses. Twice I made motions seeking sanctions for the failure to provide discovery. Norm could have been barred from presenting evidence on issues relating to the discovery. The court reserved the right to take such action, but kept giving Norm more time. The obvious solution to Norm's problems was to settle the case.

Obstructionist Tactics

Norm had another idea. He fired Ms. Herman and replaced her with Louis Cino. I think Ms. Herman was glad to be off the case because Norm refused to follow her advice. Cino was hired to be more confrontational and obnoxious. In this, he succeeded.

Norm and his new attorney wanted to distract attention from the nonpayment of support and the failure to file tax returns. Cino did this by litigating issues long since decided. Tammy's right to an apartment was part of the custody agreement and had been considered by Judge Chatsworth in determining support. Cino tried to argue that the value of the apartment should be counted towards the support obligation, and later tried to have the obligation limited to a year or two. He feigned ignorance about his client's obligation to pay for a second deposition required by refusal to answer certain questions at the first deposition.

On the eve of trial, Norm made a motion to dismiss the divorce complaint on the grounds that we did not state a cause of action. In effect they were saying that the allegations that Norm had raped his wife were not serious enough to justify a divorce. Cino was obnoxious as he minimized the seriousness of Tammy's allegations. Norm did not prevail on any of these issues, but he did manage to waste time and increase legal fees.

The case took longer than divorce cases are supposed to take because of the delays associated with the tax returns and discovery. Judges have certain standards and time limits for moving their cases. Judge Chatsworth scheduled a trial date, but agreed to permit the discovery to continue pending the trial. With the consent of the parties he appointed Judge Nicholas Morgan to hear the case. Judge Morgan was an experienced jurist in his sixties, retired but serving as a Judicial Hearing Officer. He was a patient man, but his patience was tried by this case. Cino and I were constantly fighting in front of the judge. This was mostly Cino's fault, but the judge unfairly tended to blame us both equally.

A few weeks before the scheduled trial, Norm produced seven years' worth of tax returns and some other records at the continuation of his deposition. The returns were unsigned and had not been submitted to the IRS. Norm and his attorney claimed the returns would be submitted shortly. The returns declared an income of between $15,000 and $25,000. Norm had no system in place to record receipts for his business or rental income. He provided copies of paid engineering bills, but there was no way of knowing how many bills were missing. Norm acknowledged that he sometimes received cash payments and kept no records of such payments. He said this was rare, but we had no reason to believe him. The rental income was also partly in checks and partly in cash, with no way of determining how much income was being hidden.

The deposition was contentious with numerous objections and disputes. Each attorney threatened to walk out, and twice we needed a ruling from the judge's law secretary to complete the depositions. At the end of Norm's deposition, Cino tried to have another deposition of Tammy. Tammy had already completed her deposition, and the court order said we were only doing Norm's. Tammy and I left without taking any questions.

When Louis Cino replaced Randi Herman as Norm's attorney, it became obvious that the case would go to trial. We needed an expert witness to establish the value of Norm's business and his real income. My family's accountant recommended Ellen Kaplan. I provided her with all the financial records we had and forwarded the tax returns when I received them. Ms. Kaplan did a thorough and professional evaluation of the information. Her conclusion was that Norm was earning about $65,000 per year and the business was worth over $300,000.

Judge Morgan called the parties in a week before the trial date in an attempt to settle the case, or at least to narrow the issues. After listening to the attorneys present our views of the case, the judge attempted to broker a deal. We spent several hours attempting to reach an agreement. In the end, Tammy agreed to the judge's proposal, but Norm refused to settle. Judge Morgan tried again to settle the case before the trial started, and the next day while Ellen Kaplan was present. Each attempt failed.

The first issue at trial was the grounds for divorce. Norm claimed he wanted to stay married and opposed any divorce. He hoped to avoid any financial obligations if the divorce was dismissed. The grounds for divorce were cruel and inhuman treatment. Although there were a few instances when Norm had pushed Tammy, the main issue was several incidents in which he had raped her.

This was a "he says, she says" issue. Tammy testified about the rape incidents. The pain they had caused came through in her testimony. Cino tried to discredit Tammy by showing there were no police reports or medical records. (This is a standard defense for such issues.)

Norm absolutely denied the allegations. He was confident the divorce would be dismissed. But Judge Morgan believed Tammy's testimony and granted the divorce. Cino attributed this to my "emotional closing," in which I told the judge that the pain and embarrassment of Tammy's testimony were obvious and could not have been made up. Cino did not believe Tammy, but only an insensitive boor could have been oblivious to her pain. The remainder of the first day of trial was taken up by Tammy's financial testimony. She testified about the couple's lifestyle, the property they owned, and the cash Norm collected but did not record.

The key financial testimony would come from Ellen Kaplan. She was the only expert for either side. Her analysis would help determine Norm's income and the value of his business. She was an experienced accountant and had conducted evaluations of many small businesses. It was obvious that Ms. Kaplan had spent many hours preparing an evaluation of Norm's business. During her testimony, we learned that Judge Morgan had been a tax attorney before becoming a judge. He asked several technical questions and was satisfied with her answers. The entire second day of trial was given to Ms. Kaplan's testimony.

At the start of the third day of trial, Judge Morgan asked to meet with the attorneys. He told us there was no way he would treat the business as being worth anything close to the $300,000 projected by Ms. Kaplan. He also said that he would not consider the business to be worthless, as Norm sought to claim. He thought the business was worth between $75,000 and $100,000. We could both disagree, but obviously the final decision would approximate what the judge was saying.

Cino sought to gain credit for the medical bills and tax bills that were outstanding. The tax penalties and interest had been caused by Norm and should not have been Tammy's responsibility. The remaining bills, if they were actually to be paid, would be marital debt. Cino also tried to end the free apartment to which Tammy was entitled. I vehemently objected that this had been long since decided, and Norm could not go back on providing the apartment without giving up his right to residential custody, which he had obtained in return for the apartment. We spent several hours negotiating, but this time reached a settlement.

Tammy received $100,000, including $8,000 in legal fees and $2,000 for expert fees. She received an additional year of maintenance. The existing maintenance and child support levels remained in force. Neither party could seek to change support for one year. Norm had to continue supplying an apartment for Tammy, but could move her to an equivalent apartment in the same school district. If Norm did not pay the taxes, the credit he received for the taxes would be paid to Tammy. The money would be paid to Tammy within one year, with $15,000 coming within 30 days. Norm received all the real estate and was responsible for all debts.

Norm continued his practice of not paying support. I had to bring a new contempt motion before Judge Chatsworth. When we came to court, Norm agreed to pay the back support he owed. I asked the court for legal fees and sanctions in an attempt to stop Norm from continuing these violations. Judge Chatsworth did not order sanctions, but kept jurisdiction over the payments. I was permitted to restore the contempt motion to the court with a letter to the judge. I had to do this one time. When Norm saw how easily we could bring him to court, he started making the payments. The maintenance payments are now completed, but the child support is being paid on time.

Norm sought to force Tammy to move to a smaller apartment. Instead of speaking to Tammy or having his attorney speak with me, Norm just ordered her to move. When she refused, Cino sent a letter to Judge Morgan seeking to enforce the move. In an attempt to win a humanitarian award, Norm sought to make Tammy move less than a week after her hysterectomy.

The judge ordered us to appear for a conference. At the conference I showed the judge pictures of the two apartments. The new apartment had a long, dangerous flight of stairs that would be difficult for Jill to manage. Tammy would lose her washing machine and the outdoor play area for the children. Judge Morgan concluded that the new apartment was not an equivalent apartment. He finally realized that Cino was being totally unreasonable and let him know it in no uncertain terms. I wish he had done this much earlier. Since that conference, Norm has stopped harassing Tammy, and Cino is no longer representing Norm.

A Qualified Success

Tammy had the advantage of two good attorneys who worked hard for her. The two divorce judges were fair and reasonable. The Family Court Judge, though not a favorite of mine, had little role in the outcome. Tammy came out of the case with reasonable support and enough money to invest for some income. The children are enjoying significant and positive contributions from both parents. And yet . . .

Tammy has suffered through an unhappy life. She is an intelligent woman, but her potential has been stifled. Laws could be changed and judges trained so that women like Tammy are not made to pay for a husband's deliberate decision to prolong litigation. Lawyers like Louis Cino could be discouraged and sanctioned. Tammy spent $15,000 on legal fees. Even this amount would have been more if I had not agreed to cap my fees. Most lawyers would have charged much more. She also spent about $6,000 for the expert witness. Norm was only required to pay $8,000 in legal fees and $2,000 in expert fees, even though his improper actions were responsible for most of these costs.

When Tammy was three years old, people did not speak of incest. This attitude contributed to her brother's abuse of her and her family's failure to provide treatment after it was discovered. The widespread public dissemination of information about sexual abuse, including the much-vilified TV talk shows, helps fight the kind of abuse Tammy suffered. Judge Morgan was able to believe Tammy's testimony about sexual abuse by her husband, in part because of the training judges now receive.

Tammy has grown in the time I have known her, and even more since she was a scared, three-year-old little girl. I would like to think that in sharing her story, Tammy is fulfilling her potential. It is the potential that other children will not suffer as she did.

Chapter 6

THE CUSTODY CARD

The Horowitz Case

I RENE HOROWITZ WAS A LUCKY WOMAN. She would have been horri-
fied at such a characterization, but compared to other women in
similar circumstances, Irene had accomplished much. She won sole
custody of her daughter, Bonnie, and was entitled to significant child
support plus reimbursement for medical and child-care expenses. Irene
obtained the nursing position she had long wanted. The Supreme
Court and Family Court judges in her case were fair and reasonable.
She was even pleased with her attorney. All this, however, was not
enough to save her life.

Irene made many serious mistakes that jeopardized her case, and
also suffered from major psychological problems, but her case did not
have to end in tragedy. The attorneys for her husband could have discouraged him from pursuing unnecessary litigation. The good judges
in this case could have found a way to provide the help Irene needed.
The laws should be changed to prevent parents from withholding adequate support. Repeatedly, the judges overlooked Irene's faults in order
to help Bonnie. So why must Bonnie grow up without her mother?

This case involves not physical abuse, but verbal and emotional
abuse, which is often minimized but can have serious consequences.
Irene's story demonstrates some of the very destructive tactics often
engaged in by abusive husbands in the process of a divorce. The results
of these tactics in this case were particularly tragic.

The Background

Irene first contacted me in June of 1993. She had been through several attorneys, and was now representing herself in a divorce action. A
court conference and depositions were scheduled in two weeks, and the
trial was less than three months away. I was reluctant to take the case

because I was busy with another trial that conflicted with the scheduled conference in Irene's case, but she was persistent in seeking my help.

I agreed to prepare an affirmation in support of her motion for a delay in the depositions and an award of legal fees for me. I wrote the court that if I was awarded $2500 in legal fees as a retainer, and permitted time to complete my trial, I was willing to represent Irene in the divorce. The court refused to delay the depositions, but agreed to delay the conference (with which I had a conflict), and ordered Irene's husband to pay me $2500 in legal fees. I agreed to take the case.

Irene was 33 years old when I started representing her. She thought she was short and fat, but she was actually quite pretty. She had bleached-blonde hair, used heavy make-up and perfume, and wore short skirts. Some people thought she dressed provocatively, but in fact she had had no sexual relationships during the last several years of her life. Irene was often loud and profane, but at other times could be gentle and caring. She often demanded instant gratification, but could also spend countless hours trying to help people she had only recently met. She was filled with contradictions that led to many misunderstandings.

Irene's husband, Sam Horowitz, was in the shoe business. With his family, he owned part of two shoe stores and the building that housed the store where he worked. Sam claimed his income was limited to the $23,000 declared on his tax returns. Irene believed he made substantially more money in cash that was not declared to the IRS, and sought to prove this by using the family's bank statements and expenses. The documents demonstrated that Sam deposited and spent far more money each year than the declared income could justify. Sam responded by claiming to have received substantial gifts and loans from his mother. The president of the family shoe business was Sam's brother, David Horowitz. A long battle was fought over the depositions of Sam's family, but under the circumstances, such depositions were justified.

Irene described her husband as being stupid. She knew this was a common viewpoint about estranged spouses, but promised I would find it accurate. She told me about the time he had slammed something down on a glass table and been surprised when the table cracked. On another occasion Sam had tried to give their daughter Bonnie a suppository, but could not figure out what was wrong. He had failed to remove the aluminum foil! Irene also told me Sam's family never paid much attention to his ideas because they did not respect his intellect. Irene described Sam's mother as old and distracted; she could be expected to exaggerate her health problems, and would be too easily confused to make a good witness. Dave Horowitz was the smartest member of the family. He would have some understanding of the business, but was still limited. Despite my skepticism, Irene's characterizations proved accurate.

Sam's attorney was Ralph Dunne. He was the son of a judge and used to getting his way. Dunne was professional and pleasant with me, but antagonistic towards Irene. Irene said the antagonism had started after she rebuffed his sexual advances, but Dunne claimed to be outraged at Irene's treatment of Sam. It was only after hiring Dunne that Sam sought custody of Bonnie and reduced the support he was paying.

The divorce action had started two years earlier in Putnam County, where the parties then lived. The case was assigned to Judge Harold Chatsworth. The judge awarded Irene support that was generous if based upon the $23,000 income Sam was claiming, but limited if based on the $50,000 to $75,000 Irene claimed he really made. Irene repeatedly won orders requiring Sam to pay all or part of the cost for medical expenses, preschool, child care, and other costs necessary for five-year-old Bonnie. Sam often relitigated or ignored these awards. He also stopped paying the mortgage on the marital home despite court orders to make payments. Irene and Bonnie had to move in with Irene's parents in Scarsdale. Irene repeatedly requested penalties and sanctions against Sam for his violation of several orders. Judge Chatsworth refused to take action, and Irene was sure he was biased.

Irene was vocal in her denunciation of Judge Chatsworth. She made complaints to the administrative judge, Commission on Judicial Misconduct, and many individuals. She also expressed her complaints to Judge Chatsworth himself. While denying any bias, Judge Chatsworth voluntarily recused himself. Irene requested that the new judge be from outside Putnam County (because Judge Chatsworth's colleagues might be biased) and Westchester County (because Ralph Dunne's father was a judge in Westchester). The case was therefore assigned to Judge Roger Conway in Orange County.

Ralph Dunne was fond of mentioning that I was Irene's seventh attorney. The first attorney was disqualified because she had done some work for Sam concerning his business. The other attorneys left because of personality conflicts, excessive money demands, and the dissolution of a legal partnership. Irene also had problems with the law guardian, believing he favored Sam and did not take action to protect his client. The bitter dispute between Irene and the law guardian led him to withdraw from the case. By the time I joined the case, Irene believed that she was being severely mistreated by the legal system. While she could be difficult to work with, Irene had valid complaints. One attorney had charged $19,000 for one deposition and a simple motion. The marital home had been lost to incompetence and the failure to enforce orders.

The Depositions

I prepared Irene for her scheduled deposition as I would any client. I explained that the deposition was for her husband's benefit. She needed to answer all proper questions, but there would be no benefit to volunteering information. I could object to any improper questions. If she did not understand a question, Irene was to ask that it be repeated or rephrased. I told her never to guess at an answer, because if she guessed incorrectly it would be made to look as if she were lying. She should take the questions very literally, and answer only what was asked. Irene followed my instructions and proved to be a good witness.

Sam Horowitz was 35 years old. He stood 5 feet 8 inches with a medium build, short dark hair and a thin brown mustache. His clothes were inexpensive and it showed. Sam listened to his brother and lawyer, and rarely questioned them. He generally spoke in a quiet voice. At the deposition Sam showed himself to be ignorant about his business and unfamiliar with such items as scheduling, security practices, suppliers, and financing. He often answered questions by suggesting I ask Dave.

The next witness was Sam's mother, Mildred Horowitz. She was in her late seventies, but looked and acted older. Irene sought the deposition because Mildred claimed to have given Sam substantial sums of money. This is how he sought to explain the source of his bank deposits over and above his declared income. Mildred was trying to help her son with her testimony, but was confused about the money she was supposed to have given him. She had trouble remembering the allegations in her affidavit, in which she claimed to have given Sam substantial sums of money, often in cash, to help pay his expenses. In response to my questioning, Mrs. Horowitz acknowledged signing the affidavit without knowing what was in it. She said Ralph Dunne had not been present when she signed it. This was important because Dunne had notarized her signature. Mrs. Horowitz changed her story during Dunne's questioning, but it was obvious she would make a poor witness.

David Horowitz was slightly taller than his brother, slimmer and better dressed. Dave worked in both stores owned by the family. The stores were owned equally by Dave, Sam, and a cousin, while the building in which the first store was located was owned equally by those three along with two uncles.

Dave denied that any of the partners received cash from the stores. He acknowledged that significant sums of cash were taken in each day, and there were no internal controls to establish the income and expenditures. The money was counted and recorded by one of the partners in each store. Dave claimed this assured them that all the money would be counted. He further complained that business was bad and therefore a higher income was impossible.

Dave and Sam claimed that business had been bad for several years, but only a few years earlier the partners had expanded to the second store. Two years earlier, Sam had threatened to sue his partners and dissolve the business over improprieties. We had copies of the legal documents prepared by Sam's attorney, but the case had been settled before the papers were filed. Incredibly, Dave denied knowledge of the difficulties or the proposed lawsuit.

The Conference

The pre-trial conference had been adjourned until July. Irene and I decided to drive up to Goshen the night before in order to avoid the rush-hour traffic. This was a good opportunity to discuss the custody and visitation situation, which would be the focus of the conference.

Irene had always been the primary parent. When Sam was not working, he was usually watching television or playing computer games. There was no doubt Sam loved Bonnie and would not deliberately hurt her. He was, however, irresponsible and capable of neglecting her needs. Irene complained about incidents since the separation when Sam failed to dress Bonnie for the cold weather, did not take an umbrella when it rained, and failed to give Bonnie her medicine. These failures were due more to a lack of parenting skills than to malice.

When they first separated, Irene expected she would have custody and Sam would have reasonable visitation. She wanted to promote his relationship with Bonnie. When Sam's attorney persuaded him to seek custody, the case turned bitter, with the parties trying to hurt each other. Irene wanted to limit Sam's time with Bonnie because of his mistakes and neglect.

Judge Conway appointed a psychiatrist, Dr. Felix Schmidt, to give an evaluation of the parties. I was all too familiar with Dr. Schmidt—he was the psychiatrist in the Wong case (Chapter 2). I told Irene about the Wong case. Had I been involved in this case earlier, I would have objected to Dr. Schmidt, but it was too late now. Fortunately, Dr. Schmidt's major weakness is abuse cases, and abuse was not the focus of the Horowitz divorce.

Judge Conway ordered Sam to pay for the evaluation, but Sam claimed to have no money. This would be an issue at the conference. Dr. Schmidt told the new law guardian he would recommend Irene for custody. The law guardian agreed that Irene should have custody. It was clear that Irene was closer to Bonnie and the more responsible parent. Custody should not have been an issue. Sam, or more accurately, Dunne, was using this for negotiating purposes.

I had never appeared before Judge Roger Conway, but he had a good reputation. He was rumored to be in line for administrative judge of the district when the present judge retired. He had a quiet authority in the courtroom and a kindness in his personal relationships.

The law guardian was Renee Collins. Ms. Collins was forty years old, tall, slender, and fashionably dressed. I did not know her, but she was well thought of. Ms. Collins met with Bonnie about a week before the conference.

The judge met in chambers with the three attorneys. Judge Conway told Dunne he was doing him a favor by awarding me legal fees. The case should be settled and this was only possible if Irene was represented. It was not healthy or advisable for Dunne to work directly with Irene. Dunne agreed with the judge, but was not happy about the situation.

I suggested to the judge that there was no real custody issue, but that Sam had raised the issue for bargaining purposes. Dunne vehemently denied my charge, but Judge Conway warned that if the trial supported my allegation, Sam would be required to pay all legal expenses and would be dealt with severely. I was pleased the judge was considering these possibilities.

When the case was called, I raised the issue of Sam's failure to pay Dr. Schmidt and me. Dunne claimed Sam had no money and could not make the payments. The judge looked directly at Sam and said, "When I made the orders, I expected you to obey. If you have not made payment within five days, the court will entertain a motion for contempt. The court requests the law guardian to make the motion with respect to Dr. Schmidt, and Mr. Goldstein is welcome to make a motion for his fees. I expect the payments to be made!"

We then began a discussion of the custody issues. The judge repeated his concern about playing the "custody card." He said that if there was no real custody issue, the claims should be dropped immediately. Judge Conway looked at each party and continued, "There are only two possibilities. You [pointing to Sam] get custody or you [pointing to Irene] get custody. There is no way to have joint custody when the parties are so hostile to each other." He asked the attorneys to meet in an attempt to settle all or part of the case.

Judge Conway's statement about custody was one of the most brilliant statements I have ever heard from a judge. It cannot be in the child's best interest to have joint custody when the parents despise each other. Often one parent seeks joint custody for control, ego, or negotiation purposes. Too often judges encourage this in the interests of "compromise." The law does not permit the imposition of joint custody when the parties are hostile and unable to cooperate. Nevertheless, many judges pressure parties to accept joint custody under the implied threat of losing custody if they do not agree. Judge Conway made it clear that he would not impose such an unworkable arrangement. As a result, the custody and visitation were quickly and fairly settled.

After the judge's statement, Sam agreed that Irene could have sole custody, provided he was given acceptable visitation and notification. We spent most of the day working on a settlement. Irene wanted to limit Sam's visitation because he was often irresponsible in caring for Bonnie. She also wanted to limit his access to medical providers and school personnel because Sam often interfered with treatment in an effort to save money. One of Bonnie's doctors refused to speak with Sam because of his interference over her treatment. We also had concerns about the ability of Sam's mother to take care of Bonnie.

Sam was unaware of his limitations as a father. Even Dunne referred to Sam's limited intelligence to excuse improper behavior. Nevertheless, Sam sought extra visitation as "payment" for his concession about custody. There was also a dispute over Sam's taping of phone calls with Irene.

Irene's temper added to the difficulty of the negotiations. At one point, she started screaming at me uncontrollably in response to a proposal she objected to. Another time, when we appeared before the judge, Irene started yelling at Judge Conway. She was lucky he didn't hold her in contempt. The judge exercised great patience with everybody.

The final agreement provided visitation every other weekend from Friday evening to Monday morning (Sam would take Bonnie to school). This was slightly more than normal visitation, but had the virtue of reducing the exchanges between the parties, who were best kept separated. Sam also had visitation one night a week for three hours and certain holidays, plus two weeks' vacation in the summer. Sam was given the right to information from medical and other providers, but doctors and schools had a right to deny such information if they believed he was acting inappropriately. The parties were prohibited from taping conversations with each other. Sam's mother could not be left alone with Bonnie. We tried to require Sam to have counseling or parenting skills training, but he absolutely refused.

Judge Conway asked the attorneys if any other settlements were possible. Financial issues could not be resolved because of the basic disagreement about Sam's income. I suggested that we work on the grounds for divorce. We all believed it would be psychologically helpful to get the parties divorced. Both parties consented to a divorce based upon constructive abandonment.

The trip home felt like a celebration. Irene was lavish in her praise of Ms. Collins, Judge Conway, and me. Thereafter, Irene told everybody she met what a wonderful attorney I was. She also recommended me to several women who later became clients. The conference accomplished more than we had expected or even hoped for. Although Irene had always expected to win custody, it was such an important issue that even a small chance of losing was scary. This concern had been magnified by her previous problems with the court system.

The threat of contempt meant Sam would have to pay my legal fees. I received my legal fees (which Sam had said he was unable to pay) on the last day before I was authorized to start contempt proceedings. This was a good precedent for obtaining additional legal fees at the end of the trial. Judge Conway's actions provided great hope that we would have a fair trial regarding the remaining economic issues.

The Trial

The trial was scheduled for September, and the main issue was Sam's income. It is common for spouses to allege unreported income, but rare for it to be proven to the satisfaction of the court. We subpoenaed the bank records for Sam and Irene. Irene's mother, a bookkeeper, used these records to prepare spreadsheets showing the monies deposited and the expenses paid during the marriage. Each year, there were deposits of $20,000 or more that could not be accounted for.

A few days before trial, I went to Goshen to review the bank records of Sam's mother and other documents we had subpoenaed. In her affidavit, Mrs. Horowitz claimed to have given Sam substantial amounts of cash. She sought to support this claim by producing fifteen checks made out to cash. During her deposition, Mrs. Horowitz said she had given Sam all or most of the cash from these checks. The memo on the front of each check read, "cash for Sam." Five times I asked her whether the checks had been altered. Each time she denied any alteration. On the copies of subpoenaed checks, however, the memo said only "cash," not "cash for Sam." The "for Sam" had been added after the checks cleared the bank in order to defraud the court. Irene was excited at this discovery. The attempt to mislead the court was, in itself, strong evidence that Sam was trying to hide income.

I decided to call Sam as our first witness. It is dangerous to call a hostile witness, because you do not know what he will say; anything he says gives the opposition the right to lead their witness during cross-examination. I had given this approach much thought and discussed it with Irene. Calling Sam first would make him nervous and uncomfortable. We would put his statements on the record before Irene testified. This way she could respond to anything he said. I preferred to have Sam describe his income under my hostile questioning. I was careful, however, to limit my questioning to issues concerning his income. Therefore, Dunne could not cross-examine Sam about other issues.

With Sam on the stand, I put his tax returns and bank records into evidence. I asked him to review the charts and statements prepared by Irene's mother. He was unable to dispute the material because everything was confirmed in his bank records. We established what bills were paid by check. This meant that all other bills were paid with cash. Therefore, the parties must have had resources beyond what was shown in the bank statements.

We then considered Sam's claim that the extra money had come from gifts from the couple's parents. Sam acknowledged that in his first affidavit, he had denied the expenses were more than the income. He admitted to having no evidence to support his claim that Irene's parents had supplied some of the money. In one of his affidavits, Sam submitted checks from his mother to support his claim that he had received $38,000 from her during the marriage. When we went through the checks, however, it turned out that most of the money had been given either before the marriage, as a wedding gift, or after the separation.

During the last four years of the marriage, the parties deposited in the bank account $80,000 more than their declared income could explain. During the same four years, the checks from Sam's mother were for only $3,000. Accordingly, this could not explain the deposits. Sam claimed the remaining money from his mother was in cash. He said the approximately $18,000 in checks to cash from his mother's account was only part of the cash she had given him. A review of the checks and the bank statements, however, revealed no correlation between the dates of the checks and the dates of the deposits. There was a correlation of dates, however, between times when the store was busy (back-to-school, Easter, sidewalk sales) and large cash deposits. Even these unsubstantiated claims of cash gifts could account for only a small portion of the deposits. Sam also admitted that no gift tax returns were ever filed for any of the gifts he was claiming. There was little Dunne could do on cross-examination. Sam made some general statements about business having been bad and reiterated his discredited claims about cash gifts.

The volatile Irene kept herself under control during the trial and made a good witness. She testified about the cash Sam regularly brought home, and his statements to her that he and his partners were taking cash from the business. Irene said that Sam took between $500 and $600 per week in cash. She based this upon statements by Sam and their lifestyle together. While they were married, she did not know the full extent of his income. She also explained there were certain times of year when the stores were especially busy, and additional cash was taken. This testimony taken alone would not come close to proving the extra income, but taken together with the inadequately explained deposits and the deliberate misrepresentations by Sam and his mother, the testimony demonstrated how the illegal scheme worked.

Irene testified about the family expenses during the marriage, identifying which bills were paid by check and which by cash. She also testified about her income as a nurse. While the divorce was pending, Irene often worked double shifts in order to pay bills (particularly Bonnie's medical bills) that Sam failed to pay (despite court orders). Irene worked for private patients because this provided more flexibility with scheduling. She often had to spend time on the divorce action. The work she did paid more than hospital work, in part because there were no benefits. Sam was required to maintain family health insurance, but Irene's coverage would end when the divorce was final. She testified that she would have to take a lower-paying job in order to obtain coverage.

Irene explained that she could not continue to work double shifts. It was too taxing physically and emotionally.

We put receipts for medical, school, babysitting, and other expenses into evidence during Irene's testimony. Unfortunately, some of the medical receipts were missing. Irene testified to the court orders regarding support that Sam had violated. She also testified about her outstanding debts. She wanted Sam to pay the debts because they were caused by his failure to pay full support. Irene also testified about the loss of the marital home to foreclosure. She had offered a deal to Sam that would have saved the house. Her parents were willing to pay the mortgage if he would transfer the house to Irene. When the house was sold (hopefully after Bonnie finished school), Sam could have his share of any equity. Sam had refused to make any deal unless he received $10,000 as part of the agreement. This demand killed the deal and led to the foreclosure. Irene believed that this constituted waste of a marital asset.

The cross-examination of Irene shed more heat than light. At the start of the questioning, Dunne approached Irene asking hostile questions. I objected and reminded Judge Conway about the difficulties between Dunne and Irene. The judge ordered Dunne to remain at his table while questioning Irene. He questioned her about alleged gifts from her parents. Irene testified about a $3,000 wedding gift and a $7,000 loan her parents had made to Sam when he wanted to sue his brother and cousin. Despite a court order, Sam had repaid only half the loan. Dunne tried to imply that there were other loans or gifts. At one point after the judge again sustained my objection, Dunne told the court that he had meant no disrespect. Judge Conway responded, "You do, and I resent it." Thereafter, the questioning went quickly and Dunne accomplished little.

David Horowitz was the first witness for Sam. He testified that the family shoe business was doing poorly. Numerous unpaid bills were submitted into evidence. The bills indicated a substantial debt, and payments were far behind. He said that they were considering bankruptcy for the second store (each store was a separate corporate entity). Dave testified that many stores in the vicinity of their shoe stores were empty, which reduced traffic at their stores. He supported Sam's statements that each partner was being paid only $23,000 per year. All the non-family employees had been let go.

During cross-examination, I asked about income from the building owned by the family, which housed the original shoe store. He acknowledged that he and his two uncles each received $4,000 every third year for managing the property. The uncles lived in Florida. There was little or nothing to do to manage the building because the only tenant was the shoe store. I asked about any money received by Sam for managing the building where he works. Dave said Sam was incapable of managing the building. He related an incident in which Sam didn't know enough to call a plumber when there was a leak. He had to call Dave and ask Dave to call the plumber. Dave was amused by the incident and believed it demonstrated that Sam could not be trusted with anything important. Nevertheless, Sam was usually left alone most nights in the first store to rectify the cash and receipts.

Dave admitted that there was no system in place to make sure all receipts were deposited. The partners did not keep the cash register tapes or customer receipts. The only record of the money taken in each day was the deposit. There was no attempt to compare inventory to receipts. The partners trusted each other to report all money collected each day.

The next witness was Rolly Bennett. He had been the Horowitz family accountant for many years. He sought to use the income figures supplied by Dave to claim the business was close to bankruptcy and of no value. Bennett quickly demonstrated that he had no credibility. He testified that he had verified the income for the shoe stores, but when the judge pressed him for details, he quickly admitted that he had done no such verification. In the middle of his testimony, he started to tell a joke about lawyers. Judge Conway interrupted by saying, "I know a lot of accountants who are in prison." The courtroom erupted in laughter and Bennett's testimony was soon over.

During cross-examination, Bennett admitted that in all the years he worked for the Horowitz family, the shoe stores never finished with a profit of more than $5,000 or a loss of more than $1,000. In other words, the profit varied little between good years and bad years. One likely explanation was that the available profits were being taken out in the form of cash. Bennett had become our best witness and I hated to see him leave.

Mildred Horowitz was the next witness. She tried to explain how the checks had been altered. She claimed that she wrote on the checks after they came back so she would know what the cash was for. She could not explain why she made the notation on the checks instead of in the check register. She said she had not remembered the alteration when I questioned her at the deposition. She looked relieved to leave the stand.

Sam was called as his side's final witness. He had already testified, but Dunne wanted to cover some other areas. Sam testified that business was bad and that the partners were considering bankruptcy. He claimed not to have received most of Bonnie's medical bills. This was his excuse for failing to submit the bills to the insurance company. He said that Bonnie did not need to go to preschool and that he could not afford to pay for it. He admitted having taken a loan from Irene's parents. He had repaid half of the loan and wanted Irene to pay the remaining half.

Judge Conway asked the attorneys to prepare written summations. The parties were also given permission to make written applications for legal fees. We wanted Sam to pay my legal fees because he was better able to afford them, and his improper behavior (seeking custody and hiding income) had caused Irene to incur more legal expenses than necessary. We also wanted him to pay the legal fees from the prior attorneys. The papers were duly submitted and Judge Conway's decision came a few weeks later.

The Decision

The decision was fifteen pages long and at first glance appeared favorable. The judge agreed with our important points and concluded that the parties had substantially more resources available than the declared income could justify. Sam's stated explanations were not credible. Accordingly, the court determined Sam's income to be $49,000 ($23,000 declared and $26,000 in cash). The court also found Sam responsible for much of the unnecessary legal expenses, because of his attempt to play the custody card and his failure to declare his full income.

While the factual determinations were favorable to Irene, the decisions by the court were less helpful. The benefit of proving Sam's full income was offset by an unfavorable determination of Irene's income. In 1993, Irene earned $40,000 but, at the time of the trial, she was on a pace to earn $46,000. This included large amounts of overtime and double shifts that she could not sustain. Her compensation did not include health insurance; she would have to accept less income in order to obtain such coverage. The court found her income to be $46,000. Irene had been forced to earn the extra income because Sam failed to pay expenses required by court orders—so the decision rewarded Sam for violating orders and penalized Irene for acting responsibly.

Under the child support standards in New York, the nonresidential parent pays roughly 17% of his gross income minus social security taxes (the actual formula is more complicated) as child support for one child. Sam was ordered to pay $139 per week in child support instead of the $150 per week he would have paid on his full income. The judge justified this decision by referring to the substantial debt of the parties (Sam had deliberately stopped paying bills to support his claim of only $23,000 in income).

In addition to the weekly child support, Sam was ordered to maintain his health insurance for Bonnie (the insurance was supplied by his business) and to pay his share of unreimbursed medical expenses and part of the child-care expenses for Irene to work. The unreimbursed medical payments were conditioned on Sam's prior approval of non-emergency medical expenses. This was particularly unwise because Sam had a history of restricting Bonnie's medical treatment in order to save money. Renee Collins promised to write the judge to ask him to remove this provision. She never wrote the letter, and this was the beginning of a rift between Irene and Ms. Collins.

Despite the findings against Sam, Judge Conway ordered him to pay only $5,000 of the $15,000 in legal fees Irene owed me. Sam was not made responsible for any of the earlier legal fees incurred by Irene. With the exception of some bills Sam had been ordered to pay, the remaining debts were divided 53%–47% (proportioned to the two parties' determined income). Sam was ordered to submit the medical bills paid by Irene for reimbursement, but was not required to pay his share of the unreimbursed medical expenses. Irene had been counting on this money. Sam was also not required to reimburse Irene for Bonnie's school expenses.

The court accepted the accountant's statement that the business had no value. This opinion was based upon income of $23,000 to the three principals. The court concluded that Sam actually received $49,000 (presumably the other partners also received extra cash). This should have made the accountant's opinion invalid. Nevertheless, Irene received no part of the business. Sam was ordered to repay the remainder of the loan from Irene's parents.

Irene was furious when she heard the decision. She could not understand how she could gain so little from proving Sam's real income. Her anger was directed at Judge Conway, to whom she referred in the most vile terms. She complained to Aaron Markowitz and many others. I told Irene that some parts of the decision were unfair, but they were well within the judge's discretion.

While there was some basis for an appeal (namely the fact that the court found Sam's business to be worthless based upon income representations the court had found to be false), I recommended against it. I believed a successful appeal would provide limited benefits to Irene. It was important for her to let this battle go and get on with her life. The support provided by the decision would permit her to have a decent life. Irene wanted to pursue an appeal, but continued to be extremely complimentary about me and my work. She filed a notice of appeal, but could not afford the trial transcripts necessary. Periodically she developed schemes to obtain the transcripts, but eventually she realized that she did not have the resources to pursue an appeal.

More Troubles

The end of the trial did not end the litigation. Sam failed to pay the $5000 in legal fees awarded to me. We had to submit an order to show cause seeking to hold him in contempt. The court gave him a deadline. If he did not pay by the deadline, he would be held in contempt. On the last day, Sam paid the $5000.

The relationship between Sam and Irene continued to be difficult. Irene complained about hang-up phone calls from Sam and about his neglect of Bonnie during visitation. He would not dress her properly, failed to give required medication, and fed her inappropriately. On one occasion, Bonnie's doctor recommended that her cholesterol be limited because of a problem she was having. Irene explained this to Sam, but he took Bonnie to Friendly's for a hot dog, fries, and a milkshake. He explained that "kids eat free at Friendly's." In our court papers, we responded, "Kids eat free at Friendly's, but not fat-free."

When Bonnie went for visitation with Sam, there were serious questions about who was the adult. Bonnie started referring to her father as "Poo-poo head," much to the delight of her mother. Irene also complained about late child support payments and delays in submitting medical claims. Sam complained about missing phone calls and visitations. He also said that he was not receiving Bonnie's school and health information.

These complaints led to several Family Court petitions. Sam filed three violation petitions. Irene filed a family offense petition seeking an order of protection. Before these petitions could be disposed of, Irene filed a modification petition seeking to reduce Sam's visitation. I was not involved in preparing the petition, but appeared for Irene at the first court proceeding.

During one of the preliminary hearings, Renee Collins tried to arrange a settlement of the outstanding petitions. In the waiting room, Ms. Collins told Irene she could not possibly win an order of protection based upon phone calls. She warned Irene that if there was no settlement it was possible for Bonnie to be put in foster care (if the hearing demonstrated that neither party was a fit parent). Irene reacted angrily to these statements. After calming Irene down, I told Ms. Collins that she must be careful to avoid such threats, which made it harder to reach a settlement. The violation and family offense petitions were scheduled for trial in April of 1994. The modification petition was scheduled to be heard in May.

Judge Carla Ponzini was the presiding judge and one of the best Family Court judges in Westchester County. Judge Ponzini conferenced the case with the attorneys and clients in an attempt to reach a settlement. The attorneys explained what they believed the evidence would show. I concluded that Sam would be unable to prove the violations, but Irene could prove a family offense. Judge Ponzini reached the same conclusion. She suggested that Sam withdraw his petitions and consent to an order of protection, without admitting the allegations. When Sam objected to this proposal, the judge warned him that he might be ordered to pay legal fees if he insisted on a trial.

Sam's new attorney, Toni Spagnolo, asked to speak with her client in private. Ms. Spagnolo was a corporate attorney, unfamiliar with domestic relations issues; she had taken the case as a favor to a friend. She was personally pleasant, but often had unrealistic expectations. She tried to persuade Sam to settle, but he obstinately refused.

The trial started with Sam as the first witness. It was obvious that Ms. Spagnolo was not used to trying cases. She had trouble framing questions and entering evidence. At one point, she asked the court not to hold her inexperience against her client. Judge Ponzini responded, "If you are seeking grounds for appeal, this is not the way to accomplish it."

During cross-examination, Sam admitted making some of the harassing calls. He didn't seem to realize that the calls were improper. At this point, the judge went off the record. She said from the evidence presented that Sam's petitions were going to be thrown out and Irene would receive an order of protection. The judge asked me what I wanted for legal fees. I told her I would accept $200. Judge Ponzini appreciated my forbearance, as I easily could have requested $500 or more. She told Sam that he would be lucky to pay only $200 and should settle immediately. By this time, even Sam could see that his situation was hopeless, and he agreed to the settlement. Irene was pleased with the settlement and could not stop talking about the wonderful job Judge Ponzini and I had done.

We thought that the events in April would help us reach a settlement in May, but Sam was a slow learner. Judge Ponzini again conferenced the case with the parties and their attorneys. She suggested a compromise in which the weekend visitation would be reduced to Saturday to Monday instead of Friday to Monday. Sam's mistakes in caring for Bonnie justified a reduction in visitation. We suggested that Sam receive parenting skills training. If he learned to take better care of Bonnie, the visitation could be restored. The judge also recommended that Sam's payment of medical expenses should not be conditioned on his approval of nonemergency expenses. Again, Sam refused to compromise. Judge Ponzini warned him that a trial could result in less visitation and another award of legal fees. Sam insisted on a trial.

This time Irene testified first because the trial concerned her petition. It was easy to put Irene's story into evidence because Ms. Spagnolo did not know when to object. Irene stayed calm and testified effectively about Sam's failings. These mistakes included failure to give Bonnie medicine, keeping her out late when she was sick, and failure to dress her properly for the weather.

Sam's testimony was again harmful to his case. He did not trust anything Irene said. Instead of checking with a doctor or consulting someone responsible, Sam used his own lack of judgment. In effect, Sam admitted to neglecting his daughter. In the middle of Sam's testimony, Judge Ponzini again interrupted and suggested a settlement. Again Sam accepted the original proposal, this time with an additional $250 in legal fees for me.

We hoped Sam's Family Court failures would persuade him to abide by the court orders. Instead, he continued to violate the orders concerning medical insurance, medical payments, child-care payments, and repayment of the loan from Irene's parents. This failure became critical when Bonnie became ill.

For at least a few years, Bonnie had suffered from physical problems. She had trouble walking and could not compete with the other children. She was knock-kneed, a condition in which an abnormal curvature of her bones caused her knees to turn towards each other. She did not complete toilet training until she was five. The doctors prescribed physical therapy and special shoes. In June of 1994, her condition deteriorated. Bonnie's toes were turning in and she had hyperactive reflexes in her feet, ankles, and knees. She also suffered from constipation.

During the spring and summer of 1994, Irene had to take Bonnie to various doctors and specialists in an attempt to learn what was wrong. The likeliest possibilities were all grim. One doctor said it was most likely cerebral palsy; another doctor suggested some kind of palsy. The doctors tested for several rare diseases, some of which were fatal. Irene persuaded the doctors to test for Lyme's Disease, and these tests were positive. After treatment Bonnie's health was restored to what it had been before the crisis.

While Irene was desperately worrying about Bonnie's health, Sam refused to cooperate about medical and other expenses. Under Judge Conway's decision, Sam did not have to pay his share of the medical expenses until the insurance company made a determination of benefits. Sam took advantage of this by refusing to submit medical bills to the insurance company (Irene was not authorized to submit the bills). This had the effect of denying medical reimbursements to Irene from either the insurance company or Sam. Many of the medical providers required payment at the time of service. Several times Irene had to cancel or delay appointments because she did not have the money for the medical providers.

Sam compounded the problem by violating other financial requirements. Irene had gone from job to job until June of 1994, when she obtained a permanent job with the School for the Deaf. It was an ideal position because it provided good benefits and permitted her to be off during school vacations. During one week in the spring, Irene was out of work. Sam decided to use this to deny payment of child care. He demanded proof of where and when Irene was working. While Sam was not obligated to pay for child care unrelated to Irene's work, there was nothing in the order permitting him to withhold money until receiving proof. Irene did not want to provide this information because she was afraid Sam would harass her at work and put her job at risk. As a result, Sam unilaterally stopped paying for child care, and Irene had less money available to pay the medical expenses.

We brought an order to show cause before Judge Conway in August seeking payment of all outstanding medical and child-care expenses, immediate submission of all medical bills to the insurance company, the right to submit bills to the insurance company directly, and a requirement that when medical providers required payment at the time of service, Sam would have to pay his share.

The order to show cause was made and decided on the basis of papers without any appearances. The court ordered Sam to make all outstanding payments. He was given a deadline to submit all bills to the insurance company. There were two or three specific doctor bills that we knew had to be paid on the day of the appointment. Judge Conway ordered Sam to pay his share of these bills by the day of the appointment. The Court, however, did not make this a general requirement. Sam made the specific payments required, but otherwise ignored the order. Irene was angry that the Court had failed to solve the problem.

Sam failed to submit the medical bills to his insurance company and did not pay any child care or past medical bills. He continued his refusal to repay the loan from Irene's parents. In September, we brought a new order to show cause seeking to hold Sam in contempt for these violations.

Ms. Spagnolo contacted me after receiving the papers to see if we could arrange a settlement. Irene was anxious to see Sam go to jail. I told Ms. Spagnolo that any settlement would have to resolve all issues and prevent constant litigation. I worked out a plan to resolve the many financial disputes and provide a mechanism including advance payments into escrow so that future payments would be paid promptly. Irene preferred to have Sam in jail, but agreed to my proposal. Ms. Spagnolo liked the idea in general, but needed to discuss it with Sam.

Ms. Spagnolo and I met with Judge Conway on September 16, 1995. Ms. Spagnolo had a check to cover most of the child-care expenses and the medical bills that were ordered paid in advance. I told Judge Conway that we wanted Sam jailed for all the violations. The judge responded that he would not put Sam in jail if he made full payment. I told the judge about my settlement plan. He liked the idea and urged Ms. Spagnolo to encourage Sam's approval. She did not have an answer from Sam, but he was complaining about the amount of money he had to come up with. Sam also had objections about my role in the arrangement. Judge Conway said Sam was lucky to have my involvement and wondered if I really wanted such a burden. He suggested I put the proposal into writing. The case was adjourned for one week to work out a settlement. The return date was for a contempt hearing, which everyone hoped would not be necessary.

I prepared the settlement proposal, but Sam refused to agree. I hoped he might change his mind during the contempt hearing. Irene's mother, Mrs. Pecota, joined us for the contempt hearing. Mrs. Pecota was needed to testify about the loan to Sam.

During a conference with Judge Conway, it came out that the child-care provider was an illegal alien. The babysitter had worked for Irene for almost four years and Bonnie was very attached to her. She was paid only $240 per week. This was a particularly helpful arrangement because of Irene's schedule (Irene sometimes had to work extra shifts in an emergency). Sam benefited from the arrangement because anyone else would be more expensive. Judge Conway urged the parties to settle, because he would have to make a report if this information were revealed in court. Sam agreed to pay the outstanding child-care expense, but Irene wanted the money and to have Sam put in jail. I tried to persuade her to accept the money and drop the hearing, but she refused. When I informed the court that we wanted to go forward with the hearing, Judge Conway adjourned the hearing one day and ordered the babysitter to come to court.

Irene started yelling, cursing, and carrying on. I was unable to calm her down. She was afraid that the babysitter would run away as soon as she heard the court's order. Irene did not have an alternative babysitter and could not afford a more conventional arrangement. She was afraid she would lose her job. The drive back was a disaster. At one point, Irene and her mother started blaming each other for the suicide of Irene's sister.

The babysitter left as soon as Irene told her what had happened. Irene was unable to locate a short-term replacement, and any permanent replacement would be much more expensive. She was in a terrible mood when we arrived at court the next day. The situation worsened as Ms. Spagnolo announced that Sam had filed for bankruptcy. There were serious legal issues about whether Sam could escape his marital debts, but Judge Conway suspended the proceedings until legal briefs could be submitted.

The parties had joint debts that Sam had been ordered to pay. Irene was afraid that if Sam went bankrupt, the creditors would come after her. The suspension of the contempt hearing meant there was no way to force Sam to meet his obligations. She felt overwhelmed and without hope. Irene started to talk about giving Sam custody over Bonnie. More ominously, she was talking about suicide.

The Downward Spiral

That evening I received a call from Irene at my home. She said she was planning to drop Bonnie at Sam's home, then go to my office (in my parents' home) to leave some jewelry and a note. She said she would then take the car somewhere to kill herself. I tried to talk her out of the suicide. She asked me to come up with a plan that would permit her to keep her job and take care of Bonnie. I made some suggestions, but none of the day-care possibilities was satisfactory. I told her that she had no right to consider suicide because of the harm it would cause to Bonnie. Irene had given this issue much thought, and we had discussed the subject several times. She believed a person had a right to commit suicide.

I called a psychologist who knew Irene and had treated Bonnie. She thought Irene was most likely using the threat of suicide for leverage. Irene had threatened to give up custody in the past in an attempt to get her way. The psychologist warned, however, that Irene was capable of going through with suicide.

My mother called to tell me that Irene had left a note and some jewelry at my office. The note was addressed to me. It asked me to hold some of the jewelry for Bonnie and sell the rest to cover some of my legal fees. Irene thanked me for my work and implied that she was going to kill herself.

I called Irene's mother. She did not know where Irene had gone, and was very worried. Mrs. Pecota went out of her way to tell me that she was not to blame for Irene's behavior. I considered calling the police or Crisis Intervention, but I did not know where Irene could be found. A few hours later, Irene called. Sam had refused to take Bonnie without a court order changing custody.

The next day, Irene called Renee Collins and asked for a change of custody. As soon as she hung up, Irene realized that she had made a big mistake. She tried to withdraw her request, but Ms. Collins continued with her order to show cause to change custody. Irene was extremely upset when she called me. She said that this time she was really going to kill herself. She was just waiting to say goodbye to Bonnie after school. Irene warned me not to call Crisis Intervention. She said it would not do any good, because her training as a psychiatric nurse would be useful in fooling them. She said that I had no right to stop her, and she would have me disbarred for violating confidentiality if I tried. Irene seemed to want my approval. I told her that I did not approve and asked her to give me some time to find another solution. I hung up and called Crisis Intervention. I was unwilling to take the risk that Irene would kill herself.

About an hour later, a team of police, technicians, and a psychiatrist came to her home. They examined Irene for two hours. A police officer called me for some information. Irene got on the phone to ask me how I could do such a thing. She was angry, but tried to control herself while the team was present. I told Irene that I was not willing to take the chance that she might kill herself. She said that it was her choice. Irene also expressed concern that my call would hurt her chances of keeping Bonnie. In fact, Bonnie's custody was transferred to Sam based upon the order to show cause.

Later, I received a call from the psychiatrist. I told her about the note Irene had left at my office and agreed to send her a copy. I warned her that Irene was a psychiatric nurse and believed she knew how to fool the doctors. The doctor said that I was right to call Crisis Intervention. They were not going to hospitalize her, but would interview her two days later to judge her condition. After the second interview, they decided that she was not a danger to herself or others.

After the Crisis Intervention team left, Irene vented her full fury on me. She was screaming and cursing while she threatened to sue me and have me disbarred. She told me she would never trust me again. I offered to withdraw as her attorney. Irene could not afford another attorney and knew the judge had high regard for me. She was afraid that another change of attorneys would hurt her position with the judge. I told Irene that she would have to cooperate with me and act civilly if she wanted me to continue. Regardless of her feelings about my calling Crisis Intervention, I had done it for the right reasons. Irene agreed to behave, and I accompanied her for a conference with Judge Conway concerning the change of custody.

Irene wanted Bonnie to be returned to her immediately. She pointed out that, even under terrible pressure, she had made sure Bonnie was well cared for. The child was never at risk. Under the circumstances, however, there was no way that Judge Conway could return Bonnie until a thorough evaluation of Irene was completed. The judge decided to transfer the case to Judge Ponzini. The Family Court had more resources for evaluations and for a determination of custody, and the parties both lived in Westchester County. Furthermore, Irene had expressed great hostility towards Judge Conway.

Judge Conway ruled that Irene could have only supervised visitation. He asked for suggestions about who could do the supervision. The judge approved Bonnie's piano teacher, a friend of the family, and Irene's parents. I offered my parents as supervisors (Bonnie knew and liked them). The judge said that this was generous, but did not want to inconvenience them when there were other supervisors available. When I gave Irene the judge's order, she ripped it up and threw it out.

Sam took full advantage of the circumstances. He scheduled appointments for Bonnie to interfere with visitation and refused to let Irene speak with her on the phone. I asked Renee Collins to intercede in order for Irene to have the phone calls. She arranged for phone calls by giving Sam permission to tape the calls (in violation of the court order). Sam stayed in the room during the calls, often whistling or talking in order to disrupt the conversation. Frequently, Sam would encourage Bonnie to end calls by offering television, movies, or other treats. Bonnie was required to spend her afternoons at Sam's shoe store. He would not take her for physical therapy or other activities. He also failed to give Bonnie some of her medication.

In the beginning of November, we appeared before Judge Ponzini. Irene wanted an immediate change of custody, but the judge refused. Unsupervised visitation was also turned down. The court appointed Dr. Thomas Galvin to conduct psychological evaluations on the parties.

The evaluations were scheduled quickly. Sam played tapes of phone calls between himself, Bonnie, and Irene that had been made when Irene had custody. Under the existing court order, Sam was forbidden to use these tapes, but Dr. Galvin did not know this. Sam accused Irene of taking Bonnie to doctors unnecessarily and inventing medical problems that did not exist. These allegations could easily have been refuted, if Dr. Galvin had bothered to contact any of Bonnie's doctors. Instead, he repeated the allegations in his report. Dr. Galvin did not give Irene a chance to respond to Sam's charges. The doctor seemed more interested in Irene's menstrual history than in the recent events that created the custody issue. Irene was angry because Dr. Galvin refused to listen to her. The resulting report was unfavorable to Irene. The false report of unnecessary medical treatment created tremendous confusion.

I was receiving several angry calls from Irene each day. She now thought that I was a terrible attorney, deliberately doing a poor job. When she wasn't yelling at me, Irene was referring to Sam, Renee Collins, Dr. Galvin, and many others in the most vile terms. Irene called Aaron Markowitz to complain about us and asked him to intervene with Judge Ponzini. Markowitz told Irene that it would be unethical for him to interfere. This caused Irene to turn her wrath on him. She threatened to take her car and injure his children. She made the same threat concerning Ms. Collins's children.

In fact, Irene did not know these children and had no real intention of doing anything to them. Nevertheless, Markowitz did not believe he could take a chance with the lives of his children. He called me to discuss the situation. I told him that I did not think Irene would do anything, and he agreed with me. If the threat had been against him, he would have let it go, but under the circumstances, he felt he must call the police. That night Irene was arrested. Given a choice of jail or treatment, she agreed to go to a psychiatric hospital.

Irene continued to call me from the hospital. She blamed me and others for her predicament and requested that I return her file. We agreed that I should withdraw from the case. I prepared an order to show cause which was returnable the next court date. Irene was still in the hospital when the court date was scheduled, and her mother was permitted to be in court on her behalf. I asked to be relieved as Irene's attorney. Ms. Collins made an oral motion to withdraw as law guardian. Judge Ponzini was sympathetic to our situation, but said it was a difficult case and our knowledge and experience were needed. The judge asked us to remain, in the best interests of Bonnie. If it became impossible for us to continue, the court would permit us to be relieved in the future.

Irene was released from the hospital after ten days. Her behavior and attitude towards me were much improved. She expressed her appreciation for all the work I had done. The final report from the hospital repeated the allegations from Dr. Galvin about the unnecessary medical treatment of Bonnie. The psychiatrist at the hospital confirmed that this allegation was false. I asked him to put this in writing. He said the report stated that Irene did not suffer from a psychosis. If she had sought unnecessary treatment, that would constitute a psychosis; therefore, the final report established that the allegations were false. I explained that the court would need something more specific, but he was unwilling to prepare any additional statements.

The visitations were being supervised by the Probation Department while Irene's parents were in Florida. The Probation Department was not available for Christmas visitation. Sam refused to approve any supervisor but the Probation Department. I offered to have my parents supervise, but even this was rejected. Irene never saw Bonnie for Christmas.

In January, Irene's behavior and mental health deteriorated. She was constantly yelling at me. One day, she left several messages for me at another office in which every word was a curse. I told her that I would not permit such treatment. She threatened to sue me and complain to the Bar Association. Under these circumstances, I could not continue to represent her. At the next court appearance, I asked Judge Ponzini to let me withdraw as Irene's attorney. Irene responded with a diatribe against me, and the judge agreed to release me.

In April, I passed by Irene's home and saw Christmas decorations. Finally Bonnie was allowed to visit her home to share Christmas with her mother. In May the custody trial took place. One Thursday, Renee Collins called me. Ms. Collins had been replaced as law guardian but had gone to the trial as a witness, and Irene saw her in the parking garage. Ms. Collins was concerned because Irene had seen her car and wanted to know if I thought she or her children were in danger. I assured her that she and her children were safe. I said if anyone was in danger, it was Irene.

On that Friday, Judge Ponzini awarded custody to Sam. That night, Irene Horowitz swallowed a bottle of aspirin. She died the next morning.

Chapter 7

GENDER BIAS

The Pollack Case

C HILD SUPPORT COLLECTION is a difficult problem in this country. Most often the mother needs to find and collect child support from the absent father. Fathers in a cash business are often willing and able to hide a large part of their income. Even after a mother wins an award of child support, judges are generally reluctant to take aggressive action to enforce the award. The choice of paying or going to jail usually results in the magical appearance of money that previously did not even exist. Nevertheless, judges usually give the recalcitrant father numerous chances before imposing such a choice. If the father agrees to pay even a small portion of the money owed, the possibility of contempt or jail quickly recedes. There are, however, some judges who are much more willing to enforce child support.

This case demonstrates how very differently a judge can act when the situation is reversed and it is the mother who is ordered to pay child support. The mother in this case was given no leniency whatsoever, in spite of the fact that the support ordered was genuinely beyond her ability to pay.

An Impossible Situation

My client, Irene Horowitz (see Chapter 6), was a friend of Emily Pollack. Irene told me about Emily and her precarious legal situation. Emily had lost custody of her four children and was ordered to pay 120% of her income as child support. Irene wanted Emily to replace her attorney with me. One day Irene came to my office and asked me to call Emily immediately. She was at the county jail for allegedly violating an order of protection. I spoke briefly with Emily Pollack and agreed to represent her in Family Court the next day. She told me that she had been arrested for giving her children their allowance at the school bus stop. Irene arranged to meet her at the jail and bail her out.

I met Emily for the first time the next morning in White Plains Family Court. Emily was a short, slim woman in her early forties. She had moderately long black hair and thick glasses and always dressed in dowdy clothing, which she often borrowed from friends.

We had a chance to discuss her situation before her case was called. A few days earlier there had been an incident in which a friend of her husband had dropped a piece of paper next to her car. Emily's daughter, Molly, picked up the paper and threw it through the car window. My client threw it back out and never read the contents. The paper turned out to have been an order of protection requiring Emily to stay away from her children. When she met the children to give them their allowance, her husband treated this as a violation and was able to persuade the police to arrest her.

The case was assigned to Judge Anthony Schinasi. Judge Schinasi is an experienced jurist with a reputation for making the parties and attorneys strictly follow the rules. I explained to the judge the circumstances as related to me by Emily. The first attempt at service of the order was invalid because the petition and order of protection were never given to the respondent. The actions by Molly Pollack could not constitute service because she was just a child. In any event, my client could not have deliberately violated an order of protection she did not know existed.

I also pointed out that the underlying petition was defective. Mr. Pollack had sought the order of protection because Emily had approached her children to speak with them. She did this because the father was interfering with her visitation rights. There was no allegation that Emily had done anything wrong when she approached the children. Accordingly, I asked the judge to dismiss the order of protection as well as the violation. We also requested an order of protection against Emily's husband for illegally causing her arrest.

Kenneth Pollack was represented by Janet Martin. She was an experienced attorney who often used aggressive tactics. She denied that the service was improper and complained that the children were frightened when their mother stopped to visit them. Ken wanted his wife to be returned to jail.

Judge Schinasi's decision was completely predictable. Emily could remain out of jail and the bail was returned. She was required to observe the conditions in the temporary order of protection. We could seek an order of protection, but would have to file a new petition. A trial concerning the order of protection and alleged violation was scheduled.

After we left the courtroom, Janet Martin asked to speak with me. I thought she wanted to discuss a settlement of these issues. Instead, she engaged in a diatribe telling me how ridiculous our position was, and promising that there was no way we would ever receive an order of protection.

I instructed Emily to bring a petition for an order of protection based upon her husband's involvement in the illegal arrest. Mutual orders of protection are often used improperly by abusers (see page 12), but Emily really needed this protection because her husband had demonstrated a willingness to fabricate charges in order to put her in jail.

By the time we were scheduled for trial, Emily had her order of protection. With the help of Judge Schinasi, we quickly reached the logical settlement. Each party received a permanent order of protection. The alleged violation by Emily was dismissed. Emily agreed not to pursue an action concerning what we believed to be her illegal arrest.

Custody and Visitation

Emily was appreciative of my work and asked me to help her enforce visitation. The existing Supreme Court order gave custody of her four children to her husband, but provided normal visitation for the mother. This visitation included every other weekend and every Wednesday for dinner. Frequently, the father denied the visitation by claiming that the children did not want to see their mother. He was planning to take them away to Washington, D.C., for a weekend when Emily was supposed to have visitation. Emily had brought an order to show cause seeking to stop the children from going out of state and to enforce the visitation. She wanted me to represent her during arguments before the supervising judge.

Emily had a daughter nine years old and three sons, ages eight, six and five. By the time of the court appearance, my client had not seen the two oldest children in three months and had seen the two youngest sons only twice during that same period. The dispute was to be decided by oral argument before the administrative judge. Janet Martin argued that the trip to Washington was a wonderful opportunity for the children. Emily was portrayed as mean and selfish for trying to deprive the children of this experience. I pointed out the history of the father's interference with visitation. If my client had received her regular visitation, we would not be arguing about one weekend. The visitation order had to be enforced.

Ms. Martin claimed that the lack of visitation was caused by Emily's failure to come on time and by the fact that the children did not want to visit with their mother. I denied the charges and pointed out that children this age do not have the right to decide whether visitation will take place. Furthermore, at the original trial, when the judge had ordered the visitation, Ms. Martin had objected that the children might not wish to go for visitation and had tried to make it conditional. The judge responded that the father had the obligation to make sure the visitation took place.

The administrative judge ruled that the children could go to Washington, but the following weekend (Thanksgiving weekend) would be a make-up visitation from Thursday to Sunday. The judge cautioned the father that any failure to provide the visitation would have serious consequences. The judge referred the remaining custody and visitation issues to Judge McLaughlin, who had tried the prior custody action. The children enjoyed their trip to Washington, but the following weekend, they remained with their father in violation of the court's order.

The first thing Emily ever told me about custody was that she had made a horrible mistake. Ken had started a fight with her while she was teaching Molly piano. Emily was very upset and started yelling at Molly. Ken taped the verbal abuse and used it effectively in court. The law guardian and the judge were convinced that Emily was an abusive mother, and Ken won custody. I pointed out to Emily that she had been given normal visitation. The court could not award unsupervised visitation to an unfit parent. Therefore, implied in the court's decision was a determination that she was a fit mother.

Emily wanted to seek a change of custody based on the denial of visitation. The court had conducted a full trial only a few months before and was unlikely to change custody so soon after the trial, so I persuaded my client to seek instead enforcement of the visitation, mandatory counseling, and sanctions against the father. We needed to make more of a record of the father's interference in the relationship between mother and children before the court would be willing to take the extreme step of changing custody. The court would look more favorably on an attempt to make the visitation work than on one to uproot the children.

Judge Francis McLaughlin is a Family Court judge in Putnam County. He frequently serves as an acting Supreme Court Justice and sometimes hears a case in both capacities. This was a Westchester case, but the custody and visitation issues had been referred to Judge McLaughlin. Intelligent and knowledgeable, Judge McLaughlin was only in his thirties, but had been on the bench for several years. He was generally impartial at the beginning of a case, but once he decided which party he favored, he could be very unfair to the party he disliked. He had limited patience and at times could lose his judicial demeanor. I was concerned that he might have closed his mind with regard to Emily. On the other hand, the judge had been helpful to me and my clients in some recent cases.

Judge McLaughlin prided himself on being tough with parties who violated his orders. It seemed beyond dispute that Kenneth Pollack had violated the visitation orders made by both judges. We hoped he would take strong action to guarantee regular visitation. A conference was scheduled to discuss the outstanding motions; the judge met with just the attorneys.

The law guardian, Elise Mitchell, was experienced and ambitious. I had previously had only one major case with her as law guardian. She had sided with the abusive father against my client, but the children she had represented were 15 and 17 years of age and had wanted to live with their father. It is common for older children to side with an abuser for safety and other reasons. Ethically, Ms. Mitchell had to advocate for her clients' wishes because of their age. In this case, she was a strong advocate for Kenneth and was hostile toward my client.

Throughout this case, Ken Pollack was represented by two attorneys. In addition to Janet Martin, Peggy Collins was present during most of the sessions. Ms. Collins was young and obnoxious. She seemed to feel that cooperation or even civility was a sign of weakness. Her tactics did not benefit her client, but made a difficult situation even more unpleasant.

The conference was three to one against me—four to one if you include the judge. The three attorneys claimed that my client's past and present mistreatment of the children made it impossible for the father to persuade them to go for visitation. They asked that the visitation be stopped altogether.

I pointed out that both the administrative judge and Judge McLaughlin had ordered the visitation to occur despite these same claims. The children were too young to refuse visitation. I reminded the judge that he had repeatedly forced mothers of children abused by their fathers to make their children go for visitation. The charges against Emily were much less severe. I also complained about the actions of the father in denigrating my client and scheduling attractive activities to compete with the scheduled visitation. I requested counseling between the children and the parties to improve the relationship between mother and children. Such counseling would reveal the improper actions of the father in interfering with the children's relationship with their mother.

The judge made it clear he had little use for my client. He did not like her and did not believe anything she said. He would do nothing to enforce the visitation. He did not even ask the father's attorneys to encourage him to cooperate with the mother. The judge recommended that counseling begin (with Emily paying the full cost) and that scheduled visitation be reduced to one day per week. The trial of the motions would not take place for months. While waiting for the hearing, visitation would be limited. Emily was of course disappointed with the conference. It was obvious that she would never receive a fair hearing from Judge McLaughlin.

Finalizing the Divorce

The next issue before the courts was the remainder of the divorce. The custody and visitation had been tried and temporary child support established. The grounds for divorce, permanent child support, equitable distribution, and the validity of a prenuptial agreement still had to be determined. Emily wanted me to represent her in the divorce, but was reluctant to ask because she had no money. She promised to pay when she could.

As an advocate for victims of domestic violence, I often represent women pro bono or at a greatly reduced rate when they have little or no resources. It was obvious that a grave injustice was being perpetrated against Emily. I knew it would be a difficult case, but I wanted to help. I never asked Emily for any money. Periodically she insisted on giving me a few dollars. Over the course of my representation, she paid me a total of a few hundred dollars.

Emily was a piano teacher. Most of her students were children whom she taught after school. She worked in a wealthy community and drove to her students' homes. She was a popular and well-respected teacher. When I took her case, many prominent people, the parents of her students, contacted me to offer any help they could provide. Their testimonials to her ability and character were most touching. Many provided food, clothing, money, and other help when Emily was forced out of her home.

Kenneth Pollack owned his own wholesale meat and seafood business at the Hunts Point Market. He came from a wealthy family and maintained an expensive lifestyle. A few years before meeting Emily, Ken had been involved in a fraudulent financial arrangement. He was convicted of a felony and served a brief jail term.

The parties lived together for four years before marrying. They married shortly before the birth of their third child. Ken wanted Emily to abort their third and fourth children. In order to get Ken to marry her, Emily had to agree to provide him with at least $35,000 per year. This was later raised to $1500 per week (or $78,000 per year). He also required her to convert to Judaism.

Ken was verbally and emotionally abusive throughout the relationship. Even his attorneys would acknowledge that he was sometimes loud and profane. On a few occasions, he had slapped Emily and kicked her. During the final incident before they separated, Ken pinned Emily to the car with his body, slapped her face, and repeatedly kicked her legs and buttocks. When she left the house, he threw out all her clothes and she was left with only the clothes on her back. One friend even had to lend her money for undergarments.

Emily borrowed over ten thousand dollars from her sister to hire Theodore Johnson as her attorney. Johnson is an experienced attorney, but has a reputation for taking advantage of his clients (see Chapter 1). He failed to prepare Emily for her testimony and did not interview potential witnesses. He told Emily that claiming the highest income possible would improve her chances for custody. This caused Emily to make a mistaken guess about her income, which would haunt her for the rest of the case. The harm caused by Ted Johnson's work would never be overcome.

By the time I agreed to represent Emily in the divorce action, the case was already scheduled for trial. Johnson had done nothing to prepare for trial. I was able to arrange a deposition of Ken Pollack, but only on condition that it not delay the case. There was no time or money for further discovery. Under the system in effect at the time, the parties came to the trial assignment part, where a judge would be assigned at random.

The attorneys met with the administrative judge's law assistant,

Aaron Markowitz. Markowitz was well respected by all the attorneys, in part because he was so good at finding settlements in very difficult cases. His magic was of no help in this case. The parties' versions of reality were too far apart for a settlement to be possible. I asked for a delay because I had had so little time to prepare the case. Markowitz could not grant the delay because the case had been scheduled for trial months before, but privately he assured me that the trial would not start for at least a week because there were no judges available.

Ms. Martin requested that the case be assigned to Judge McLaughlin because of his familiarity with it. I strongly objected and complained that he was biased against my client. Markowitz stated that the fact that one side specifically sought a certain judge would cause him to make sure that judge was not assigned to the case. We were advised to call each day in the afternoon to see if a judge would be available the next day.

Ten days later we were told to come to Court for the trial. The judge assigned to the case was Francis McLaughlin. Markowitz took me aside to apologize for the assignment. The day before he had had a meeting in the city and Judge McLaughlin had come to Westchester seeking an assignment. We were the next case to be assigned. Markowitz felt very badly about what had happened, but he could not change judges. I believed his explanation, but that would not help Emily. We had a judge whose mind was already made up.

Judge McLaughlin conferenced the case in an attempt to reach a settlement. None of the issues could be settled. He decided to try the issue of grounds for divorce first. Assuming there were grounds, we would then consider the validity of the prenuptial agreement. Finally we would try the financial issues.

During the conference, I told the judge that I believed he was biased against my client and should not hear this case. He asked for the basis of my belief. I repeated some of his statements from the last conference, which demonstrated his hostility towards Emily. The judge stated that any negative views he had were based on the prior trial and totally appropriate. I told him his statements suggested that he had already made up his mind and was unable to listen to the new evidence with an open mind. Judge McLaughlin said he would not recuse himself, but promised to consider whatever evidence was presented. I informed the judge that I would make the motion for recusal on the record.

An attorney is generally reluctant to seek a judge's recusal. There is a danger that the judge will take such a motion out on the client.

Furthermore, it may hurt the attorney in future cases with the same judge. I discussed these issues with Emily prior to the conference. The judge was already all out against her. We hoped that making a record of the recusal motion before the start of the trial would put him on notice that his behavior towards Emily might be reviewed in the future.

Emily was the plaintiff in the action and therefore required to present evidence first. She was seeking a divorce based upon cruel and inhuman treatment by her husband. Abusers usually commit their deeds in private to insure that there are no witnesses. Accordingly, a hearing on the grounds of cruel and inhuman treatment is usually a question of which party to believe. Verbal and emotional abuse can be more harmful than physical abuse, but the law in New York State requires at least some physical abuse to justify a divorce based on cruel and inhuman treatment.

Emily testified about the final incident in which Ken had pinned her against the car, slapped her face, and kicked her legs and buttocks. She told of a few other incidents when he had pushed and shoved her. We had pictures of the bruises on Emily's legs from the last beating. This was the strongest evidence because the bruises were unlikely to have been caused in any other manner.

Emily also testified about an incident in which the family went out for dinner. Her husband yelled, screamed, and cursed her in front of the children. He told the children that they did not have to listen to her because she was a "stupid bitch." Ken had engaged in this kind of verbal abuse throughout the marriage.

The verbal abuse was not critical to the determination of cruel and inhuman treatment, but we hoped to spring a trap on Ken. We rested our case on the grounds after Emily had testified and the pictures had been introduced into evidence. Ken admitted that he was sometimes loud, but denied all the other allegations. He specifically denied denigrating Emily in front of the children or calling her a "stupid bitch" at the restaurant. We hoped he would give this testimony, because a prominent member of the community had witnessed the incident and overheard the statements made by Ken.

The defendant rested, and I announced that we wished to present a rebuttal witness. Ms. Martin immediately requested a conference. (The trial was scheduled a day or two at a time to accommodate the judge's schedule and lasted almost five months. During this time, we had several conferences.) Ms. Martin requested an offer of proof (a statement of what we expected to prove) and I gave it. She then suggested that the case was really about financial issues, and in the interest of time they would agree to the divorce if we used less inflammatory grounds. I insisted that the grounds be cruel and inhuman treatment. I told Judge McLaughlin quite frankly that I wanted him to hear the next witness because I thought it might make him reconsider the relative credibility of the two parties.

The judge told Ms. Martin and Ms. Collins that he could not force me to accept other grounds. They then agreed to consent to a divorce based upon cruel and inhuman treatment. I still wanted to present the witness in order to demonstrate the defendant's lack of credibility, but the judge ruled that if the defendant agreed to the grounds, the proposed testimony would be irrelevant. We put the consent to the grounds of divorce on the record and the divorce was granted. Ms. Martin expressed fear that Emily would use the grounds to harm Ken's reputation in the community. The judge responded by ordering that the transcript be sealed and that the parties not reveal the grounds to any nonparties. This highly unusual ruling demonstrated the complete sympathy the judge had for the defendant.

The next issue concerned the purported prenuptial agreement between the parties. The agreement said that in the event of a divorce, the wife would receive nothing but a share of the marital home. She would not receive her share of the house until and unless the husband decided to sell the house. If the house was sold, after the mortgage was paid, the husband would receive the first $200,000. The remainder would be shared equally. The agreement stated that the parties were each represented by counsel, there was complete disclosure of all financial circumstances, and they were entering the agreement freely and voluntarily.

On its face, the agreement appeared valid. Emily told me that she had signed the agreement, but not in front of a notary. Her signature was notarized on the document, but she claimed that the notary had not witnessed her signature. Emily also told me that her purported attorney had been selected by Ken, and she had never met the attorney. We also disputed the claim that full financial disclosure was made. Emily had been pregnant at the time and wanted to get married. It was not a voluntary transaction.

Although there were factual disputes, legal issues predominated. The judge asked both sides to research the issues and submit legal briefs. We had a weak case, even under the best of circumstances. On its face the document was valid. That meant that we had the burden to prove fraud or undue influence. There was no way the court was going to believe Emily. In effect, she was accusing not only Ken but his attorney and the notary of committing fraud. Neither the attorney nor the notary could be found. Accordingly, the court ruled that the agreement was valid.

Child Support

The main issue remaining was child support. This would be based upon the incomes of the parties, which was greatly in dispute. The temporary child support order required my client to pay over $30,000 per year in child support. This was more than she earned. As a result, she was tens of thousands of dollars in arrears. The child support and arrears could be adjusted if the court decided the existing support order was excessive.

Ms. Martin and Ms. Collins repeatedly requested that Emily be immediately jailed for violating the support order. Judge McLaughlin stated that he could not do so until it was established whether the violation was deliberate, but in conference, he repeatedly stated that he did not expect to reduce the support, and if the arrears remained, Emily would be jailed. Repeatedly, the judge sought a compromise support figure, but all of the figures suggested were way beyond Emily's ability to pay. Among the other issues were whether the denial of visitation should reduce or eliminate child support; the use of the equity in the home to pay outstanding bills; support; and legal fees.

The following excerpt from the transcript of the previous trial was the basis of the statements by the defendant and the court that Emily's income was between $63,000 and $78,000.

Ms. Martin: How much did you pay your husband each week?
Emily: Fifteen hundred dollars.
Ms. Martin: Fifteen hundred dollars per week would come to
$78,000 per year?
Emily: I believe that is correct.
(. . .)
Emily: I did not pay him over the summer vacation.
Ms. Martin: How long was the summer vacation?
Emily: Ten weeks.
Ms. Martin: So the total for the year would be $63,000?
Emily: Whatever the math is.

Whenever we tried to prove Emily's real income, these statements were repeated over and over. Emily took the stand needing to make the court look beyond this testimony.

We started with the joint tax returns for the last five years of the marriage. The returns were signed by both parties. Ken acknowledged that they were accurate copies of the returns actually filed. The best year Emily ever had income-wise was the year before the couple separated. She earned $37,000 that year according to the sworn return. The incomes for Emily ranged from $15,000 to $37,000. Ken's declared income varied from $10,000 to $20,000, except for one year when he sold some property.

Normally, joint tax returns constitute very powerful evidence. Since each party swore to the truth of the information contained in the returns, courts are reluctant to permit either party to challenge its truthfulness. A party who benefited from declaring less income for tax purposes will rarely get away with claiming greater income in a divorce. Even when one party had no knowledge of their spouse's income, challenging the information in a tax return is difficult.

Emily described her business as a piano teacher. With a few exceptions, all of her students were children. She would teach them in their homes after school and sometimes on Saturdays. During the week, Emily would leave home a little before 3 P.M. and return home about 10 P.M. She had to drive to each lesson; the average drive between lessons was fifteen to twenty minutes. She charged $30 for a 30-minute lesson and $42 for an hour-long lesson. Unlike therapists who have 50-minute hours, Emily gave each student the full amount of time.

When the children were on vacation from school they were not available for lessons. Lessons were often cancelled due to other circumstances, such as when the children became ill, had other appointments, or needed to study for exams, or because of bad weather. Sometimes cancelled lessons could be made up or rescheduled, but often Emily lost the potential revenue. All of these factors limited the amount of income she could make. None of these circumstances was disputed by the defendant.

My client had significant expenses associated with her work. The major expense was for transportation. She was driving an old, broken-down vehicle with almost 100,000 miles on it. This created significant expenses for gas, oil, insurance, and especially repairs. If the car broke down, she could not make it to her classes. She also had expenses for the phone and music materials.

Emily testified about the financial and other arrangements she had with her husband. Ken controlled all the money in the marriage. When Emily was pregnant with her third and fourth children, he wanted her to have an abortion. In return for keeping the children, she had to agree to give Ken $1500 per week. He kept all her financial records and pressured her to produce the desired income. When Emily did not earn enough money, she gave him the rest from an inheritance. The year that she earned $37,000, Emily was forced to work 60 hours per week. She could not keep up that pace and had reduced her workload even before the separation.

When Emily was forced to leave her home after the last incident of abuse, she left with just the clothes on her back. All of her business records remained with Ken. The testimony at the custody trial was taken at a time when Emily had no access to these records. Ken had pressured her to pay him the $1500 per week for so long that she used this figure in answering the cross-examination. She should have said that she wasn't sure, but instead tried to guess at the answer. This was certainly a mistake, but it did not justify ending all other inquiry as to the truth about her income.

In addition to Emily's misstatements at the custody hearing, Ken relied on rosters of her students. Ms. Martin took lists of all the students taught by Emily in a year, multiplied the total by $42 (the rate for a one-hour lesson), and claimed this to be her weekly earnings. We put into evidence both the rosters and the actual schedules. Some of the students took only 30-minute lessons; some took lessons every other week. Several students took lessons for one semester and were replaced by other students for the spring semester. Ms. Martin's calculations did not allow for any of these circumstances.

The schedules contained notations of actual lessons given and demonstrated that Emily did not, and, in fact, could not possibly have seen every student on the roster each week. During the cross-examination, Ms. Martin repeatedly asked questions assuming a particular student was taught every week for both semesters. She appeared shocked when Emily explained that a student had stopped the lessons or took them less frequently.

The trial went on for five months. Ken had plenty of time to contact any of the students discussed in Emily's testimony. Our case could have been destroyed if just one student had contradicted this testimony, but no such witness was ever presented.

We presented Emily's individual tax returns for two years. This included the year she left her husband and the following year. The year before the parties separated, Emily earned $37,000. The year of the separation, her income was down to $20,000. The next year, she earned only $12,000. It is common for the income of a noncustodial parent to be reduced when a couple separates. Sometimes this is done deliberately in order to reduce child support obligations, which is not permitted. A court will look suspiciously at such an income reduction, and the parent will have to justify the loss of income.

There were good reasons for the reduction in Emily's income. She had cut back on her hours even before the separation because she could not maintain the 60-hour weeks. Furthermore, she wanted to spend more time with her children. Once the parties separated, there were additional obstacles to maintaining her income. Emily's scheduled visitation was on Wednesdays and weekends. Accordingly she did not schedule classes at these times.

Repeatedly, she had to cancel lessons in order to be in court. Also, the last winter had been unusually severe, forcing the cancellation of several days of lessons. All of these circumstances were unchallenged by the defendant. Emily had also lost income when her car broke down and she had no money for repairs, and when Ken called students to tell them what a bad person she was. Ken denied that he had done this.

Emily's financial circumstances were precarious. She was paying $160 per week in child support (out of the $600 per week she had been ordered to pay) when she was working. This did not even leave her enough money for rent (in fact, she lost her apartment during the trial) and she often went without eating. Many of her friends and her sister lent her money and gave her necessities, including food, clothing, shelter, and medical treatment. Her friends were prominent citizens in the community and parents of her students; they wanted to help Emily in any way possible and agreed to testify on her behalf. I wanted Judge McLaughlin to see the high regard they had for Emily and the extent of charity she needed to survive. Clearly, this was not a woman capable of earning $60,000 or $70,000 per year, as the defendant pretended. Several of Emily's friends testified on her behalf. I could have brought in more witnesses, but during the conferences, the judge made it clear that he was unimpressed with the testimony and did not want to hear any more such witnesses.

Judge McLaughlin had agreed to consider evidence concerning Ken's attempt to poison the children's minds against their mother.

Repeatedly Emily took a witness with her when going to pick up the children for visitation. Ken orchestrated scenes in which each child walked up to the mother, stated that he or she did not want visitation, and went back into the house. The older children also pressured the younger children not to go for visitation. On one occasion, the youngest child, Matt, told his mother that he wanted to visit her, but was afraid of what the others might do. The father scheduled fun activities to conflict with the visitation. When Emily insisted on her visitation, she was put in a position of taking away their fun activities.

Just before we were scheduled to try this issue, the judge conducted a conference with the lawyers. He said that the evidence from the custody trial provided reason for the children to dislike their mother. Accordingly, no matter what evidence might be presented, he would not say that the father was the sole cause of the denial of visitation. Therefore, there was no way we could win on this issue. Reading between the lines, it was clear that seeking a reduction in child support based on the denial of visitation would only antagonize the judge further without accomplishing anything. I discussed the situation with Emily and we decided to drop this issue.

Kenneth Pollack was the only witness for the defense. He acknowledged the genuineness of the joint tax returns, but claimed that the information about Emily's income was inaccurate. He wrongly tried to claim that his signature on the returns swore to the truth of his income only. For some of the years, Ken said he did not know Emily's income was wrong at the time, but other years he was aware of the misinformation when he signed the returns. He stated that Emily gave him $1500 per week from her earnings and that he kept the records for her business and sent out the bills.

Ken stated that his income from his business was $10,000 per year. On cross-examination, he acknowledged that he was sometimes paid in cash. In reviewing his records, it was established that he received between $20,000 and $30,000 per year in checks from his business, made out to cash. He claimed that he used this cash for business expenses, but was unable to produce any documentation. He acknowledged that he regularly brought home food from the business for the family. He did not consider this as additional income, and did not report the value of the food. According to Emily, they regularly enjoyed large quantities of steak, lobster, and other expensive foods from his business. Ken also acknowledged selling flowers at his home. He claimed that this did not constitute income because he took his profits in flowers instead of cash. This income was never reported on the tax returns.

The defendant also sought child-care expenses from my client. According to his net worth statement, the woman taking care of the children while Ken was working was being paid $12,000 per year. Accordingly, Ken was paying more for child care than he was earning at his business. He never explained the logic of this arrangement, but Emily testified that the woman was actually his lover.

At the end of his testimony, Ken sought to place into evidence new information about Emily's class schedule. He thought it supported his claim about her income, but in fact it was an update of the previous information. The interesting issue was how he obtained the document. The schedule had been in Emily's car only two days earlier. Their oldest son made a point of coming into the passenger seat to kiss Emily good-bye after a visitation. He had not done so on any of the previous visits. The boy did this in order to take the schedule in an attempt to help his father's case. We do not know if Ken asked the child to do this, but, at the very least, the incident demonstrates the improper information Ken provided to the children. Judge McLaughlin should have been outraged at this incident, but he did not seem to care.

By the end of the trial, the parties had been separated for almost two years. During this time, Emily paid child support of $160 per week. This was substantially less than the $1500 Ken claimed to have been receiving during the marriage, but despite this shortfall, he never altered his lifestyle. Shortly before the separation, Ken secretly took a $150,000 equity loan on his house. This money was used to maintain the family's lifestyle.

The Judgment

At the close of testimony, Judge McLaughlin asked the attorneys to prepare written closing arguments. He specifically asked us to propose what the final terms of the divorce should be. Each side was also authorized to make a written application for legal fees.

It was physically and mathematically impossible for Emily to make the kind of income the other side claimed. In my closing argument, I tried to focus the judge's attention on the realities of her work. I thought we had an overwhelmingly strong case, but the judge was so hostile towards Emily that I was afraid he would ignore the evidence. A child support award of anything much more than what Emily was already paying ($160 per week) was likely to cause a tragedy.

I presented several potential tragic scenarios that could result from an excessive award. Emily could get sick from overwork and failure to take proper care of herself as she tried to make more money. She could get into an accident as she pushed herself and her broken-down car beyond their limits. With no hope of satisfying the demands, she could run away, depriving the children of a mother and support. She could kill herself (as her friend Irene did shortly thereafter). She could go to jail, which would destroy her business and her ability to pay any support. Nothing good could come from the court blindly burdening her with greater obligations than she could handle. I begged the judge to find a way to avoid a tragedy. I even addressed the envelope to him as "Hon. Francis McLaughlin, Committee to Prevent Tragedies."

The judge repeatedly stated that when someone swears under oath that they earned a particular income when it was to their advantage, he would not listen to them say they earned less when the lower amount suits their new objective. In fact this is exactly what Ken Pollack had done when he swore to the truth of the tax returns. Unlike Emily in her original testimony, when Ken signed the returns, he had all his records and time to consider what he was doing. Furthermore, Ken was much more sophisticated in financial matters. On the evidence presented at trial, the issue was no longer *whether* a party could change his or her story, but *which* party would be allowed to do so.

There was strong reason to question Ken's credibility. He had a felony conviction for financial fraud and admitted that he had failed to declare income from the meat, seafood, and flowers that he kept. Ken also acknowledged that he had arranged for the home equity loan prior to the separation without informing Emily. The defendant handled all the financial records for Emily's business. Furthermore, I caught him in several contradictions concerning the checks for cash that he regularly took from his business, but could not account for. I also believed that his claim to pay the babysitter (his lover) $12,000 per year in order to go to work where he claimed to make $10,000 per year was not credible. Even with Emily's misstatements, I believe most finders of fact would have found her much more credible.

I argued that the home equity loan secretly taken by Ken could be used to improve the situation. Anything above the first $200,000 in the home's equity was half Emily's. The fact that Ken had taken this loan without telling Emily in no way changed her right to the money. He claimed to have used the money for living expenses and legal fees for his attorneys and the law guardian (the parties were ordered to share the law guardian's fees, but Emily had not paid her share). In effect, Emily's equity had paid for living expenses and legal fees. She should receive credit for one-half of the money paid. This would have wiped out all arrears and given Emily a credit, which would give her the opportunity to fix her car, buy some necessities, and generally get her finances in order. In the long run, this would place her in a better position to earn money in order to pay child support. Accordingly we requested that Emily receive credit for one-half of the home equity loan.

During the trial, when the defense complained that Ken had no money, I pointed out that he had the resources to use two attorneys throughout the trial. They responded by representing that they were charging him only for Ms. Martin's time and giving a discount at that. In their papers, however, they sought their full legal fees from Emily and included separate fees for the work done by Ms. Collins.

Ms. Martin and Ms. Collins also went out of their way to include personal attacks against me. They accused me of trying to create controversy and prolong the trial. They also stated that I served only to increase the animosity in the litigation. This was ironic because early in my representation, Emily informed me that Ms. Martin had had an affair with Ken. She wanted me to use this fact to embarrass them. Unfortunately, there was only limited evidence of such an affair, and if the affair had occurred, it was several years earlier. Accordingly, I refused to pursue the matter. To this day, Ms. Martin is unaware of the evidence we had.

I told the judge, "If you are going to create a tragedy, at least tell us how you could calculate the income in excess of what she is capable of earning." This would be our only request the judge honored. He decided that her income was $57,000. In order to reach this number, the judge decided that she could work 48 weeks per year—despite Emily's original statement in the custody hearing that she could not work during the summer or other school vacation periods because her students were not available. The court also decided that there were zero expenses associated with Emily's work. The judge never explained how he came to that conclusion.

The judge ordered Emily to pay $17,000 in child support and another $6,000 toward the salary for the babysitter. The court refused to give Emily credit for the home equity loan. She was ordered to pay most of Ken's legal fees and half of the law guardian's fees. Once the judge decided to maintain the fiction of substantial income, the details did not matter. Emily was buried in debt she could never hope to overcome. I hoped she would not soon be buried another way.

Perhaps the most bizarre part of the decision was to grant Emily a divorce on the grounds of constructive abandonment. The agreement was that the divorce would be on the grounds of cruel and inhuman treatment; no evidence of constructive abandonment was ever presented. The court records would never have been sealed if the grounds had been constructive abandonment. At first I thought the judge had made an inadvertent error, but when I wrote to him in an attempt to correct the mistake, Judge McLaughlin refused to correct his decision.

The Inevitable End

The only hope for Emily was in an appeal. I believed she had good grounds for appeal. I have had little experience with appeals and advised her to find an attorney who could prosecute her appeal. I made several calls on her behalf in an attempt to find an attorney to represent her without charge. Irene Horowitz was trying to help Emily with her legal problems. I had stopped representing Irene when she became abusive after suffering a mental breakdown (see Chapter 6). Irene convinced Emily that I should not be trusted and I had no more contact with Emily.

Several months later, the local newspaper reported that Emily had been jailed for non-support. A few days after that, the paper reported that a new attorney had won her release from prison by an appeal, but a few weeks after that, Emily was back in jail. It was considered a newsworthy event because the deadbeat parent was a mother. Some months later, in a story about powerful women attorneys, Ms. Martin was mentioned for her ability to put Emily in jail. Perhaps she should have been in the story for her ability to win child support in excess of the mother's income. The fact that the child support award was excessive did not appear in any of the articles.

Recently, I represented a mother attempting to enforce a child support award. The father had failed to pay support for over five years. No one would ever have bothered him if he had not contacted my client in violation of a court order. This led to a proceeding for his violation of the child support order. The trial before the hearing examiner resulted in a finding of deliberate violation and a recommendation of three months in prison.

Under the law, the hearing examiner cannot impose a jail sentence. The case has to be submitted to a Family Court judge to confirm the sentence. We had to return to court five times before the judge took action. Each time the court gave the father another chance and more time. The judge practically begged him to make some payment. If the father had paid just one dollar, I am sure he would have avoided jail. Finally, on the fifth appearance a jail term was imposed. Comparing Emily and this father, it is clear which one should have been given a chance.

Chapter 8

MARITAL RAPE
The Kowalick Case

Domestic violence is not a new phenomenon, but only recently has it become a public issue. It has taken even longer for the law to recognize sexual crimes within marriage. In 1978, Oregon became the first state to prosecute marital rape, and in 1984, sexual assault between spouses first became a crime in New York State. No man had ever been tried and convicted of sexually assaulting his wife in Westchester County until Stanley Kowalick broke into his estranged wife's home and attempted to rape her in 1989.

An Abusive Husband

Barbara Kowalick was a beautiful, petite blonde in her early thirties who worked for an employment agency. Her husband was 32 years old, 5'10", a muscular 170 pounds with brown hair and a tattoo on his arm. Stanley worked as a carpenter in a business he owned with his brother.

Barbara and Stanley had dated on and off for five years before getting married. He had been physically and emotionally abusive throughout the relationship. His abuse escalated after the marriage, and especially after Barbara became pregnant. It is common for abusers to hit their wives during pregnancy, particularly in the stomach. Stanley threw Barbara down and kicked her stomach while she was expecting a baby.

Throughout the relationship, Barbara frequently suffered bruises and black eyes from Stanley's attacks. He slapped, punched, and kicked Barbara in her face, stomach, arms, buttocks, legs, and groin. He also threw things at her. Embarrassed by his abuse, Barbara would hide her injuries or make excuses instead of seeking help.

Domestic violence is all about control. Physical abuse is just one of the methods abusers use to control their victims. Stanley constantly criticized Barbara in order to reduce her self-esteem. He made her believe that she deserved the abuse and was at least partially to blame for it. Other common methods of control include isolating the victim from friends and family and controlling the family finances, which Stanley also did.

Many of the assaults took place after Stanley had been drinking. He often stayed in bars late at night and came home under the influence. It is a common fallacy that drinking or drug abuse causes abuse. In fact, they are two separate problems. Although an abuser may drink to gain the "courage" to commit an assault, solving the substance problem leaves the abuse unchanged. Law-abiding men respect boundaries. There may be times when they would like to hit their spouse, but nevertheless, they do not choose to do so, whether they are drunk or not. The abuser's belief system and societal acceptance permit him to assault his wife or child. Too often, judges mistakenly believe that ending a substance abuse problem will end the violence. Many women and children have been the victims of this error.

By the late spring of 1989, both parties had decided they did not want to be married. The couple owned a house in Mamaroneck, New York. Stanley moved out and was staying with friends. Barbara changed the locks and bolted the doors to keep him out, but periodically he broke into the house. On several occasions, Barbara woke up in the morning to find her husband sleeping on the couch. She called the police a few times, but never pressed charges.

The Assault

In the early morning hours of August 20, 1989, Barbara was sleeping in her bed. The baby was asleep in another room. Stanley stayed up late drinking and then broke into the house. He went up to the bedroom, slammed the door, and yelled at Barbara, "I'm going to kill you, you f— bitch." Stanley said that he was going to rape her first, although that was not the word he used. He grabbed her by the throat and started choking her. She could not breathe and was gasping for air, but managed somehow to scream loud enough that the neighbor across the street heard her and called the police.

Stanley pinned Barbara down and pulled off her nightgown. In the past she had always given in to his sexual demands because she was afraid of him, but on this night, she fought to make him stop. The force of his anger made Barbara believe she was fighting for her life. She thought she was going to die. Stanley attempted to put his penis in her mouth, anus, and vagina. Throughout the assault, Stanley told Barbara to shut up and repeated that he was going to kill her. He ejaculated all over her naked body. In the middle of the attack, however, the police rang the doorbell.

Stanley was stark naked when he went downstairs and opened the door. The police arrested him and took him to the precinct. A policewoman went upstairs to help Barbara. The officer had been to the house only a week before, after Stanley had broken into the house, but Barbara had refused to press charges. This time, she quickly agreed to sign a complaint. She arranged for her mother and father to meet her at the police station and take care of the baby while she spoke with detectives.

Stanley was also at the police station, which made Barbara very uncomfortable. She did not want to see him. At one point, she heard an officer ask Stanley if he wanted anything from a nearby restaurant. The detectives took pictures of Barbara's injuries and took her statement. Then they brought her to the hospital for a rape exam.

The doctors and nurses were considerate, but the experience was embarrassing and unpleasant. At the time, Barbara did not understand what they were doing, and no one had explained it to her. She had bruises on her arms, legs, face, and inner thighs; pictures had to be taken of all these areas. Some of her pubic hair was pulled out for sampling, and they scraped under her fingernails for evidence. Several years later, Barbara described the experience as painful. She was particularly embarrassed because the hospital staff knew the attack had been made by her husband. Barbara did not feel safe in the hospital, even though it was located in a good neighborhood.

Deciding to Prosecute

A week after the attack, Barbara had a meeting with Oliver Jansen, the local assistant district attorney in Rye Brook. (Local courts have jurisdiction over misdemeanors and the initial arraignment for felonies. When the district attorney decides to prosecute a case as a felony, the evidence is presented to a grand jury and prosecuted in the County Court in White Plains.) Mr. Jansen suggested that they should not prosecute because it would be hard to obtain a conviction. He explained that there was no way to proceed against a husband. Barbara accepted this statement and assumed this was the end of the case. Stanley was charged with attempted rape and assault in the Mamaroneck Village Court the night of the crime. The charges remained until the main office of the Westchester district attorney decided what charges would be presented to a Grand Jury.

In the late 1970s, the Westchester district attorney formed a domestic violence unit. This was the first such office in the country. The office has an outstanding reputation and has been emulated by many DAs around the nation. A few weeks after the Rye Brook office recommended against prosecuting, Denise Carlucci of the county domestic violence unit called Barbara and told her she wanted to prosecute her husband for the attempted rape. Ms. Carlucci had nine years' experience in the district attorney's office, including six years in the domestic violence unit.

Sex crimes are generally difficult to prosecute, especially when there is an issue of consent. The problems are compounded when the crime is committed by a friend or relative. Ms. Carlucci was not sure if a jury would be willing to convict when they learned Stanley was Barbara's husband, but the fact that the couple had separated made it a stronger case. Ms. Carlucci warned Barbara that pursuing the case would be unpleasant and the chances of conviction no better than fifty–fifty.

The New York statute concerning rape and sexual abuse says there can be no crime if the assault is committed by the woman's husband. However, in 1984, the state's highest court, the Court of Appeals, changed the law by upholding the conviction of a husband for raping his wife in front of their three-year-old son. The court stated, "A marriage license should not be viewed as a license for a husband to forcibly rape his wife with impunity." (Ironically, the decision was written by Chief Judge Sol Wachtler, who later went to jail for harassing and stalking his former lover.)

Barbara agreed to cooperate in the prosecution of her husband. She was nervous about pursuing the case, but wanted Stanley to obtain help for his problems. Although the marriage had no future, Barbara was concerned about their daughter, Lindsey. Barbara had to testify before the grand jury investigating her case. This was uncomfortable because she had to answer the jurors' questions about a painful and embarrassing episode.

Barbara's father helped support her emotionally with his optimism. He was a gentle man and the parent she felt most comfortable discussing her problems with. She depended on his support when things in her life went badly. He told her that Stanley would be indicted. A few days after the indictment, Barbara's father died.

As part of the criminal proceedings, Barbara received an order of protection. This kept Stanley away from her except for visitation exchanges. His mother used every chance she could to pressure Barbara to drop the charges.

After her father's death, Barbara had second thoughts about the prosecution and told Ms. Carlucci that she did not want to continue the case. The district attorney offered a generous plea bargain of assault. This would have permitted Stanley to avoid any jail time. Stanley and his lawyer contemptuously rejected the plea bargain and said they wanted to go to trial. Barbara felt that she had no choice but to proceed with the prosecution.

The Trial

More than a year elapsed between the crime and the trial. Ms. Carlucci helped prepare Barbara to testify before the jury. She advised Barbara to answer the questions explicitly, although the subject matter was uncomfortable and humiliating. There is a natural tendency to speak in generalities or euphemisms, but the evidence must demonstrate exactly what was done in order to secure a conviction. Barbara could not speak about the history of abuse, but the defense attorney could ask about the history of their sex life together. Ms. Carlucci warned Barbara that the defense attorney would be aggressive and unpleasant. Barbara says this was quite an understatement.

The judge assigned to the case was Paul Zingaro. Judge Zingaro had moved up to the County Court two years earlier after several years as a Yonkers City Court judge. He was a pleasant man of about forty with a reputation for fairness, but not necessarily toughness.

As the trial started, Stanley faced an eight-count indictment. He was charged with sodomy, attempted rape, attempted sodomy, three counts of sexual abuse by forcible compulsion (oral, anal, and vaginal), assault, and harassment. All of the charges were felonies except the assault, which is a misdemeanor, and harassment, which is a violation. The sodomy charge referred to his forcing his penis into Barbara's anus. The attempted sodomy referred to his attempt to force oral sex.

Barbara was the main witness at the trial. Her testimony lasted two and a half days. She wore conservative suits as she had been advised to do by the prosecutor. Barbara described the attack in graphic detail. She identified the pictures of the various bruises. Barbara was uncomfortable with Stanley's viewing the pictures. He was laughing and smirking as if he were admiring his work. Barbara testified that in no way were the sexual activities consensual; she had been afraid for her life. She had attempted to fight Stanley off, but he had held her down and punched her face.

The cross-examination was long and brutal. The defense attorney, Sidney Klein, used the typical strategy of trying to blame the victim. He tried to show that Barbara had worn a sexy dress at a party the night of the alleged rape. This backfired when the actual dress proved to be rather conservative. Klein tried to offer alternative explanations for the bruises. The explanations were implausible and easily denied by Barbara. He questioned her ad nauseum about her past sexual activities with her husband. These had been varied and consensual, but the past consent did not justify the attack in question. Klein confronted Barbara with tapes of an argument between her and Stanley's mother, trying to make Barbara look bad, but the argument was irrelevant to the issues in the case.

Barbara held up well under the interrogation. There were times when her voice cracked, but she never lost her composure. Klein was never able to make her change or abandon her story. The jurors would later say that they never doubted the truthfulness of Barbara's version of the events.

Two of the police officers testified about coming to the house and the statements made by the defendant. They described Stanley's opening the door while still naked. They also testified about Barbara's condition after the attack. Most damaging was an admission by Stanley at the time of his arrest. He told the police, "I kind of went too far, but I'm her husband." Stanley did not realize that his statement summed up what the case was all about. This was strong evidence because it corroborated Barbara's version of the attack.

The doctor and nurse testified about the gynecological exam performed the night of the rape. The bruises and injuries were consistent with a rape. They validated the pictures in order to place them in evidence.

Stanley did not testify for the defense. His attorney called three of his friends as witnesses. They said that Barbara had been dressed provocatively at a party the night before the alleged rape and that she had already had the marks and bruises on her face and arms before the attack. They also tried to suggest that Stanley was not the kind of person ever to commit such a crime.

The Verdict and Sentencing

The jury deliberated for a day and a half before reaching a verdict. Barbara had stayed away from the trial except for giving her testimony and was not present for the verdict. Stanley remained confident, even cocky, throughout the trial. The jury found him guilty of the three counts of sexual abuse by forcible compulsion. These were all felonies. He was also convicted of the assault misdemeanor. Stanley was acquitted of the more serious felony charges, sodomy, attempted sodomy, and attempted rape. The harassment charge had been dismissed before the case went to the jury. After the verdict, Klein said that they were pleased that his client was found innocent of the most serious offenses, but in reality, Klein and his client were shocked by the verdict.

The jurors later explained that it was a compromise verdict. They always believed Barbara and had no doubt that she had been forcibly attacked. The sexual abuse convictions established that Stanley had attempted rape and sodomy by forcible compulsion. It was a relatively older jury, and Barbara and Ms. Carlucci had been concerned that they would be offended by the subject matter or have a traditional attitude about the rights of a husband. The jury decided that they did not want Stanley punished too severely; this is why they found him not guilty of the most serious offenses. There was no doubt in their minds, however, that the evidence required a conviction.

Stanley was scheduled to be sentenced two months after the trial. Today, the victim of a crime such as this would have the opportunity to meet with the probation officer preparing the sentencing report and to speak to the court. This way, she could explain the impact of the crime and her opinion about sentencing. In January of 1991, when the sentencing occurred, only the defendant was permitted to provide information about himself. Judge Zingaro received fifty-five letters in support of Stanley, asking that he be spared a jail term. Ms. Carlucci asked the judge to sentence Stanley to some jail time, but she had serious doubts he would do so. Sidney Klein argued strenuously against imprisonment, claiming Stanley had been punished enough by the conviction and publicity.

A jail sentence is important in cases such as this in order to counter the abuser's belief that such behavior is permissible against a close family member. Stanley had no prior record and would never have committed such a crime against a stranger, but somehow he believed that it was acceptable if done to his wife. It is important to let such an offender know that society does not agree with him. A jail term tells him that society takes his behavior seriously. No other penalty will get this message across.

Judge Zingaro sentenced Stanley to five years of shock probation, which included six months in jail. This meant he would actually have to spend four months in jail. The judge said that a jail sentence was necessary because of the "cold and calculating part of your personality. There is no doubt you did it and you have no remorse," he admonished Stanley.

For the sentencing, Barbara was in the courtroom for the first time since giving her testimony. She was pleased with the sentence because she thought it would force Stanley to get help. Today, Barbara says, "Stanley took a part of my life I can never get back. He created a fear. I am still afraid of him." She does not regret what she did, but if this ever happened again, she would not go to court. The process was too painful.

Family Court Issues

Stanley was not jailed immediately because he appealed. During one of the visitation exchanges, he started an argument and pushed Barbara. The district attorney prosecuted him for this violation of the order of protection. The case was again tried before Judge Zingaro. The evidence demonstrated that a violation had occurred. The judge could have found a violation without imposing further punishment, but he decided that this was a minor issue and refused to convict Stanley again.

While the criminal case was pending, Barbara needed child support for Lindsey. Stanley refused to pay anything. Barbara filed a petition for support and hired an attorney she knew from her work. She was fortunate to have Stanley's business records at the house and used them to win a substantial child support award. Stanley responded by closing the business he ran with his brother and refusing to pay any support.

Under the law, a father cannot deliberately avoid work in order to reduce his child support payments. Barbara responded with a violation petition seeking to jail Stanley for deliberately violating the order. In practice, the courts rarely send someone to prison for nonpayment of child support unless he continues to be recalcitrant. Usually, when the court finds someone in contempt, the deadbeat suddenly finds the money, and the court does not jail him. This practice encourages deadbeats to play games because they can most often avoid jail by paying in the end.

The hearing examiner found that Stanley had deliberately violated the order and recommended that he go to jail. A hearing examiner is an attorney appointed by the courts to hear support and paternity cases, and does not have the authority to send someone to jail. Therefore, the case went to the Family Court judge, Ronald Washington, to confirm the determination. Judge Washington had served in the Yonkers City Court with Judge Zingaro and had been elected to the Family Court only a year earlier. This judge has a great memory and is known to go out of his way to help people. Unfortunately, he also had a reputation for inappropriately yelling at litigants and attorneys. This was unprofessional when he was in Yonkers City Court, but an absolute disaster when he dealt with victims of domestic violence in Family Court.

Stanley told Judge Washington that he was unable to pay the support because he was out of a job and had no money. Furthermore, he claimed to be deep in debt because of the criminal case. The child support violation should have been an easy case to understand. For over a year, Stanley had not paid one penny, even during the time he admitted to having work. He might be unable to pay the full support, but his failure to pay anything demonstrated bad faith. He also had a family to help him. If the court had confirmed the sentence, Stanley would have paid the support in order to avoid jail. Instead, Judge Washington yelled at Barbara for being vindictive by seeking a jail term and refused to force Stanley to help support Lindsey.

Barbara again went before Judge Washington on the issues of custody and visitation. Although it never became a serious issue, Stanley initially petitioned for custody. The court ordered psychological tests and a probation report. Each report concluded that Stanley was a danger to Barbara, but not to Lindsey. Nevertheless, shortly after the reports, Stanley consented to give Barbara sole custody.

The sole dispute before the court concerned the type and extent of visitation. Barbara's attorney was hindered by family problems and forced to withdraw. She replaced him with Theodore Johnson. Johnson did no better for Barbara than he had for Melanie Brewster (see Chapter 1).

There have been many studies about the effect on children when their father abuses their mother. Fathers who abuse their children's mothers are about 33 percent more likely to abuse their children than those who do not. The abusive behavior is harmful to the children even when they are not direct victims of it. Children are traumatized by seeing and hearing their mother abused. Even if they do not witness the abuse, the fear and other negative effects on the mother inevitably have an impact on the children. Many types of dysfunctional behavior in children, as well as academic and social problems, have been shown to be caused by their fathers' abuse of their mothers. As a result of these studies, the law in New York State now requires the courts to consider domestic violence when determining custody and visitation. This law did not exist in 1991, and Judge Washington was ignorant of this research.

Stanley wanted the full range of normal visitation, but Barbara was concerned that Stanley might hurt Lindsey, and was also concerned about the exchanges. The incident in which Stanley had pushed her during a visitation exchange reinforced her belief that protection was needed. Barbara preferred supervised visitation with a neutral observer. She wanted Stanley to obtain professional help before receiving normal visitation. She was particularly concerned about his anger after the conviction.

Judge Washington wanted the visitation gradually to increase to normal visitation. Normal visitation usually means every other weekend, shared holidays, a few weeks' vacation, and sometimes a few hours during the week for a lunch or dinner. Initially, the visitation exchange was handled by Stanley's mother. She was hardly a neutral observer and unlikely to protect Barbara in the event of a problem. There was no supervision during the visitation.

During one visitation, Stanley was observed drinking on a boat in violation of the conditions of his probation. After another visitation, Lindsey came home with a red mark on her bottom, presumably from an excessive spanking. When Barbara complained about the drinking incident, Judge Washington said that as long as the baby came home safely, she had nothing to complain about. During her testimony, Barbara mentioned the attempted rape. Washington responded by yelling at Barbara. Every time the judge yelled at Barbara, Stanley would grin from ear to ear. Judge Washington was abusing her in ways Stanley could no longer do.

A Change of Attorneys

Ted Johnson wanted Barbara to agree to normal visitation; he yelled at her and called her an idiot when she refused. Barbara hired me to replace Johnson shortly after this incident. He took his revenge by refusing to return her file.

Stanley sought an order of protection for himself. He claimed that Barbara had harassed him by calling him names, particularly in front of the baby. The allegations were false, but Stanley received the protective order *ex-parte* (without Barbara or her representative having a chance to respond to the charges). Orders of protection are routinely granted as long as the allegations, if true, would constitute a crime. The law requires, however, that the granting of a protective order support the purposes of the law, which is to protect family members who may be in danger.

Judge Washington knew that Barbara had an order of protection because of a serious crime committed against her. Stanley's order could be used, in effect, to nullify Barbara's order. Such an order should not have been granted on unsubstantiated accusations of minimally illegal behavior. In motion papers, I wrote, "It is unconscionable for the court even to consider an order of protection under these circumstances." Stanley withdrew his petition before the hearing for a permanent order.

Stanley frequently missed visitation or came late. On two occasions, Barbara failed to provide visitation. She was afraid for two-year-old Lindsey's safety and openly angry at Stanley and the court over her mistreatment. Stanley responded by filing an order to show cause seeking to hold Barbara in contempt.

Of the three allegations on his desk, Judge Washington was not eager to pursue Stanley's nonpayment of child support for over a year, nor did he care about all Stanley's missed visitation. Instead, he gave the contempt petition the top priority. Judge Washington held Barbara in contempt; the feeling was mutual. He did not jail her or otherwise impose punishment, but in the decision he stated that any further violation would result in a jail term.

Barbara wanted to fight for supervised visitation. She did not want to permit visitation with a dangerous man who refused to engage in counseling. I sympathized with Barbara's feelings, but I doubted our chances to succeed in court, especially in light of Judge Washington's statements that he wanted Stanley to have normal visitation. Any attempt to stop this would only cause the judge to penalize Barbara.

I took the time to listen to my client's concerns. I gave her support and validation, but also advised her to accept the normal visitation. Barbara realized that nothing better could be accomplished in Judge Washington's court. The settlement was reached, and she never entered his court again.

Stanley filed a petition seeking a reduction in child support. He claimed to be out of work and unable to pay support. Barbara filed a petition seeking to punish him for not paying child support. The trial was held before the hearing examiner. We believed that Stanley was doing repairs and other work in his own business. Such income, mostly cash, is notoriously hard to prove. The mother has the burden to prove the income, but all the information is controlled by the father. In this manner, many children are denied adequate support.

Stanley was the first to testify at the hearing. On cross-examination, I asked him if he had done work at any homes or businesses for which he was paid. He denied doing this. I asked if he ever went to a particular bar to drink. Again, he denied this. When our turn came, I called a private investigator to the stand. He was a retired New York City police detective and a friend of Barbara's father; he had worked for her as a favor to the family. He had followed Stanley for several days and seen him do repair work at three homes and one business. No income was reported for this work. The investigator had also found Stanley drinking in the bar I mentioned, in contradiction of his testimony and in violation of his probation.

Short of a Perry Mason–type confession, it is hard to imagine stronger evidence to prove unreported income and dishonesty by a party. I awaited the decision with complete confidence. The hearing examiner announced that she did not believe our witness. She gave Stanley a substantial reduction in support and dismissed the violation petition. I do not know whether she was influenced by the decision of Judge Washington, refusing to send Stanley to jail for the previous violation.

Stanley served his four months in jail for the attempted rape. After the jail term, his mother took Lindsey for most of the visitations; Stanley now sees his child only occasionally. Lindsey enjoys spending time with her grandmother. Barbara is now remarried to someone she describes as a wonderful man. Lindsey is doing well, and they have a happy family life.

The psychic scars produced by her abuse at the hands of Stanley Kowalick and Judge Washington are still present. Seven years after the divorce, Barbara went to the courthouse on another matter. She ran into Judge Washington in the corridor, and their eyes met. "I shook," Barbara said. "It had been seven years, and a wave of fear ran through me."

Chapter 9

THE BEST INTERESTS OF THE FATHER

The Morgan/Richardson Case

OST JUDGES PRIDE THEMSELVES on treating all parties fairly. Such sentiment is noble, but judges should remember the difference between *fairly* and *equally*. Surprisingly, this distinction is often lost in domestic violence cases. In a custody case, each party should receive a fair hearing, but treating the victim the same as the abuser is unfair to the victim and the children.

Repeatedly, I have witnessed supposedly learned judges equate the victim's normal reaction to abuse with the predator's violence and control. Both parties are responsible for the problems their children are having and they should learn to cooperate, the judges sanctimoniously pontificate. I would much rather see a child raised by someone like *The Cosby Show*'s Claire Huxtable than the NBA's Latrell Sprewell, but in courts like the one presided over by Judge Ronald Washington (see Chapter 8), even a Mrs. Huxtable type would have a hard time gaining custody, and her children would have more difficulty reaching their potential.

A Model Mother and a Deadbeat Dad

Gloria Morgan was a well-spoken and attractive African-American woman in her mid-thirties when I first met her. She was a single mother with a five-year-old son, Raymond, whom she had raised without any help from the boy's father, Skunk Richardson. Gloria had made a successful career for herself in public relations and devoted herself to little Ray. She was, and is, responsible, intelligent, honest, and a classy individual in every way.

Skunk Richardson was a short, heavyset, well-dressed African-

American in his early forties. He had five children from three separate relationships and rarely paid support for any of them. Since the birth of Raymond, Skunk had been convicted of crimes against Gloria three times, including assault, aggravated harassment, and violation of an order of protection. He had been out of work for most of Ray's life. Skunk was rude, lewd, obnoxious, and dishonest.

I sometimes thought that Gloria was the type of person Judge Washington would have enjoyed meeting at a party and Richardson was someone the judge would have been afraid to meet on the street. A more lopsided custody battle would be hard to imagine, until Judge Washington decided to treat the parties "fairly."

By the time Gloria first phoned me, she was a litigation veteran. Custody, visitation, and support proceedings had dragged out in Westchester Family Court for almost four years. An application was also pending in Steuben County Family Court based upon Gloria's residence in upstate Corning, New York, for over a year. She had been represented by several lawyers over the years, with mixed results. Some domestic violence agencies recommended me to Gloria, and she made an appointment to see me.

The pitch of her voice rose and she shook her head in disbelief as she described the unbelievable turns her case had taken. Gloria could not understand how the courts could treat her so badly, and her shock was justified. Repeatedly, Skunk had been caught in lies, criminal behavior, and violations of court orders, but this seemed to make no difference to Judge Washington.

Gloria had not intended to have a child with Skunk and left him eleven months after Ray was born. Skunk was emotionally abusive before and during her pregnancy. His aggression escalated after Raymond was born, especially after Gloria decided to leave. Although the physical abuse was limited to pushing and a few slaps, he threatened to kill her if she left and repeatedly stalked her thereafter. She pressed criminal charges for assault and harassment.

The criminal court initially worked as it should. Skunk was convicted of aggravated harassment and was forced to serve a few weeks in jail. Gloria received an order of protection. Several months later, she had to call the police because Skunk was yelling and cursing at her during a visitation exchange. He sat in his car, refusing to leave, until the police came.

The police officer started to open the car door to speak with him, but Skunk attempted to get away by hitting the accelerator while the officer was holding onto the door. This foolish behavior could easily have resulted in a serious injury. The police wanted to charge Skunk with assault and resisting arrest, but the district attorney accepted a plea bargain whereby Skunk admitted only to violating the order of protection. He spent just two more weeks in jail.

Gloria filed a petition in Family Court seeking custody, and Skunk countered with a petition for visitation. Before making any decisions, the court ordered the Probation Department to conduct a home study of the parties' residences. Skunk refused to reveal his address until the judge told him he could not receive visitation without the home study. The loving father responded by providing a false address, which was in reality a friend's apartment. Judge Washington ordered supervised visitation as a result of the deception.

Richardson appeared for two of the five scheduled visitations and provided a second false address to the Probation Department. Thereafter, Skunk agreed to accept Gloria as the custodial parent and to drop any claims for visitation in return for having Gloria withdraw all the charges against him. She notified the court and the Probation Department that she was leaving the area in order to take a job so she could support Ray and herself.

Gloria had previously sought child support in the Family Court. Skunk conducted a campaign to delay any determination of child support. He sought adjournments based on pretended illnesses and to seek an attorney. At times, he failed to appear for scheduled appointments and then claimed he had had no notice. Perhaps the most bizarre delay came when he claimed to be unable to appear because he had to fight in Desert Storm. This spectacular lie was revealed when it turned out he wasn't even in the military, but the court never punished him for his deceit.

Ultimately, Gloria won a judgment for support, but Skunk rarely if ever paid any support to Gloria. Over the more than six years that the parties fought over custody, Skunk continually failed to pay and sought to be relieved from his child-support obligations. Whenever Gloria tried to enforce the support order, he claimed poverty. He always had money for expensive clothes, legal fees, and travel to harass Gloria, but never anything for his son.

Court-Ordered Harassment

My client moved to Corning, New York, to start a new life for herself and her son. She worked in the public relations department of a large corporation and quickly won their respect and admiration, despite several calls from Skunk attacking her character. If the court system worked, the story could have ended here, but Judge Washington does not permit happy endings. Contrary to the settlement, the court dismissed all of Gloria's charges against Skunk, but reinstated his petition for visitation.

Skunk filed a writ of habeas corpus (requiring her to produce the child), claiming that Gloria had illegally removed Raymond from Westchester and prevented visitation. The court required Gloria to leave work and travel 250 miles in order to bring her son to the judge. My client shook her head and her voice rose to a soprano as she explained, "There was no visitation order, I personally told Judge Washington I was moving to Corning, and Skunk had been caught lying umpteen times, but none of it mattered to Washington."

Years passed before Gloria was given any opportunity to answer the wild charges against her. Judge Washington is notorious for permitting custody and visitation litigation to drag on for years. In an attempt at being "fair," the judge gives litigants every opportunity to prove even the most ludicrous charges. The case is scheduled for a day or two of trial, but often interrupted with other emergencies. When the trial cannot be completed in the time allotted, additional trial time is scheduled, but the dates are usually two to three months later. In the interim, new incidents inevitably occur that must be fully explored at the trial. As a result, Judge Washington presides over many "career cases." This case continued for four years in this manner.

The court initially awarded Skunk visitation supervised by the Probation Department. After a few months, unsupervised visitation was permitted and Gloria was required to do most of the driving. Washington justified this burden because the mother had "voluntarily" moved out of the area. The fact that Gloria moved to get away from her abuser and to obtain employment to provide for a child the father refused to support had no weight with the judge.

The bad situation became worse with the appointment of Bill Skinner as Skunk's attorney. Skinner was a tall, thin African-American in his early forties when he was first appointed. This ethically challenged attorney is adept at ingratiating himself with judges and other influential people while being obnoxious to everyone else. Despite the harm to the child, Skinner encouraged Skunk to keep the case going. On three separate occasions Gloria and Skunk agreed to settle the proceedings, only to have Skinner sabotage the agreement.

Abusive men such as Skunk often seek custody or visitation as a means to continue their abuse against a former lover, but courts assume that the request is made out of love for the child. Judge Washington confidently predicted that the visitation order would reduce the friction between the parties, but Skunk was only interested in punishing Gloria. Repeatedly, the father refused visitation; then he filed another writ of habeas corpus seeking an immediate change of custody and the production of the child, based on his claim of being denied visitation. The judge had a hard time believing that Skunk would deliberately refuse visitation in order to file charges against Gloria; accordingly, the charges were taken seriously. More incidents had to be litigated, and visitation was increased without any substantiation of the charges.

Gloria knew that Raymond would never be protected by Judge Washington. She also could not afford the legal and travel expenses necessary to litigate in Westchester. Accordingly, Gloria submitted an order to show cause in Steuben County seeking to modify the visitation and give the child's home county jurisdiction. The convenience of the child and the proximity of potential witnesses strongly supported jurisdiction in Steuben County. The judge in Steuben County agreed, took jurisdiction, and required future visitation to take place near the child's home. Gloria allowed herself to dream that her nightmare might be over. Skunk responded in the only way he knew, by filing still another writ of habeas corpus in Westchester, seeking to punish Gloria for filing court papers in her home county.

Gloria hired me to represent her in the Westchester proceeding, after Skunk's latest writ and before the judge's decision. She believed that Judge Washington had mistreated her throughout the many proceedings and wanted him off the case. Skunk had never proven any of his allegations, but the judge treated each new claim as if it had merit. Gloria was also afraid of Judge Washington because he had yelled at her in addition to making unfair decisions. The judge was notorious for his courtroom outbursts as a Yonkers City Court judge, but it was especially harmful that he verbally abused victims of domestic violence who came to Family Court for protection.

I explained to Gloria, "When it comes to custody, you have a big advantage because Ray has lived with you his entire life and you are a good mother, but when it comes to visitation, Skunk is favored." Ronald Washington was an African-American judge being called upon to decide custody and visitation for an African-American family. Aware of the widespread problem of absentee African-American fathers, he was bending over backwards to keep Skunk in Raymond's life. I knew Washington to be a compassionate person, but he would have helped the child far more by forcing Skunk to act responsibly.

My first appearance in the case was to respond to the latest writ. Gloria had to bring Raymond to the court because Skunk claimed he did not know where his son was living. Ray was uncomfortable in the waiting room because both his parents were present. Skunk exacerbated the situation by trying to keep his son away from Gloria. The child wanted to spend time with his father, but only in small doses.

The law guardian for Raymond was Mary Lucas. Although I had never met Ms. Lucas, she was an experienced attorney and the law partner of another law guardian I knew and liked. She was professional and personally pleasant, but refused to take sides. Ms. Lucas knew that Gloria was a good mother and there was no reason to change custody. She regarded the case as mostly about visitation and wanted Skunk to have as much visitation as possible. The law guardian tried to be "fair" to both parties, but ignored many of Skunk's serious shortcomings in order to avoid an appearance of bias.

I calmly explained all the reasons it was in Raymond's best interest for any custody or visitation litigation to occur near his home. Skinner responded with a diatribe about what a terrible mother Gloria was and how she had repeatedly interfered with his client's visitation rights. He requested an immediate change in custody and wanted my client punished for filing papers in another court.

In response, I pointed out that a basic purpose of the court system is for disputes to be decided in court instead of through violence. A party's pursuit of her legal rights in a court of law should not be made an excuse to punish that person. Judge Washington stated that he was fully familiar with the case after more than three years and, therefore, was better placed to decide the outstanding issues. He had spoken to the Steuben County judge, and all proceedings would be conducted in Westchester.

Going to Trial

The obnoxious behavior of Skunk and Skinner made the trial unpleasant. I had not said one word to Skunk the entire afternoon of the first day of trial, but as Gloria and I were waiting for the elevator Skunk yelled at me, "I'm going to get you, you fag." When I mentioned this to Judge Washington at the next court appearance, he made no effort to restrain Skunk. A few months later, when there was a problem with the return of Raymond's clothing after a visitation, I tried to solve the problem with Skinner. I started to say, "I would appreciate it if you could have your client return the clothes after the afternoon session." Before I could finish, Skinner interrupted by saying, "I do not care what you would appreciate." This was the most honest statement I would ever hear him utter.

Skinner called Gloria as his first witness at the trial. He tended to ask long, convoluted questions that often were only remotely connected to the issues before the court. Skunk had told his lawyer a series of lies, which Skinner fully believed. Repeatedly the attorney was surprised at Gloria's answers to his questions.

Two basic rules of good cross-examination are (1) do not ask "why" questions, and (2) do not ask questions to which you do not know the answer. Skinner would repeatedly ask questions like, "Why did you deny Skunk a particular visitation?" only to find out that Skunk had called to cancel the visitation or had failed to appear when the visitation was scheduled. Accordingly, Skinner accomplished little with the witness, but managed to waste four days of court time over the course of several months.

The disadvantage of calling the adverse party as a witness is that the party's attorney can ask leading questions on cross-examination. In previous hearings, Gloria had never had the opportunity to answer Skunk's wild charges. My questions gave her the opportunity to explain that she had not interfered with Skunk's visitation. Each missed visitation was caused by his cancellation or refusal to promise to return the child to her home. On one occasion, the visitation was canceled because Raymond was sick. Gloria notified Skunk of the illness, but he came to pick up the child anyway and sought to involve the police. She tried to testify about the history of abuse, but Washington was not interested.

My client accepted the need for visitation, but did not want to carry the brunt of the transportation burden. Skunk was out of work and refusing to pay support; the least he could do for his son was to provide transportation. Gloria had trouble seeing to drive at night, which she was required to do to comply with the court's order. She also wanted the exchanges to be either at her home or at her parents' home in Westchester for her own safety.

Raymond suffered from lactose intolerance, which required that he take medication and avoid milk and chocolate. Failure to follow this regimen would result in painful constipation. Gloria testified that she had repeatedly explained Ray's condition to Skunk and provided the medication; this concerned father frequently gave the child chocolate, but failed to give him the medicine. As a result, Raymond often came home sick from visits.

The previous December, the court had ordered that Skunk have visitation the first week of Christmas vacation and return Raymond on December 26. Richardson traumatized the child by refusing to return him until January 2. Ray was clinging to Gloria for months after this incident and often refused to speak to his father on the phone. Skunk blamed my client when his son would not speak with him.

Trial sessions were often scheduled a month or two apart. In the interim, the visitation order continued. Raymond was required to visit with his father one weekend every month, and more during holidays or summer vacation. While the trial was recessed in the middle of Gloria's testimony, Skunk lost his temper during a visitation, slapped Ray and locked him in the bathroom. At first, when the child returned home, he did not tell his mother what had happened, but again clung to her more than ever before. After a few days at home Raymond revealed what had happened. Angry with his father, the boy told my client he never wanted to speak with his father or go for visitation again.

Gloria filed a report with the Child Protective Service (CPS). The worker investigated the complaint over several weeks and believed the complaint to be valid. This opinion was supported by the child's therapist, who recommended that the visitation be suspended. CPS ruled the case "indicated," which means there is strong, credible evidence to sustain the allegation. One week while the case worker was on vacation, Bill Skinner pulled some strings and the case was expunged. We never learned how Skinner managed to distort the outcome, but, to this day, the case worker believes the decision was improper.

Judge Washington was not concerned about this incident. Once the report came back expunged, he concluded that Gloria was at least as much to blame for the child's anger at his father as Skunk was. Aside from a slight decrease in the visitation and providing the child with the right to call his mother, Washington did nothing to protect Raymond after this incident.

Gloria was a reasonable and articulate witness. Although she expressed her frustration a few times at the court's failure to protect her son, she kept her composure and told her story. Gloria had tried to encourage the relationship between Raymond and Skunk and understood the benefit of such a relationship to her son. She wanted the judge to force the father to act more responsibly and share more of the burden. With Skunk not working or paying child support, he could at least provide the transportation for visitation. He could also help the child by ending the constant litigation.

While waiting to finish her testimony, Gloria learned that her job was being terminated, but she had the opportunity to continue working for the company as an independent contractor. In order to do so, however, she would need to move to the Washington, D.C., area. Her new home would actually be slightly closer to Westchester and easier to get to because of better transportation. Washington also has fewer snow problems than Corning, New York. Gloria told Skunk of the impending move and even let Raymond visit with his father while she looked for a house. Skunk responded by filing still another writ of habeas corpus, claiming Gloria was trying secretly to spirit the child out of the state.

Skunk was the next witness and he reiterated the litany of past charges. According to Skunk, Gloria had continually interfered with visitation, phone calls, and the transmission of information from schools, doctors, and babysitters. He told many stories, mostly fictitious, of his attempts to gain information and maintain a relationship with Raymond. In Skunk's view of the world, the police, teachers, babysitters, and almost everyone connected with Gloria or their dispute was out to get him. Although Skinner had frequently claimed to have evidence supporting the allegations, the entire case consisted of Skunk's unsubstantiated accusations.

During cross-examination, Skunk testified that he was seeing a therapist to work on past relationship problems and parenting skills. He claimed to have become a better father as a result of his treatment. I asked for the name and address of the alleged therapist, but Skunk refused to answer. The judge forced him to provide the information, but when I attempted to subpoena the therapist, we learned there was no such person.

Skunk repeated a claim from one of his writs of habeas corpus that the police in Corning, New York, had told him that Raymond was in school at a time when Gloria claimed the child was too sick to go for visitation. He also claimed that the police had threatened to arrest him if he ever came to Corning again. Skunk used this allegation as an excuse to avoid traveling to Corning to pick up or drop off the child.

Based on this unsubstantiated claim, Judge Washington refused to permit the convenience of exchanges in Corning. As part of Gloria's case, we called a detective from Corning who was familiar with the alleged incidents to testify. He confirmed that no one from the police department had told Skunk that Raymond was in school or had threatened him in any way.

We also called the police officer from Tuckahoe (Westchester County), New York, who had been involved in the incident mentioned earlier that took place during a visitation exchange. The officer testified that as he was talking with Skunk, Skunk had started to drive away while the officer was holding onto the open door. Although his injuries were minor, the policeman believed he had been lucky to escape a more serious injury. In the "he said, she said" case before the court, testimony from two disinterested police officers showing Skunk to be a liar and a dangerous individual should have made an impression, but not with Judge Washington.

In the closing arguments, Skinner repeated all of Skunk's charges as if they were gospel and continually referred to Gloria as a liar. I reminded the court that Skinner had repeatedly promised proof of the various allegations but, in the end, had only the testimony of a convicted criminal who had been caught in lies many times.

Most importantly, I asked Washington to think of the best interests of the child. The child might benefit from having a relationship with his father, but the question of whether Raymond would grow up to be a responsible member of society like his mother or a dysfunctional failure like his father would in the end be determined by the relationship with his mother. The court and the father needed to understand that by supporting Gloria and lightening her burden, they would be helping Raymond. Custody in this case should not be considered a serious issue, and the judge should place the transportation burden on the father. The law guardian also favored continued custody for Gloria, but with more visitation and shared transportation.

I received the decision a few weeks after the closing arguments. Gloria continued to have custody, but the remainder of the decision was unfavorable. Judge Washington required my client to drive to Westchester every month for visitation, and sometimes more often for holidays. Skunk was given an additional weekend per month of visitation, but had to drive to Washington for it. As expected, he never exercised this visitation because he was not interested in seeing his son, but only in harassing Gloria. Worst of all, the judge ordered that any future dispute be decided in Westchester, which guaranteed the litigation would go on forever.

The Last Straw

Gloria was disappointed, but not surprised, at the results. I did not hear from her for several months, and then she called to tell me what had happened. Skunk had fired Bill Skinner as his attorney, but submitted still another writ of habeas corpus. A major snowstorm was predicted for the court date and Gloria was afraid she would be caught in the storm if she came to court. Accordingly, she faxed a letter to Judge Washington explaining that she could not come because of the weather. The snow had not yet started falling on the morning of the court appearance. Gloria's new attorney was also unable to appear.

Skunk asked the judge for an immediate change in custody. The law guardian strenuously objected because of the trauma such an order would inevitably cause to seven-year-old Raymond, but Washington gave the father temporary custody. Without warning, the police came to Gloria's home and took the child away, kicking and screaming.

When Gloria called me, she had contacted a reporter for the *Westchester County Weekly* and asked me to speak with her. I spoke with the reporter about Gloria's case and also put her in touch with Barbara Kowalick (see Chapter 8). Many of the other sources were afraid of Judge Washington and did not wish their names to be used. The resulting article told the story of Judge Washington by discussing his effect on the lives of Gloria and Barbara (who used a pseudonym for protection). Interviews with Washington (who was ethically barred from discussing the merits of the cases), as well as the presiding Family Court judge, representatives from the district attorney's office and some women's groups, and a social worker familiar with the courts, led to a fair but critical article.

The judge was criticized for a lack of judicial temperament based on his predilection for yelling at parties and their attorneys, as well as for his insensitivity regarding domestic violence issues. In a campaign statement about women leaving their abusers made when he first ran for Family Court, Washington had stated, "The court must use authority and power sensitively to make the victim secure and steadfast in her decision." The judge had brought intelligence, diligence, and compassion with him to the bench, but had failed to fulfill his promise to help protect victims of domestic violence. The article suggested that this failure was not due to malice, but to a lack of understanding. In one case, Washington had left observers bewildered when he ordered the victim of a brutal beating to supervise the visitation of her assailant.

The power of the article came from the courage and eloquence of Gloria and Barbara as they explained the overwhelming pain and fear Washington had caused them. They are both now married and, to all outward appearances, doing well. In another era we might have said that they lived happily ever after, but their experiences with Washington are seared into their souls. There will always be a pain in their hearts because they came to the court for protection, only to be abused all over again.

I was apprehensive appearing before Washington just a few days after the article appeared. I hoped he would be touched and changed by my clients' words and undeniable suffering. In fact, he has improved as a judge since the article appeared. Washington no longer yells unprofessionally during court sessions, but he remains ignorant about domestic violence issues.

I did not learn the final outcome for Raymond until I read the article. The judge's decision was never made into an order because Skunk fired his attorney. Gloria's new attorney discovered there was no order that had been violated. Accordingly, there was no basis for the change of custody, and Washington had to restore custody to Gloria at the next hearing.

Skunk angrily accused Judge Washington of having an affair with Gloria. Why else, he implied, would a judge permit Raymond to live with his mother?

Chapter 10

JUSTICE DENIED

The Jensen Case

S UPREME COURT JUSTICE Daniel P. O'Connor was familiar with the work of Joseph Sullivan, a successful and well-respected attorney and town justice. Both men were active in the Republican Party and often met during their campaigns for judicial office. Sullivan complained that his ex-wife had destroyed his relationship with his children and prevented any visitation. He asked O'Connor for a divorce—from his children. Judge O'Connor believed a distinguished judge and attorney could not possibly be an abusive alcoholic—the situation had to be the ex-wife's fault. This is how one family lost their support.

A Damaged Relationship

I first met Annette Jensen when she came to my office for a consultation during the spring of 1989. Annette was a suburban housewife in her mid-forties. She had a problem because her ex-husband had stopped paying child support and maintenance, with the approval of the Family Court.

Annette's divorce had taken only eight months from summons to judgment, but the litigation consumed the family for many years. The parties were divorced in 1984, with Annette receiving custody of the parties' four children. Sullivan received normal visitation and was required to furnish child support and maintenance. However, problems developed because the children did not want to see their father.

In 1984, Jessica was 17, Matthew was 15, Josh was 12, and Sarah was 8. Throughout the marriage, Sullivan spent little time with the children and was frequently emotionally abusive. During this time, he was an active alcoholic. The alcoholism did not interfere with his professional career; he waited for evenings and weekends before starting to drink. This behavior, however, created a bad relationship between Sullivan and the children, which was further damaged by incidents in the spring of 1984 when he assaulted Annette and Jessica. The last such attack, in June of 1984, resulted in a Family Court order removing Sullivan from the marital home.

The judgment of divorce made no provision for repairing the relationship between father and children. Instead, the children were expected to suddenly spend substantial time with their father. Sullivan made it clear that he would withhold needed support if he were denied any of his visitation. Under the circumstances, it is not surprising that problems developed.

The children rebelled at going for visitation. Sullivan knew only two responses: he threatened to go to court, or he went to court. In the fall of 1985 he obtained a Supreme Court order requiring visitation. In January of 1986, Judge Harriet Dunston ordered a change of custody. This was done without the benefit of a law guardian, psychological evaluations, or even a full hearing. The children were brought to their father for one night, but quickly returned to live with their mother.

In April of 1986, Judge Dunston issued an order permitting Sullivan to withhold support in proportion to the visitation he was denied. From October 1986 until February 1989, the visitation took place. The children believed they were being exchanged for the payments and were uncomfortable during the visitation. This discomfort was worsened by Sullivan's sexual activities during the visitation. Although Sullivan was in another room, the children complained they could hear what he was doing.

Support Denied

In March of 1989, the children refused to go for visitation and the support stopped. Annette wanted to know if there was any way to force Sullivan to pay support without compromising her children. Under the April 1986 order, Sullivan had the right to withhold support whenever the visitation order was not complied with.

I suggested that we attempt to modify the visitation order. When Annette came to see me, Josh was 16 and Sarah was 13. Older children are often given a say in visitation decisions, especially if a parent has behaved abusively or inappropriately. I advised Annette to seek a Family Court order conditioning the visitation on the desires of the children. The children could then decide whether to go for visitation, and Annette would be in compliance with the visitation order. Such compliance would prevent Sullivan from withholding support.

Annette filed a modification petition in May of 1989. Sullivan responded with a petition seeking custody. Judge Carla Ponzini was assigned to the case. Judge Ponzini was an experienced jurist with a reputation for fairness and toughness; I was pleased to have her as the judge. She ordered psychological evaluations of the parties and appointed a law guardian for the children.

The court assigned Dr. Felix Schmidt (the psychiatrist in the Wong case, Chapter 2) to perform the evaluations. I would have objected to Dr. Schmidt, but the appointment was made between court sessions. By the time we returned to court, the evaluations were finished. The parties were ordered to share the cost of the evaluations. Annette had not received support for several months and had no money to pay for the evaluations. I was not permitted to see a copy of the evaluation until the money was paid.

Denise Puglia was appointed as the law guardian. She was a 35-year-old, well-respected and experienced professional. When we returned to court, Ms. Puglia approached me with a proposal for the parties to waive the trial and permit the judge to make a decision based upon Dr. Schmidt's evaluations. Ms. Puglia assured me that the evaluations were favorable to Annette. She said the doctor had concluded Sullivan was an active alcoholic with serious personality disorders.

We trusted Ms. Puglia and agreed to permit Judge Ponzini to make a decision based on the evaluations. The judge dismissed Sullivan's petition for custody, saying, "It would be unwarranted to change custody against the expressed wishes of older children and in the face of a damning evaluation of Mr. Sullivan." Annette's petition was granted. All future visitation would be at the discretion of the children. I asked the court to order Sullivan to resume payment of support. Judge Ponzini agreed he would have to pay the support, but she could not order payment because no petition was before her.

I spoke with Sullivan's attorney after the court session. He claimed to have a legal theory by which Sullivan could avoid payment. I warned him I would demand legal fees if he made us go to court in order to collect the support. Sullivan acted like he was doing Annette a favor, but he did resume paying support. This time the court had worked perfectly.

Divorcing the Children

The new arrangement worked for eighteen months, until Sullivan brought an order to show cause in Supreme Court. Sullivan's claim was most unusual. He alleged that his children had abandoned him and therefore, in effect, he wanted to divorce them. The purpose was to eliminate all child support and maintenance. Sullivan claimed that Annette's behavior had poisoned his relationship with the children.

Sullivan relied on a recent decision in which a father had been permitted to terminate all child support because the child refused to have anything to do with him. The case cited was actually very different in its facts. The child refused to go to counseling with her father to improve the relationship (it was Sullivan who refused counseling in our case); there was no contact between father and daughter (in our case, Sullivan saw the children, but did not have all the visitation he said he wanted); and the other father attempted to promote a relationship with his daughter (Sullivan never called, sent cards, or made any overtures to heal the relationship).

Annette gave me a copy of the order to show cause in early June of 1991. I explained that orders to show cause are routinely signed even when their claims are weak. The order merely requires the opposing party to demonstrate why the relief sought by the moving party is not justified. I confidently prepared a written response to the order. In addition to the facts mentioned above, we had the last Family Court order. Sullivan misrepresented the facts of the Family Court proceeding, claiming to have consented to the withdrawal of his petition and the new order. I informed the court of what had really happened, and suggested Sullivan's misrepresentations damaged his credibility.

The presiding judge was Daniel P. O'Connor. He was an experienced judge, having served many years as a Family Court judge before being elected to the Supreme Court. He was known as a no-nonsense ex-Marine with a strong sense of integrity. I expected the motion to be denied, but Judge O'Connor ordered a trial. Annette thought that bias was involved—a belief that was strengthened by the timing on the motion. The order was presented on May 31; the response was on June 26, and the court ordered a trial for July 28. It is unusual to receive a trial so quickly on a nonemergency issue.

Annette had experienced similar circumstances with her divorce in 1984, which Judge O'Connor also handled. The complaint was served on March 8, the answer on March 19, the reply on March 27, and on

March 30 Sullivan filed his net worth statement and a note of issue. The note of issue places the case on the trial calendar and says all discovery has been completed. In fact, no depositions had been held and there was no time to review Sullivan's financial statement. Annette's attorney made a motion to cancel the note of issue in order to have discovery. The court permitted a deposition, but refused to delay the trial. The trial was scheduled for November 2 and resulted in an unfavorable settlement, at least in part because of the inadequate time to review Sullivan's assets and income.

I did not believe Judge O'Connor would deliberately favor a party. The judge knew Sullivan, but there was no personal relationship between them. I told Annette that there was a discrepancy in the factual claims of the parties. The judge probably wanted to resolve the factual issues before dismissing the motion.

Annette asked if I would mind her having people at the court to support her during the trial. I had no objection, and Annette arranged for members of the Coalition for Family Justice to come to court. The Coalition is an organization founded by Monica Getz to help people (mostly women) who have been treated unfairly by the court system. Monica Getz had been married to jazz great Stan Getz. They were involved in a terrible divorce, exacerbated by greedy attorneys taking advantage of his alcoholism. This resulted in a frightful emotional toll and hundreds of thousands of dollars in wasted legal fees. Monica formed the coalition in the hopes that other people would not have to be victimized by the court system.

At the start of the trial, Monica and a few other members of the Coalition were present to support Annette. Also present was a reporter for a local newspaper. The paper was interested in the case because Sullivan was a town justice. Sullivan represented himself for the order to show cause, but was represented by Paul Burton at the trial.

Burton immediately made a motion to bar spectators (especially the reporter) from the courtroom. The courts are generally supposed to be open to the public. Judges have discretion in rare cases to bar the public when sensitive testimony is being presented (such as testimony by a child concerning sexual abuse). The case at trial had no such sensitive issues; it was basically about financial matters. Accordingly there was no proper justification for barring spectators, especially considering that one party wanted the spectators to be present.

I vehemently opposed the motion. Judge O'Connor called a recess during which he called the reporter's boss in an attempt to kill the story. The judge was angry about the spectators and particularly the reporter. When he returned to the courtroom, O'Connor barred everyone but the parties and their attorneys from the courtroom. Since this case, the rules have changed so that the public can no longer be removed.

I expected the trial to take a few hours. The last court determination had been only eighteen months before, and not many incidents had occurred since. Sullivan would be the only witness his side presented. He sought to go back through the entire history of the case. I objected to any evidence from before the last Family Court proceeding, but Judge O'Connor permitted him to testify about everything that had happened since the divorce. I told Annette the judge was probably trying to understand the context of the problems during the last eighteen months.

Annette became less assured as Sullivan went into great detail concerning every incident for the past seven years, and my objections were all overruled. Sullivan and his attorney seemed to deliberately drag out his testimony. The first day of trial concluded with Sullivan still on direct examination. I tried to reassure Annette. Most of the testimony was only marginally related to this motion. Sullivan probably had a psychological need to perform this way.

Sullivan finished his direct testimony the next morning. Aside from the long history of missed visits and frequent court actions, the evidence presented was limited. He claimed he had had no contact with Josh and Sarah during the last two and a half years. He said Annette had poisoned the children against him. Sullivan also presented a note he had received from Josh that said, "Hey asshole—This is your son Josh. Hide, I'm coming to kill you! You better start looking over your shoulder! I know you're a millionaire and it's time to die! Death = Big Bucks $$_____$."

During the cross-examination, Sullivan admitted he had had several contacts with the children, including phone calls and visits. In fact, the note from Josh was in response to a meeting in which Sullivan had refused to help Josh with college expenses. Sullivan acknowledged that unless he received the full visitation set forth in the original divorce judgment, he did not count it as any contact. Therefore any phone calls or visits for less than a weekend were not considered contact with his children.

I asked Sullivan if he was familiar with his children's therapist, Barbara Finkel, who stated, "The various court orders are not solving the problem because the court is unaware of what the real problems are as they relate to the children. Accordingly I would recommend the gradual rebuilding of the relationship." He did not remember the exact quote, but admitted the recommendation of therapy between himself and the children. He stated that he had an order requiring visitation, and therefore there was no need for therapy or any type of graduated visitation. Sullivan admitted he had made no effort to promote a relationship with his children, except by court actions and threats of court actions.

Sullivan denied he had a problem with alcohol. He falsely claimed to have consented to the last Family Court order. Sullivan denied that the evaluation by Dr. Schmidt was unfavorable or that the evaluation had led to Judge Ponzini's decision. He maintained his position that Annette was the sole cause of his poor relationship with the children.

After Sullivan finished his testimony and rested, I made a motion to dismiss his order to show cause. "By his own testimony," I confidently argued to the court, "Sullivan has admitted that he has enjoyed substantial contact with his children. Furthermore, his failure to agree to counseling with his children (contrary to the case relied upon by Sullivan) or alter visitation to make it more acceptable to the children demonstrates that he has substantially contributed to the bad relationship with the children. You heard him say that the only efforts he made were to go to court or threaten to go to court. It is obvious that this rigidity caused the problems with his children.

"The Family Court, even after all the prior proceedings, had the opportunity to review the visitation with the help of evaluations. Judge Ponzini specifically chose to give the children a choice in visitation. The children have tried to work out a relationship with their father. They saw and spoke with him several times by phone and in person. His inflexibility has thus far caused these attempts to fail. Now he goes back to the only method he knows, another court action. This method does not work for the children and it cannot be made to work for him. By his own testimony, Sullivan has demonstrated that the children have not abandoned him. He now seeks the court's help. This court should help him and help the children by dismissing this unfortunate motion."

Sullivan's attorney responded by reiterating the long history of problems with visitation. It did not matter what he said; Judge O'Connor quickly rejected my motion.

We were disappointed with the judge's decision. I thought my motion should have been granted. Monica Getz suggested that

O'Connor was biased against Annette. Others suggested he had been bought off. I explained to Annette that there is a heavy burden of proof to have a case thrown out without presenting our side. Even weak cases can survive such a motion. For the purpose of the motion, the court must consider the evidence in the light most favorable to Sullivan, but this should not be true for the final decision.

Annette was called as our first witness. Paul Burton, Sullivan's attorney, objected to testimony about Sullivan's abuse of Annette. I reminded the court that Sullivan had been permitted extensive testimony about visitation problems that had occurred long before the present visitation order. The children knew about Sullivan's abuse of their mother and it was only natural it would affect their feelings towards him. Judge O'Connor limited the testimony to incidents occurring in the presence of the children, and made it clear he did not think this was an important subject.

Annette testified about Sullivan's history of alcoholism. He had had little involvement with the children even when they lived together as a family. He spent his weeks at work, his weekends with his cars, and evenings drunk. He was always very rigid; he referred to himself as "Master of the Universe" and expected to be treated as such. When the divorce occurred, the children virtually did not know their father.

Sullivan made no effort to make the visitation enjoyable for the children. Once when Sarah asked to go home he responded, "You have to stay here—it says so in the judgment." As a result of his behavior, Annette had to force the children to go for visitation or they would not go. After the Family Court order in April of 1986, the children were forced to go for visitation. Annette testified, "Sarah and Josh were exchanged for maintenance and child support."

In February of 1989 the children rebelled and refused to go any more. They were particularly upset about the alcohol abuse and sexual activity that occurred during the visitation. Mr. Burton made a hearsay objection because Annette had not been present during the visitation. This objection was properly sustained, but it meant we had to call the children if we wanted to present this evidence.

Since the divorce, Annette had become active in the fight against domestic violence and unfairness in the courts. As part of these activities, she had spoken before a state commission and written a letter to the local paper at a time when Sullivan was running for reelection. She complained about how Sullivan manipulated the courts in order to avoid support and maintenance.

Burton sought to question her about these statements. I strongly objected on the ground that it was not relevant to the issues in the case. The issue was whether she sought to harm the children's relationship with Sullivan. Unless it could be shown that these activities affected the children, this was unrelated to the issues before the court. Even if Annette had harmed Sullivan's reputation (perhaps rightfully), her actions would not justify the termination of child support or maintenance. If Sullivan were slandered or libeled, he could sue Annette, but these activities were irrelevant to the case on trial. I was shocked when O'Connor permitted the questions and obviously took the subject seriously. The judge asked to see a copy of the newspaper article and read it through.

Under the circumstances, we decided we had to call Sarah as a witness. She was the only one who might make the judge understand the real reason there was such a bad relationship between Sullivan and his children. Sarah Sullivan was a pretty fifteen-year-old with brown hair and a sweet smile. She was nervous and spoke in a soft voice. I limited my questions in order to make it easier for her. She testified that during the visitation her father had several drinks of alcohol. She was embarrassed by his behavior with his girlfriend. They would hug and kiss in front of her and then have sex in their bedroom. She could hear the sounds while they made love, and it disturbed her.

Sarah stated that her mother had done nothing to interfere with her relationship with Sullivan. She thought it was still possible to have a relationship with her father if he would take it slow and make an effort. She hoped he would do this. Sarah was on the stand less than five minutes, and I was about to ask my last question when she burst into tears. The judge immediately called a recess, saying, "This is why I asked you not to have the children testify."

When she walked out of the courtroom, Sarah told us that her father had been mouthing words and mocking her while she was testifying. I was not looking at Sullivan and did not see it. Obviously, neither did the judge. When Josh heard what Sullivan had done to his sister, he ran into the courtroom and started cursing his father. This was reported to the judge when the recess ended. When Sarah resumed her testimony, she told the court what had caused her to cry. At the end of her testimony, we rested our case.

The recess lasted almost an hour, giving me plenty of time to prepare my closing argument. I wanted to put the evidence together for the judge so he could see that Sullivan had no right to the relief he sought.

Sullivan's testimony that he had had no contact with the children for two and a half years had been refuted. Sarah had expressed a willingness to work on her relationship with her father. Only Sullivan refused to show any flexibility with his children. Under the circumstances, the facts were totally different from the case Sullivan was relying on. As I gave my closing arguments, Judge O'Connor paid little attention and spent part of the time writing.

An Unfair Decision

As soon as I finished, the judge read his decision. He believed everything Sullivan said and nothing from our side. He said Sarah was a naive girl who could not possibly have known the sounds from her father's bedroom were associated with sex. (In this the judge was partially correct; she did not know what the sounds were until she asked Josh.) Judge O'Connor said that although not perfect, Sullivan was a good father who did not deserve such treatment. He blamed Annette totally for the problems between Sullivan and the children. The judge again referred to Annette's letter to the editor about Sullivan. He thought it proved Annette to be vindictive and hostile to the relationship between the children and their father. Judge O'Connor said to Annette, "If it were in my power, I would put you in jail for six months."

The court canceled all maintenance and all arrears. He ordered Sullivan to pay $3,000 per year per child, on a six-figure income. The father was also required to pay college expenses not to exceed the cost of a state-financed school. On top of everything else, Annette was ordered to pay $5,400 for Sullivan's legal fees.

We were all devastated by this unfair decision. The length of the trial meant Annette could not possibly afford to purchase the transcripts for an appeal. Sullivan had found a successful way to avoid paying the support to which his family was entitled.

I spent much time thinking about how Judge O'Connor could make a decision so at variance with the evidence. This was especially puzzling in light of his behavior when he was assigned to some of my other cases. On other cases, he was much more reasonable and helpful. I did not believe he had been paid off. I believe Judge O'Connor knew Sullivan as a competent professional and an honored jurist. He could not imagine that someone with such a successful professional life could have an alcohol problem or be such a monster in his private life. In fact, such a pattern is all too common.

My theory about Judge O'Connor was strengthened by another case in which the judge appeared biased in favor of a husband who was also a lawyer. Judges can be much like mental health professionals without training on abuse issues. Inevitably they will encounter abuse cases. They try to use common sense, but this often does not work in a domestic violence case. As a result, they make the wrong decision. They then consider themselves experienced in abuse cases and keep making the same wrong decisions. I believe this is what happened to Annette and her brave family.

Part II

COURTING DISASTER

Enlisting the Courts in the Fight Against Abuse

Chapter 11

THE HARM OF
DOMESTIC VIOLENCE

IMAGINE MEETING TAMMY BOYD when she was three years old. She has not stopped her brother from abusing her. Tell her why she deserves the abuse. Fifteen-year-old Fran Wong did not prevent her sister's husband from fondling her. Thirty-year-old Karen Thomas was an alcoholic who remained with her husband despite many beatings.

I believe few people would blame Tammy, more would blame Fran, and many would blame Karen, but none of these women deserved their mistreatment. We could suggest better ways for each woman to handle her circumstances, but one hundred percent of the blame must go to the abusers. Perhaps this is easier to see when considering the three-year-old.

Until society stops entertaining the possibility that the victim at least shares in the blame, progress in fighting this plague will be limited. Repeatedly, I have seen judges equate the women's normal but inappropriate reactions to the violence with the men's abuse itself. The judges suggest that each party did something wrong and that both are relatively equally to blame. This approach sometimes hastens the end of a case, but it perpetuates the violence. Instead, the courts must consider whether each decision will promote or discourage domestic violence.

Society pays a high price in crime, economic loss, and social upheaval for tolerating domestic violence, but the steepest price is to the victims and their families. Tammy Boyd sat with me for three hours answering all my questions about the abuse she had suffered and its effects on her. After I wrote her chapter, I sent her a copy in case she had any suggestions or corrections. It took me a long while to reach her, and finally Tammy explained that she had tried to read the chapter several times, but could not get past the first few sentences. She cooperated in this book in hopes of helping others in similar circumstances, but her own story was too painful for her to read.

Tammy is an intelligent and caring woman, born with great potential. This potential has gone unrealized, and her life has been one of great pain and sadness, because of the abuse she suffered. Perhaps telling her story will accomplish more than she otherwise would have done with her life, but her potential should never have been limited in that manner. Tammy is a good mother to her two daughters, but inevitably these girls have been diminished by never having known the confident, happy, and successful woman Tammy might otherwise have been.

The courts systematically stripped Emily Pollack of custody of her children, visitation, money, and then her freedom. The judge did not seem to care about the harm he caused Emily, but he should at least have considered the damage he was doing to the four children. Judge McLaughlin deprived the children of the love, support, and example of their mother. The children learned quickly to take the side of the abuser in order to protect themselves and be on the winning side. They saw the great power of the court come down on the side of the abuser. I believe these children are in great danger of having relationships in which men abuse women when they are older, and of other dysfunctional behavior. In other words, the court failed to break the cycle of violence.

None of the stories in this book described murder or life-threatening physical injuries, and yet the consequences of the men's abuse and the courts' failure to respond appropriately are devastating for the women, their families, future generations, and the people who will come in contact with them. A calculation of the extent of domestic violence in this country depends on the definition used. One study found that two to four million women are abused by their partners each year, and between one-fifth and one-third of all women are abused by a partner during their lifetime. Another study, which defined abuse to include slapping, plate-throwing, or shoving, found that two-thirds of American husbands abuse their wives at some point during the marriage. Still more people are affected by child abuse.

The economic costs of domestic violence in this country cannot be calculated. One study put the cost of absenteeism from domestic violence at three to five billion dollars. (This does not consider women like Tammy Boyd who never developed careers.) Ninety-six percent of female inmates serving time for murder were victims of domestic violence. Numerous studies have shown a correlation between domestic violence and crime. Children who witness men abusing women have significantly higher rates of juvenile delinquency, including burglary, arson, prostitution, running away, drug use, and assault. One-half of all homeless women are on the street because of domestic violence. My aim is not to overwhelm the reader with statistics, but to demonstrate the foolishness of continuing to tolerate abuse.

Domestic violence makes a huge difference to our society. It is easy to see the effect on those killed and seriously injured. We have no trouble imagining the effect on the families and close friends of such victims. The public can also understand the tremendous impact of child sexual abuse. These are the headline victims of family violence. Such behavior is universally considered unacceptable.

Less extreme examples of domestic violence are largely hidden from society, but they have a significant impact on all of us. What happens when wives suffer through years of put-downs and physical abuse? How does it affect the children who witness such behavior? What becomes of the children who suffer similar mistreatment?

There are those who say that many people have grown up with serious abuse, but have overcome the mistreatment to become responsible, productive adults. This is true, but it does not change the fact that a significant percentage of our criminals and others who live dysfunctional lives were abused or witnessed abuse as children. Some politicians make a career out of appearing tough on crime, but even a five-percent drop in domestic violence would do more to reduce crime than all of their proposals.

The women and children described in this book are not likely to adopt a life of crime. Most are or will become productive citizens. Nevertheless, their lives have been diminished by the abuse they have suffered. Even for those who have recovered their self-esteem, years of their lives were lost while they accepted their abusers' poor opinion of them. Most will never reach their full potential or enjoy the happiness they would otherwise have experienced. Society has lost significant contributions from these and other victims of domestic violence.

Perhaps the most long-lasting effect of abuse is on relationships. When a person is abused by someone he or she is close to, trust is destroyed. Even when they leave their abusers, the effect on their ability to trust can persist and destroy new, otherwise healthy relationships. These problems can in turn affect a party's children, creating a whole new set of problems. Research shows that both abusers and victims of abuse tend to minimize the abuse. We must make sure not to emulate this example.

The remainder of Part II will discuss the various issues involved in domestic violence cases and present numerous ways that the system for dealing with domestic violence, and those who work within that system, might be improved to provide greater protection for victims of abuse and to hasten the end of domestic violence in our society.

Chapter 12

THE ISSUES

THE MAJOR ISSUES INVOLVED in domestic violence cases are custody and visitation, grounds for divorce, orders of protection, criminal issues, offender education programs, and financial issues, including child support. The last is such a large and important topic that we will devote an entire chapter to it; the other issues will be considered here.

Custody and Visitation

If society wants to break the cycle of domestic violence, changing the way we handle custody and visitation is the best opportunity to do so. Children learn about family life from their own homes and have limited ability to compare their own family with others. They understand more about the abuse happening in their homes than we give them credit for. The response of authorities, such as police and judges, sends a powerful message about the normalcy and acceptability of domestic violence. The child's future will often be compromised when the wrong message is sent.

At one time men could beat their wives and children with impunity. Laws concerned with cruelty to animals were used for the first child abuse cases because no child protection statutes existed. As discussed in Chapter 8, spousal abuse was considered irrelevant to custody and visitation decisions in New York only a few years ago. New York and other states have improved the process by requiring that evidence of domestic violence be considered in custody and visitation decisions. The model code prepared by the National Council of Juvenile and Family Court Judges recommends taking stronger action to protect children in homes where domestic violence has been committed by creating a rebuttable presumption against custody (the nonoffending parent always receives custody unless clearly unfit) for someone guilty of family violence. Several states have adopted this reform. I believe we should take it a step further.

Researchers have now established that spousal abuse is as harmful to children as child abuse, even if the child does not directly witness the abuse. In fact, some states, as a result of this research, have increased the penalties for domestic violence crimes witnessed or heard by children. The dysfunctional behavior promoted by child abuse is equally prevalent in homes where men abuse women. In other words, spousal abuse is another form of child abuse. Throughout my career, in domestic violence cases, judges have asked me if there was also child abuse. If I say no, they conclude that there is no reason to limit visitation. If spousal abuse were treated as child abuse, as it should be, children would be protected for the first time.

Most judges (but regrettably not all) would treat someone who abused his child as an unfit parent. An unfit parent would not be considered for custody and would receive no more than supervised visitation. A court would consider a parent who used illegal drugs to be unfit and would limit visitation. If that parent received treatment and kicked the bad habit, normal visitation would be permitted. I believe domestic violence should be treated similarly.

Domestic violence is different from substance abuse because there is no test to determine whether a man has changed his behavior. Ethical experts will acknowledge that completion of requirements such as therapy, counseling, anger management or domestic violence classes in no way suggests a man will not be abusive again. Courts must therefore approach custody and visitation decisions involving an abusive father with the understanding that unsupervised visitation risks further harm to the children.

Courts should weigh the harm to the children of seeing their father with and without supervision. The court must consider possible abuse during exchanges, improper messages conveyed during visitation (not only verbal attacks on the mother, but comments about how bad the father feels being alone, general sexist comments, and complaints about money problems), and the real risk that the father will abuse other women in new relationships. Before considering any relaxation of the supervised visitation, the courts can take into account a father's completion of parenting-skills and domestic-violence–education classes, as well as his willingness to acknowledge to the children what he did and that he was wrong. If any unsupervised visits are allowed, the victim must be protected during the exchanges, and if the man commits any further abuse, the unsupervised visitation must be stopped immediately.

It may seem that a father who abuses his partner should be permanently denied unsupervised visitation. Advocates for victims of domestic violence would be unlikely to persuade judges and legislatures to adopt such a policy, but even if we could win their approval, the policy would cause more harm than good. The inevitable result would be that many fathers would take no further role in their children's lives. Many children would believe that they were being punished for some misbehavior, and this would seriously harm their development. If abusive fathers were instead given the opportunity to win back unsupervised visitation (even though there is no reason to believe they would be "fixed"), we would avoid the effects on children of growing up without a father and in the process send some very important messages. The requirement that the fathers go to class tells both the father and child that society takes domestic violence seriously and that there are consequences for abusing one's partner. Acknowledging the father's abuse validates a child's reality and reinforces the idea that the father's behavior is wrong.

I often use an analogy comparing the determination of visitation with abusive fathers to a farmer's response to pests. Although farmers would like to eliminate all pests, this is not usually a good idea because of the expense and the collateral harm that can be caused. Accordingly, farmers instead try to keep the pests under control, knowing they will inevitably do some harm. Similarly, when dealing with abusive men, we don't have the option of preventing all harm, but rather must make choices to limit the harm done. When a man abuses his child, he should lose the *right* to visitation; instead, visitation should be determined based solely on the best interests of the child.

Domestic violence needs to be carefully defined because of the serious consequences involved. I would include any physical or sexual attack, regardless of the resulting injuries. Any nonconsensual touching is unacceptable, within or outside of marriage. I have heard too many judges state that a "minor" incident like a push, grab, or pat should not be taken seriously. If someone knows or should know that the contact is unwanted, he must refrain from such behavior. Even the most limited unwanted contact involves violating someone's boundaries. The research proves that once such boundaries are violated, the abuse is likely to become more severe until there is effective intervention.

Verbal and emotional abuse should not be minimized, because they often have more damaging effects than physical abuse. However, the law must be careful about restricting custody and visitation based on verbal and emotional abuse because of the danger such requirements would be misused. Abusers and their supporters would likely claim their victims yelled at them or cursed them, in order to gain an edge. Such accusations would be difficult to prove or disprove. A parent who threatens death or grave bodily harm, destroys property, throws items at someone, deliberately harms pets, interferes with an attempt to call the police for help, or is guilty of a long pattern of verbal and emotional abuse should be considered unfit.

The courts would have to be vigilant to make sure that abusers cannot misuse this policy in unintended ways. Studies show that a majority of men seeking custody have abused their wives and sometimes their children. They use the courts and the threat of winning custody as a method of controlling their former partners. At best, the mother will have to waste substantial resources in legal fees, lost wages, and therapy. The emotional harm is even worse as the mother has to see her abuser in court, submit to questions by his attorney (in which she is beaten up emotionally yet again), and work with her husband on visitation and child-rearing issues that he never cared about before the breakup. Courts will need training and the use of certified domestic violence experts to recognize this.

Creating a rebuttable presumption against custody for abusers, as some states have done, or treating them as unfit, as I recommend, would reduce the ability of these men to misuse the court system. Courts should be aware of these improper legal tactics and should respond aggressively to make the abusers reimburse their victims for legal fees, economic losses, and therapy. Judge Washington pressured Barbara Kowalick and Gloria Morgan to give the abusive fathers excessive visitation. Barbara was found in contempt and threatened with jail, while Gloria saw her son removed from his home. Clearly, Judge Washington was putting pressure on the wrong side.

JOINT CUSTODY

Joint custody is a terrible idea that has caused great harm to families. The idea has been particularly misused in the courts, creating mischief and damaging children. Some states have started to bar or restrict joint custody in cases of domestic violence. I cannot understand why states have taken so long to adopt such an obvious policy. The victim of abuse should never be required to negotiate child-rearing issues with her abuser. Some states have recognized this principle by exempting abused spouses from mediation requirements.

Joint custody can mean an arrangement to share time with the children or to share the decision-making on significant issues. Most experts would agree that having children constantly going back and forth between homes (as in spending half of each week with each parent, or six months at each home each year) is harmful to the children. Joint custody can only work when the parents live close together and get along well. Of course, in those circumstances, why would they have divorced in the first place?

In practice, courts and attorneys have misused the concept of joint custody in a scandalous manner. Courts are always looking for compromises that can settle cases. With the crowded dockets, this is quite proper. In a typical case where both parents want custody and the mother has been the primary parent, the only middle ground the court can see is joint custody with the children living with the mother. The mother is most likely to have residential custody because she has been more involved in raising the children. Therefore, the court would not expect the mother to agree to less than residential custody. The father would not agree to give the mother sole custody, because if he lost the trial that is the worst that would happen anyway. Many judges like this compromise because they think it encourages the father to pay child support. Unfortunately, some states encourage joint custody in their laws.

The appropriate compromise in such a case is for the mother to have sole custody and for the father to be given access to school, health, and other similar records. If there is no abuse, the agreement could say the father will be consulted before major decisions are made. If the parties can cooperate, the father's suggestions made for the benefit of the children will be fully considered. If the parties cannot cooperate, joint custody will be a disaster.

In the case of joint custody, what happens if the parties cannot agree on a decision concerning the children? Going to court is expensive and time-consuming. Often, the court cannot make a decision until it is too late. The mother can be forced to accept the father's decision in order to have any decision. Sometimes joint custody agreements provide for a therapist or trusted third party to help make decisions, but this can be inconvenient or impractical. In the Boyd case (Chapter 5), the father refused to meet with the therapist or pay for his services; he continued to make his own decisions.

Dozens of my clients have "agreed" to joint custody (many before they became my clients). Many have felt pressured into the agreement, and every one has been sorry to be involved with such an arrangement. Inevitably, the judge asks the client on the record if she is entering the agreement voluntarily. Under the threat of losing custody, paying legal fees they can't afford, paying for evaluations they can't afford, and other implied threats from the judge (and sometimes threats from their own attorneys), the women have "voluntarily" agreed to joint custody.

Abusers and their attorneys regularly use the concept of joint custody to cause mischief. Frequently abusers who never had much interest in the children seek custody as a way of harassing and hurting the mother. Judges are so anxious to find a father who cares that they will treat the fathers as if they are acting in good faith. When the judge in the Horowitz case told the parties that joint custody would not be considered because of the hostility between the parties, he quickly brought the case to settlement. Sam Horowitz had little parenting experience or expertise and had no chance of getting sole custody. He was seeking joint custody in order to pressure Irene into making concessions on the financial issues. Significant resources were wasted in Sam's frivolous effort to obtain joint custody. These assets were not available when the child became sick, and this fact substantially contributed to Irene's suicide. These tactics should be outlawed and their practice severely punished.

At one time, fathers automatically received custody of the children because the law favored men. More recently, women were favored as custodians either because they were women, or under the "child of tender years" doctrine, which suggested young children would do better with their mother. With the attempt to treat the sexes equally, such distinctions have been outlawed. Mothers still receive custody more often than fathers because they are usually the primary parents. "Father's rights" advocates sometimes cite this as proof that the courts favor women, but in fact, fathers win a majority of contested custody cases. I believe this is caused by greater resources on the part of fathers and by sexism on the part of too many judges. I hope some of my other suggestions will eliminate this bias, particularly in domestic violence cases.

VISITATION

Visitation, like custody, should be decided based upon the best interests of the child. Frequent access to both parents is generally in the best interests of the child. Traditionally, courts have treated a parent's desire for visitation as a right and not a privilege. A parent guilty of the most harmful acts of child abuse would be limited to supervised visitation, in order to physically protect the child, but some visitation was required no matter how psychologically harmful it might be. In no other circumstance would a girl be forced to spend time with her rapist week after week. In some cases, mothers have been jailed or otherwise punished for failing to make their children go for visitation. The Wong children were forced to endure long years of unwanted supervised visitation until their father agreed to permit their adoption in order to save child support.

When parents divorce, children often blame themselves. Similarly, if a parent is removed from the home for abuse or other misconduct, or simply decides to abandon his family, children will often believe they are being punished for some misdeed. The denial of a parent's support, companionship, and love is detrimental to a child. Often, a child is better off visiting a flawed parent than losing the relationship altogether. When a parent is unfit, the benefits and harm of continued visitation should be weighed and the child's desire considered in determining whether supervised visitation should go forward. An unfit parent should not have an automatic right to visitation. Such decisions should be made in the best interests of the child.

Many judges believe that if the abuse of the other parent was not too "severe" or if the parents are no longer together, there is no harm in giving the abusive parent full visitation rights. Implied in this attitude is the idea that the victim has contributed to the abuse. In fact, the abuse occurred because the abuser does not respect boundaries; he is extremely likely to engage in the same behavior in future relationships. The children will likely experience new incidents of domestic violence and the same harmful attitude. Furthermore, the court's action of providing normal visitation sends a terrible message that society condones domestic violence and that there is no price to pay for engaging in such reprehensible behavior. Research demonstrates that children given such a message are significantly more likely to engage in dysfunctional behavior. Accordingly, unsupervised visitation with such parents is not in the best interests of the children.

As we have seen repeatedly in this book (see Chapters 2, 8, and 9) judges tend to be prejudiced in favor of unrestricted visitation for fathers. If a woman seeks to limit visitation, most judges assume the request is made out of vindictiveness rather than because of the abuse committed by the father. Judges need to avoid the mistakes of Judge

Pauling and Judge Washington and instead treat the victims' claims very seriously. Judges should see their role as protecting children. In one case the parties agreed on normal visitation, but Judge Moakley refused to approve the agreement because the evidence suggested the father had harmed the children. This should be the normal response of judges, but in fact this judge's actions were most unusual.

Domestic violence must be considered in determining visitation arrangements. Several states have recently added this protection to their laws. A court should consider not only what visitation is good for the child, but how to protect the custodial parent during the exchange. Abusive parents often use the visitation exchange to attack or harass their victims. Just seeing her abuser can be traumatic for an abused woman, creating fear and anxiety that cannot be hidden from the child. I have worked on many cases where we spent several days of testimony trying to determine which party was to blame for the difficult visitation exchanges. Often, the child is emotionally harmed by the exchange and does not want to go for visitation as a result; then the victim of abuse is blamed for interfering with visitation.

These problems could be avoided if the judge would be sensitive to the inevitable exchange problems. If possible, the parents can keep their distance and the children can walk from one parent to the other while their parents watch. Exchanges can be effected at a police station, mall, or other public and safe location. Setting specific rules and restrictions is important in controlling the behavior of abusers. Avoiding unsafe or unpleasant exchanges is well worth any inconvenience engendered by strict enforcement of these rules and restrictions.

Some communities have had the foresight to provide visitation centers. These can be used both for visitation exchanges and for supervised visitation. These centers have been a huge success and should be expanded as much as possible. In the past, the lack of adequate and affordable supervised visitation has encouraged courts to take chances with the safety of women and children. Often, when the courts had a choice between no visitation or unsupervised visitation for an abuser, the judges have been prejudiced in favor of visitation. Some courts have ordered the victim of abuse to supervise the visitation, endangering both the parent and child. Close friends or relatives of the abuser have also been used as supervisors, creating limited protection for the child. The visitation centers have trained workers and strict rules to protect everyone involved. Security is provided and a close relationship with the police is maintained. Pleasant surroundings and toys are provided to encourage an enjoyable visitation. In a subject full of tragic stories, the visitation centers are programs that work.

Normal visitation tends to include every other weekend from Friday to Sunday, possibly one day during the week for a few hours (for lunch or dinner), sharing the holidays, and at least a few weeks of vacation. Unusual schedules or circumstances can be adjusted accordingly. Frequently, noncustodial parents, and especially abusive fathers, seek much more visitation.

Too many judges believe that the custodial parent is getting so much more time that any extra visitation will benefit the child. In my experience, the reality of visitation does not support this view. During the week, the custodial parent is often working and the children in school. They must use the evenings and weekends for all the responsibilities involved in raising a child. After these obligations are considered, the noncustodial parent often has more time with the children, especially for fun activities. Any attempt to give the noncustodial parent extra visitation creates a worse imbalance.

Often, abusive parents seek extra visitation as proof that they are not abusive and as an attempt to control or harm their victim. The courts need to be careful to avoid being used in this manner. In fairness, I have noticed a phenomenon which I have not heard anyone comment on. Many fathers who never spent much time or effort on the children before the divorce nevertheless seek custody or extended visitation. In order to win their court battles, the fathers start spending more time with the children and in the process learn to be better parents. Although they started for the wrong reason, in the process of spending time with their children they learn it is a rewarding experience, and they continue the improved relationship after the litigation is over.

Grounds for Divorce

New York is an unusual state in that it recognizes only fault grounds for divorce, such as abandonment, adultery, and cruel and inhuman treatment. Most states permit no-fault grounds such as irreconcilable differences. An interesting combination of liberal feminists and religious conservatives opposes no-fault divorce. Feminists are concerned that an abusive or uncaring husband can easily opt out of a marriage without providing a fair economic settlement. If the husband does not have grounds for divorce, he would have to agree to a reasonable settlement before the wife would permit a divorce. Conservatives are worried about the breakup of the family and do not want to make divorce too easy.

Cruelty or abandonment may affect custody issues, but otherwise the grounds do not change the other results of a divorce. Most of my cases involve cruel and inhuman treatment because I regularly represent victims of domestic violence. The vindication and catharsis of proving cruelty is important to some of my clients, and they insist on trying the grounds issue if necessary.

Initially, victims are often afraid they cannot prove their husband's abuse because there are no witnesses. I assure them that they can testify and be believed. I have had many trials in which my client testified about the abuse she suffered and her husband testified to deny his behavior. In every case, despite the common bias against women and victims of abuse, my clients have won the hearing about grounds for divorce. Most judges know that a woman would not go through the pain and humiliation of discussing very personal events if the abuse had not actually occurred. The demeanor of the parties generally confirms the truth. The courts are also reluctant to keep people married who are obviously so hostile to each other.

Unlike Dr. Wong, most husbands strongly object to the grounds of cruelty. If the parties are agreeable, as part of the overall settlement, the grounds are often changed to constructive abandonment for more than a year. (This is another term for the denial of sexual relations.) In practice, this is New York's no-fault ground. No one knows what occurs in the privacy of a couple's bedroom (assuming Ken Starr is not investigating them!), so if one of the parties is willing to say they haven't had sex for a year and the other party does not challenge the claim, the divorce will go through without a problem. Judges encourage such arrangements because it helps reduce their caseload.

I believe it is a mistake to force parties to discuss and lie about their sex lives in order to obtain a divorce. Fault grounds should be required for contested divorces, but not when both parties want the divorce. A party should not be able to leave a marriage without resolving the financial issues, but once the issues are settled, the legal fiction of constructive abandonment should not be required. In order to avoid hasty divorces that the parties might later regret, a waiting period of a few months between filing for the divorce and the final judgment would be appropriate.

Orders of Protection

The public usually hears about orders of protection only after a
tragedy has occurred. The tragedy will consist of a man murdering a
woman either after she tried and failed to obtain protection, or despite
her having an order of protection. Accordingly, court decisions regarding such orders can literally be a matter of life or death. Even under less
dramatic circumstances, a court's decision about an order of protection
determines whether the victim and her children remain in their home,
whether further abuse can occur, and whether the children remain with
the victim or the abuser.

Protective orders can be obtained in criminal courts or in civil
courts that handle domestic relations and family issues. When someone
is assaulted or otherwise abused by a family member, the victim is usually given a choice between criminal and civil action. Criminal charges
in domestic violence cases will generally result in a temporary order of
protection, which will become permanent if the charges result in a conviction or guilty plea. Even after spousal abuse became a crime, police
were encouraged to steer such cases towards a Family Court instead of
bringing criminal charges. Assaults between family members were thus
treated as less serious than violence between strangers. The idea was
that each party bore part of the responsibility and they should work it
out together. Unsurprisingly, this approach was not successful. Violence
in the family needs to be taken more seriously because the victim will
see the attacker on a regular basis.

As society has learned more about domestic violence, the approach
towards these crimes has changed. Most states now give the victim the
choice of pursuing the case criminally or civilly, and many permit the
use of both forums. Orders of protection are an appropriate response
to domestic violence crimes. The primary consideration in such cases
should be the health, safety, and welfare of the victims of such crimes
and their children.

A standard order of protection prohibits the abuser from assaulting, harassing, or threatening the victim. Additional protections such as
restricting telephone or personal contact, removing weapons, and
requiring treatment can be included in such orders. The most controversial issue is often whether the abuser should be removed from the
family home. Anne Scripps Douglas and many other women may have
been murdered because a court failed to remove a dangerous criminal
from the family home.

Judges have been reluctant to remove someone from his home, especially before a trial, because of the tremendous hardship such removal can cause. Issues of safety, however, should take precedence, and an alleged abuser should be removed from the home if there is credible evidence of abuse. The accused should be entitled to a hearing within two weeks of removal from his home. This should provide protection in the rare cases where false accusations are made. When the court concludes that someone is guilty of physical assault or threatening serious injury, permitting the abuser to remain in the home constitutes an improper use of the court's discretion.

Abusers and their defenders have developed a strategy for defeating the benefits of orders of protection by seeking their own protective orders. The abusers use the actions the victims take in self-defense, or just invent an allegation in order to obtain their own order of protection. Judges who are ignorant of domestic violence issues are often happy to provide mutual orders of protection, with the idea that the orders merely forbid the parties from taking actions they should not engage in anyway. In their view, they are treating the parties equally. But why should a victim of domestic violence be treated the same as her assailant? Victims receive no protection from such orders because the abuser can use his order as a shield. If a wife calls the police after being slapped by her husband, the husband tells the police his wife hit him, and the police will offer to arrest both or neither. In this way the protection intended from the orders is nullified.

Some states have gotten wise to this legal stratagem and have barred mutual orders of protection or required a separate petition to be filed. New laws permit a court to consider who is the primary aggressor. I believe the courts should go further and consider the purposes of the law. In order to obtain an order of protection, a party must prove the technical legal requirements for an order and demonstrate that an order is necessary for the protection of the party. Courts should have such a tool in order to deny protective orders to aggressors who are bigger and stronger than their victim, and have no real need for a protective order except as a shield for their own misbehavior.

Criminal Issues

Barbara Kowalick succeeded in winning the conviction of her husband for sexually assaulting her, but said she would not prosecute if she had it to do again. Arrest and imprisonment are the best methods of discouraging abusers from committing their violence. We cannot permit victims like Barbara to be deterred from pressing charges if society wants to make progress in reducing domestic violence.

States and local police departments are starting to make progress in responding to domestic violence cases. Most police departments provide training for their employees about family violence. The trend in most departments is toward mandatory arrest policies where there is significant evidence of physical abuse. In some states, arrests are made and prosecution pursued even if the victim tries to withdraw the complaint. This is a good idea because it prevents the abuser from threatening, intimidating, or just sweet-talking the victim into dropping charges.

Another positive trend is to arrest the primary aggressor instead of both parties. In the past, and even today in some states, the police would come to a home and find physical injuries or bruises on both parties. If the abuser and the victim each claimed that the other started the fight, the police would give the parties a choice of having them arrest both or neither. Often the parties' size and strength, injuries, statements, and other evidence made it possible to establish the primary aggressor, but the law or police policy required both parties to be arrested. Such a policy discourages the reporting of domestic violence and does not permit police intervention until the violence becomes more severe.

The criminal justice system must handle rape and other sexual abuse cases with the utmost sensitivity. After the Marv Albert case, in which the defendant agreed to a plea bargain in mid-trial, some attorneys blamed this outcome on the unfairness of rape shield laws. In doing so, however, they failed to understand or explain the history or need for such laws. Traditionally, a woman would be blamed if she was raped, even if she was a grandmother, nun, or young child. The defense attorney would be permitted to beat up the witness with questions about her real or imagined sex life. Many rapes are never prosecuted because the victim fears going through such an inquisition. Much of this material is of little or no relevance to the actual case, but it can do much to prejudice a jury. The standard defense strategy is to put the victim on trial. Rape shield laws were designed to protect the victim by limiting the private information a defense attorney can use, thereby focusing the trial on the evidence in the actual case. These shield laws will encourage victims like Barbara Kowalick to come forward and help take predators like her ex-husband off the street.

Throughout this book I have discussed the fact that allegations of domestic violence are rarely fabricated. Victims attempting to pursue such claims in criminal court or civil court are required repeatedly to tell a painful and embarrassing story. They often face hostile and unpleasant questions and attacks. Few people would submit to such abuse unless they believed in their charges. The public as well as judges should be aware of these facts. Jurors especially should be aware that claims of domestic violence are rarely deliberately falsified. It is hard to stop defense attorneys from attacking victims, but if jurors responded to such attacks by holding the attorney's behavior against the defendant, such aggression towards the victim would quickly stop.

While such false charges are rare, they do occur, particularly in cases involving celebrities. The opportunity for fame and money can be a motivation for bringing false charges despite the embarrassing questions the plaintiff has to answer. In the William Kennedy Smith rape trial, the alleged victim answered any question about her honesty when she fell for an old lawyer's trick. The defense attorney started to ask a question about when the prosecutor had prepared her testimony, but the alleged victim jumped in to volunteer that the prosecutor had not prepared her testimony. She was the chief witness in the most important case of the prosecutor's career. Obviously, the testimony had been prepared and the witness was lying. While a juror should know that deliberately false charges are rare, such lies can be told and mistakes can be made.

Special offices like the one started in Westchester by Jeanine Pirro to prosecute domestic violence crimes should be encouraged. In these offices family violence is taken seriously, the issues are understood, and the victims are supported. In cases where there is not enough evidence to prosecute, the prosecutors will call the abusers to warn them that their behavior is being monitored. Such actions can prevent crimes because abusers learn that the authorities take their behavior seriously. I believe all prosecutors should have a section of their offices to specialize in such cases.

Most prosecutors keep careful records of their conviction percentages, and many seek to avoid bringing charges which may end in an acquittal. However, prosecuting domestic violence crimes sends an important message that society does not tolerate such behavior. When a victim wants to press charges and the domestic violence unit has explained the chances of success and the drawbacks, the case should go forward, even if the chances for conviction are fifty–fifty or slightly worse.

Frequently, domestic violence crimes are prosecuted at the same time that custody or divorce proceedings are taking place in another court. Defendants often try to delay the criminal case so that a conviction cannot be used against them in the civil cases. A defendant should be required to notify the court of any related actions pending, and the criminal court should prevent the improper use of adjournments.

We have already discussed the fact that jail time is the most effective response to domestic violence crimes. Any other penalty will permit the abuser to believe that he has gotten away with his crime and that such behavior is tolerated. Accordingly, judges should be encouraged to provide jail terms in domestic violence cases. Similarly, if a defendant is given probation and violates the terms of the probation, he should be brought before the judge immediately and sentenced to jail time. The public would be surprised and angered if they knew how often probation violations result in light or no penalties.

Some cases in which women have killed their abuser in some degree of self-defense have attracted publicity. Many such women were convicted before domestic violence was commonly discussed. Evidence of prior abuse should be admitted in such trials. Women who killed out of self-defense should be acquitted, and others who killed under less immediate threat should at least have their penalties reduced.

Less well-known are crimes in which battered women commit robbery or other crimes in order to avoid beatings. Significantly, these women would rather take their chances with the justice system than with the sure and violent punishment of their partners. Police and prosecutors need to look for such cases and treat such women as the victims they are.

Court-Ordered Offender Education Programs

In the domestic violence classes for men that I instruct, we teach that domestic violence is a societal problem and not the result of men being "crazy" or "bad." Men growing up sometimes learn that they have a male privilege to abuse and disrespect their wives and girlfriends. Frequently men in the class object by saying that no one ever said, "Go ahead and beat her." We tell them that the actual messages are not so direct. Boys may see their fathers abusing their mothers without penalty. Other messages come through movies, TV, videos, music, commercials, and other media that objectify women; schools in which boys and girls are treated differently, with boys taken more seriously; clergy who misuse the Bible to support the mistreatment of women; businesses where men are given more and better opportunities than women; and courts that often minimize men's violence against women. This is why otherwise "good" men often commit horrible crimes against their partners.

We must hold men accountable for their crimes, but we must also build a coordinated community response to eliminate institutional and cultural support for domestic violence. By "community" we mean people who come together, whether by relationship, activity, ethnicity, employment, or through some other connection. Each community needs to consider the direct and subtle messages they send out about how men should treat women. Men are often surprised when we tell them that the classes are a very small part of the solution to domestic violence. Only when all communities are working together to end men's domestic violence will women and children be safe at home.

Some batterers try to avoid the consequences of their criminal behavior by seeking marriage counseling or psychological treatment, preferably with a therapist ignorant of domestic violence issues. Many victims of abuse ask only that their partner obtain therapy, in the unrealistic expectation that the problems are likely to be solved with this intervention. Advocates for domestic violence victims, however, say such an approach is useless because the violence is not caused by mental illness. Frankly, discussing this issue with respected professionals in the course of researching this chapter has raised some basic and disturbing questions.

When clients first contact me, they often have unrealistic hopes that their husbands will voluntarily stop their abuse or that marriage counseling can help. *As long as an abuser minimizes his actions or seeks to accept less than one hundred percent of the responsibility, his violence will not stop.* Marriage counseling usually involves both partners sharing the responsibility for the marital problems, which is a premise doomed to fail in abuse cases. Furthermore, in relationships where men have committed domestic violence, such sessions are dangerous for a woman, who must either hide the real problems in the marriage or risk a beating for revealing even a part of her partner's abuse to the therapist.

In the course of custody battles, abusers such as James Wong often enter therapy to obtain favorable witnesses and create an illusion that they are working on their problems. Often the mental health professionals selected have little or no training or understanding of domestic violence. Much of the "therapy" consists of discussing how badly the abuser was treated by his partner and how "provocative" she was. Even if an abusive man starts treatment to save his marriage, there is little chance for significant change in his behavior with such inadequate professionals.

The situation is more confusing when substance abuse, mental illness, or other problems are present in addition to male violence. Substance abusers and mentally ill women can and do become victims of domestic violence. Inevitably, such a woman's partner tries to use her other problems to attack her credibility when she reports his abuse. Many judges and others in the court system have succumbed to these tactics. It is important for judges, lawyers, and mental health professionals to separate the domestic violence from the other issues. Similarly, substance abuse and mental illness are not the cause of domestic violence. If the substance or mental problem is solved, the violence problem will still be present.

Domestic violence is a learned behavior. Children who grow up in homes where domestic violence occurs are more likely to experience relationships in which men abuse women. When authority figures such as judges, police, and parents condone or encourage violence, children learn that these behaviors are acceptable. This is why it is so important for judges in custody cases to take abuse seriously. A decision to give an abuser normal visitation, or worse, custody, tells a child there are no penalties for abuse. Children may know other families, but they learn about family life from their own home. Whatever the children experience in their home will be internalized as "normal." The lesson is compounded by media and societal messages of unequal power between the sexes, women being treated as objects, and other more subtle suggestions that men have certain rights or entitlements over women.

This understanding of the roots of abuse is supported by studies that found abusers and nonabusers to have an equal rate of mental illness. Accordingly, the response to battering should not be therapy, but punishment and re-education. Therapy suggests that the behavior is not the fault of the abuser. Sanctions make clear that the abuser is at fault and such behavior will not be tolerated. Therapy implies that a patient can complete treatment and solve the problem. In fact, ethical professionals running batterers' education programs say that they cannot know how an offender will behave after completing the program. Therefore, judges should not assume that someone completing a program will be safe for his family or children to be near. Ultimately, all segments of society must work together to teach people that domestic violence is unacceptable.

A convict who commits rape, assault, or other similar crimes should be punished. If the criminal has other problems, such as mental illness or drug or alcohol abuse, treatment for these separate problems would be appropriate, but should not be a substitute for the punishment. Violence by husbands and fathers is particularly harmful because it involves a violation of trust. This should not be an argument for less severe punishment. An abuser can get therapy or other help if needed, he can be educated about the harm and unacceptability of his actions, but he must also be penalized to get across the message he missed as a child: *Society does not permit men to beat women and children!*

Chapter 13

CHILD SUPPORT

and Other Financial Issues

COLLECTION OF CHILD SUPPORT and maintenance payments is a serious problem in many divorce cases, not only in those involving abuse. However, abusive spouses have a strong tendency to use the withholding of payment as a way to punish and/or control their victims. The courts rarely provide as much help as they could to families deprived of support.

Determining Child Support

In New York, the child support formula requires the noncustodial parent to pay roughly 17% of his or her gross income (less social security taxes) for one child (25% for two children, 29% for three children, etc.) plus a percentage of medical and child-care expenses (the exact formula is more complicated). Other states have different formulas, but similar results. The problems occur not with the formula, but with parents hiding income and assets, refusing to work, or failing to make court-ordered payments.

Parents who own their own businesses, particularly cash businesses, can easily avoid some of their child-support obligation. Although the business owner generally has control of the records and knowledge of the finances, the spouse of the owner has the burden of proving the amount of income. Irene Horowitz had a mother with a bookkeeping background and a husband of limited intelligence, but still it took great perseverance, expense, and more than a little luck to prove his actual income. Most defrauded litigants are not as fortunate.

Sam Horowitz was given a free shot at stealing his daughter's child support. Although the court determined that Sam had understated his income by half, his perjury and misrepresentations went unpunished. He was not required to pay extra legal fees, nor an amount of support determined by the income calculations least favorable to him; nor did he lose his credibility when he later lied about his ability to pay medical bills. We must design a system to make it easier to determine a parent's actual income and to discourage parties from hiding income and assets.

Accountants and other financial experts are regularly used to determine the value of businesses and other assets. Parties have to pay for these experts, whether they are appointed by the court or chosen by the parties themselves. The courts could hire financial experts permanently and use the expert fees paid by parties who can afford the expense to cover all or most of the expense for those who cannot pay. The financial analysts would then be readily available to help courts determine when a party is hiding income.

The burden of proving income should be shifted to the party with the records and other information. If a party claimed to be earning significantly less than other similar businesses, he would have to prove why the business was making less income. The parties should be required to provide all necessary information, and any deliberate attempt to hide income should be severely punished. If a party was shown to have misled the court about income, the calculation of income should be based on assumptions most favorable to the innocent party. Judges should treat such parties as if their credibility were questionable. Once Sam Horowitz was proven to have lied about his income, his later claims to be unable to pay medical bills should have been discounted.

Legal fees made necessary by the deception should be paid by the party attempting to mislead the court. If lawyers know that their client's case can be severely prejudiced if they are caught hiding income, the attorneys will discourage their clients from such behavior. Presently, my profession has no reason to stop this practice apart from the fact that it is unethical, which obviously has not been a sufficient incentive.

Similar burdens should be placed on parents seeking to avoid paying adequate child support because of unemployment, underemployment, or a sudden lack of the usual overtime. Unemployment insurance regularly requires the applicant to prove how the job was lost and that he is attempting to find a new job; the same protection should be in place for children. Custodial parents will rarely be able to prove a lack of effort or deliberate reduction of income by the noncustodial parent. The party with knowledge of the circumstances and access to the proof should be the one required to furnish the proof.

Spousal Maintenance

There is no formula for spousal maintenance (alimony) in New York. Maintenance is generally awarded to a spouse without income or with inadequate income to live on. Parties tend to forget that the costs of running two households are significantly more than the costs for one. The marital income is often inadequate to maintain the family lifestyle after a separation. Parties expect to keep the money necessary to maintain their lifestyle, with any remainder going to the other spouse; therefore courts dividing the inadequate income are unable to satisfy either party.

Although the courts are theoretically trying to divide the available income fairly, the alarming trend has been that after a divorce the husband has resources for a lifestyle significantly better, and the wife significantly worse, than during the marriage. This result is often predictable, but courts rarely take adequate consideration of the parties' assets and future prospects when determining maintenance. I believe courts should be required to use equitable considerations to determine the length and amount of maintenance. Where a party sacrificed a career or earning position to help the family or a partner's career, such factors should be considered. Any attempts to hide or reduce income to avoid maintenance should be dealt with aggressively, as I discussed regarding child support.

Enforcing Payment

In recent years, society has been more concerned about support collection enforcement, and governments have tried to crack down on deadbeat parents. Among the recent enforcement mechanisms have been stricter criminal penalties, suspension of driver's and professional licenses, confiscating tax refunds, a greater willingness to jail parents failing to pay court-ordered support, and the use of government resources to find such deadbeats. While all of these methods are useful and should be expanded, more fundamental enforcement is necessary.

The penalties do not start until a parent is well behind on the support, and the family is suffering. The nonpaying parent is given many chances to pay and can always pay without penalty. Courts see the contempt procedure as a method of obtaining payment, rather than as a way to punish miscreants. Therefore, if a parent refuses to pay support for a few months and finally is brought to court for contempt, the worst that will happen is the support will have to be paid. But even this worst often does not happen. The custodial parent might not go to court or might be unable to find the nonpayer. The court might believe there is a hardship on the nonpayer and reduce the support, or arrange a compromise on the payment schedule or arrears. Judges will often say that the parent cannot pay support if in jail, so therefore it is only out of vindictiveness that the custodial parent seeks to jail the nonpaying parent.

The weakness of this system was demonstrated by Sam Horowitz. First, he attempted to hide his income and received no penalty when his wife proved the deception. Thereafter Sam repeatedly failed to pay some of the child support, especially medical and child-care expenses. In a series of enforcement actions, Sam avoided some of his obligations when Irene was unable to prove some of the expenses. The court then proposed a settlement in which Mr. Horowitz could avoid jail by paying most of what he owed.

We cannot permit these deadbeats to have a free shot at illegally avoiding their obligations. There must be effective penalties when someone is caught hiding income or refusing to pay court-ordered support. A party who lies to the court or misrepresents his income or assets should not be believed thereafter. When we appeared in court on the contempt motion in the Horowitz case, the court should have warned Sam that with his history, if the trial demonstrated that any of the nonpayment was unjustified, he would certainly go to jail. Instead, the court made it clear he could always pay whatever it was determined he owed and avoid jail. The court's approach made the difference between Sam paying the money in question to avoid jail, or having a free shot at avoiding payment. Although the judge could not have envisioned that this policy would lead to Irene's death, it was easy to foresee that the child's medical care could be compromised.

When a parent is found to have deliberately failed to pay court-ordered support, the penalties must be sufficient to prevent that parent from ever doing it again, and to discourage other parents from acting similarly. The recalcitrant parent should be forced to pay legal fees, lost wages, and any consequential damages. A fine should be imposed and used to establish a fund to help families denied support. If support is stopped because the parent is jailed, the fund can help support the family. In appropriate cases, jail terms can be limited to weekends so the parent can keep his job and still be punished. When a parent has violated a support order over an extended period of time, payment of arrears in response to a contempt proceeding should reduce, but not eliminate, contempt penalties. If a deadbeat knows he can always avoid jail by paying at the last minute, there is no incentive to pay before a contempt action is started.

Equitable Distribution

When I was in law school, the concept of equity stirred my imagination. In my naive mind, it seemed courts could use equity to make decisions fair and just. Now, Melanie Brewster always reminds me that once when she commented that a decision in her case was unfair, I responded, "The next thing you will want is truth and justice." The language of equitable distribution permits a court to consider what is fair, but the practice treats "equitable" as if it meant "equal." The usage of this term describes the problem and offers an opportunity to provide a fairer distribution.

Most states use either equitable distribution or community property as the basis for dividing the parties' property in a divorce. In general, community property provides for the equal distribution of property, regardless of when the property was obtained or whose name it is in. This makes it easier to calculate the division of property, but it can be unfair when the spouse in a short-term marriage receives half of premarital property or inheritances.

Although there are slight differences between states, equitable distribution is designed to divide marital property based upon the contributions each party made to the marriage. Under this system, marital property is defined as anything obtained from the time of the marriage until the start of the divorce, regardless of who owns the property, except for gifts to one spouse or personal injury recoveries. Property owned prior to the marriage and inheritances are considered separate property. Pensions earned during the marriage (even if not payable until much later) and businesses started or improved during the marriage are part of the marital property.

Equitable distribution was supposed to be a reform to permit courts to consider nonfinancial contributions such as child-rearing, housekeeping, and other work for which a spouse is not paid. In practice, however, little effort is made to differentiate the contributions of the parties. A husband who worked during only part of the marriage and made no contribution to the housework is likely to receive the same fifty percent of marital property as a husband who earned all the marital income and shared the housework and child-rearing responsibilities. Courts discourage any attempt to determine relative contributions of the parties because of the difficulty of proof, and trying to persuade parties to agree to a division of property other than fifty percent each would make it harder to reach a settlement.

As with child support and maintenance, attempts to hide income and assets are a major problem with equitable distribution. The difficulty is greater in domestic violence cases because abusers try to control their victims in a variety of ways, including financial deprivation. Perceptive judges should be aware of this practice and use the information to understand the dynamics of the relationship. The solutions suggested for support issues are equally helpful regarding equitable distribution.

The party in control of the assets should have the burden of proving the value of the assets. Any lack of cooperation or deliberate failure to provide documents should be taken as evidence that assets are being hidden. When a party acts improperly in trying to conceal property, the courts should routinely interpret the evidence in a light most favorable to the innocent party. Any deliberate failure to cooperate should be taken by the court to show a lack of credibility. If someone lies about his property and refuses to provide required documents, he will often receive a windfall because the innocent party will be unwilling or unable to overcome the obstacles to proof.

The courts must not give such criminals (they are stealing from their spouses) a free shot at keeping marital property that should be divided. When the wrongdoers are caught, the penalties must be sufficient to discourage such tactics. If someone illegally tries to cheat his spouse, I believe it is equitable to give the injured party more than the fifty percent she might otherwise receive. Such consequences would force lawyers to advise their clients against concealing assets and therefore reduce the practice.

I recommended that the courts hire accountants and other economic experts to help determine child support and maintenance. I would also use these experts for evaluating businesses, licenses, pensions, and other marital property. A spouse should not be forced to give up a share of an asset because there is no money to determine the value of the asset.

Equitable distribution must be interpreted to mean *fair* distribution instead of *equal* distribution. Courts should divide the property fairly based on all the circumstances in the case. Among the factors a court should consider in dividing marital property are the contributions of each party; the expected future income of the parties; separate property owned by each party; cooperation of each party in the lawsuit; needs and resources of the parties; health of the parties; waste of assets; debts; domestic violence in the marriage; and any other factor that is relevant to the fairness of the distribution.

Legal Fees and Legal Services

Why would a woman stay with an abusive husband? This question keeps appearing, and I feel the need to help provide some of the answers. Many abusers tell their wives that they have no choice but to stay. "You cannot afford a lawyer, and therefore you will lose custody, visitation, support, and property," the abuser repeats. The victims believe this because too often it is true. Judges should run their courtrooms so that this prophecy will never be fulfilled. The policy of the courts must be that the outcomes of domestic violence cases, and particularly the issues of custody and protection from abuse, shall not be determined by the relative wealth of the parties or the ability of one party to be better represented. Victims of abuse must have access to representation by attorneys knowledgeable about domestic violence.

My Sisters' Place, the domestic violence organization with which I was long associated, recently opened a legal services program for victims of abuse. This had long been our goal because of the tremendous need for this assistance. I often represent women in domestic violence cases on a pro bono or reduced-fee basis because of the tremendous need for this service. Frequently, I have replaced other attorneys who have made a bad situation worse. Ted Johnson took huge fees from Melanie Brewster while losing her order of protection and failing to prepare her case. He failed to prepare Emily Pollack for trial, causing her to lose custody, to give testimony that led to an excessive support award, and ultimately to be incarcerated. Irene Horowitz had a succession of attorneys who succeeded only in charging outrageous fees. Although nationwide, programs of legal services for abused women are expanding, the supply is still far short of the needs.

Lawyers must understand domestic violence enough to know what questions to ask their clients and how to overcome the negative effects of years of abuse. The attorneys must learn to empower women who have been controlled too long. Many of my clients have complained about lawyers pressuring them into unfair settlements, particularly regarding joint custody. We must find ways to provide effective representation for women with limited resources. The legal clinics should be expanded and more attorneys should volunteer to represent victims of abuse.

The courts can help domestic violence victims obtain good attorneys by making realistic awards of legal fees. In cases in which there are allegations of domestic violence and one party controls most of the marital assets, the court must act aggressively to level the playing field. The party with the assets can afford to pay his attorney a significant retainer and keep making payments on the continuing bill. The court will sometimes make a retainer award at the start of the lawsuit, but generally will not require further payments until the end of the case. Naturally the party with the assets is better able to attract and keep a more skilled attorney. There is no reason that the party controlling the marital assets is entitled to better representation, or that the attorney representing the victim of abuse should receive less money or have delays in receiving payment that his counterpart does not experience.

The courts should secure the marital assets so that they cannot be wasted or disposed of during the case. Orders should be made at the start of the case so that each attorney can be treated equally regardless of the relative wealth of the parties. This will serve to attract good attorneys on both sides and discourage wasteful litigation in which the richer party runs up legal fees to force a favorable settlement. All disputes over legal fees should be resolved before the property is divided.

In cases where both parties can afford their own attorneys, the courts should be quick to award legal fees when one party causes unnecessary legal expenses. In the Horowitz case, for example, when it was proven that Sam Horowitz had hidden income and failed to cooperate on discovery, he should have been ordered to pay all or most of the legal fees. Similarly, he had no business seeking custody when Irene was the primary parent and he had very limited parenting skills. He used the threat of obtaining custody to pressure his wife on economic issues. This is an unfair tactic that should have resulted in an order requiring him to pay legal fees related to the custody issues. Judges should be sensitive to the use of economic pressures in domestic violence cases and should aggressively award legal fees to discourage improper tactics.

Perjury

In the course of the partisan battle over the impeachment of former president Clinton, the public has been given a misleading view of the judicial system's response to perjury. Perjury occurred in most of the cases discussed in this book, but prosecution for perjury was never seriously considered. The instances of perjury convictions cited in the debate about impeachment were rare and came about under far different circumstances than the allegations against the president. The press did a poor job of providing the full facts or putting the cases into some kind of context.

Like Clinton, the man I call James Wong lied about sex, but in his case the sexual activity in question was the paramount issue in determining his fitness for custody, because it occurred with his daughters, aged four and six. As part of the settlement in which he gave up custody, Dr. Wong admitted kissing his daughters on the vagina, which he had earlier denied under oath. His lawyer permitted this admission because he knew there was no danger of a perjury charge.

Sam Horowitz and his mother both lied about his income and the money she was supposedly giving him. We caught them submitting into evidence checks that had been altered after they had cleared the bank. This would have provided strong evidence for fraud and perjury, but criminal charges were never considered.

Judge McLaughlin was sure Emily Pollack was perjuring herself when she contradicted her earlier testimony concerning her income. He was so certain of his belief that he stopped listening to the evidence. Emily ultimately went to jail, but not for perjury. At the same time, Kenneth Pollack testified at the trial under oath that he had signed tax returns that he knew were false. He knew that even this admission of perjury would not create a risk of criminal prosecution.

I once had a bitter custody trial in Rockland County in which each parent had some significant flaws. The husband had physically abused the wife, and they each at times had mistreated the children. The wife admitted her mistakes, but the other issues were disputed in the trial. The willingness of the wife to be honest about her failings, along with other evidence, strongly suggested the wife's version was much closer to the truth. The judge, however, decided that he didn't know the truth of the disputed matters, and since the wife had admitted some mistakes, the husband should get custody. The judge's failure to look for the truth in the disputed issues can only encourage perjury.

It is certainly wrong to lie under oath, and perjury should not be condoned. Realistically, however, perjury is hard to prove, and prosecution of such cases will always be rare. I would be satisfied if the courts created some consequences when it is established that someone has lied to the court. A judge should give little credibility to someone who has been caught lying.

After Irene Horowitz proved her husband's income was double what he had claimed, the court should have placed a heavy burden on him to justify his failure to pay his support obligations. The court in the Pollack case should have refused to consider Kenneth Pollack's testimony about his wife's income after he admitted to swearing to the IRS that her income was lower.

I would make an exception for a battered wife who lied to escape further abuse or who didn't have information about the family income. Judge McLaughlin tried to create consequences for someone he thought had committed perjury. Unfortunately, his gender bias caused him to hurt someone whose testimony had been truthful.

Chapter 14

THE PLAYERS

T HERE ARE VARIOUS GROUPS OF PEOPLE involved in the fight against domestic violence. Some are truly part of the solution; others are part of the problem. Following are some suggestions for how these people could best contribute to the prevention of abuse and the protection of its victims.

Judges

Most of the judges described in this book have damaged lives and failed to protect innocent women and children. Many of my clients remain haunted by their abuse at the hands of judges, in some cases more so than by the physical abuse they suffered. With the exception of the judge I call Albert Pauling, however, none of the judges is truly ill-intentioned.

Judge Washington has stopped his intemperate outbursts since the newspaper article appeared, and is capable of compassion and sensitivity. Unfortunately, he still does not understand domestic violence or place a high priority on discouraging it. In a recent case, the lawyer for an abusive father argued that he should have custody because "only the father is not afraid of the other party." I cannot imagine a greater insult than to suggest a judge would reward an abuser for his abuse, but several months later we were still waiting for a decision.

Judge Hirsch seemed to be making great progress in protecting victims coming to her court for help. In one case she was brilliant in seeing right through a husband who was using the standard batterer's tactic of asking for a retaliatory order of protection. She repeatedly asked why he needed the order, and he had no good response. I thought she had learned to be a good judge until she refused to hear a custody case that had been pending for five years, and then chose to punish a victim of years of horrible abuse for her normal and reasonable reactions to her partner's abuse.

Despite too many sickening stories, I believe judges in general are getting better at handling domestic violence cases. When I started practicing twenty years ago, only one or two of the six Family Court judges in Westchester were women. Recently, only one was a man. Although women are sometimes more sensitive to these issues, I do not want to suggest that the judges are better because of a change in gender. Rather, the increase in women on the Family Court bench suggests that the judges are being selected based upon experience and interest in family law issues instead of a generalized desire to be a judge. Judges are now required to receive training in domestic violence issues. I would like to see more education about these vital topics, particularly sessions run by organizations fighting domestic violence. Such groups should not be viewed as partisans, but as a resource for the courts.

Should judges be elected or appointed? The appointment of judges permits the decision-makers to investigate candidates and know the background and ability of those under consideration. Such appointments involve little public scrutiny, however, allowing partisan leaders to make selections for political or financial reasons. On the other hand, judicial candidates for election are limited in what they can say or how they can campaign. As a result, voters often go to the polls with little knowledge of judicial candidates. Voting your party preference makes little sense when picking a judge, but unfortunately, because of the limited information available, voters are most likely to vote for judges based on party identification or ethnicity. Ideally, judges could be appointed by a nonpartisan group with knowledge of the candidates and the skills needed. This is impractical, however, because the politicians will never give up their power.

A few years ago, Judge Pauling ran for the Supreme Court. I sent a letter to many of my friends and clients asking that they vote against him because of the Wong case and other atrocities he has committed against women. Many people thanked me for the information. They had no other way of learning what a terrible judge he was. Voters do not want judges who fail to protect victims of domestic violence.

Just as bar associations rate judicial candidates, advocates in the fight against abuse must organize to rate judicial candidates and disseminate the information. Such a rating must be based solely on qualifications on domestic violence issues; abortion or other feminist issues cannot be considered. I believe voters would be influenced by such ratings, party leaders would be reluctant to nominate pro-abuse candidates, and sitting judges would know that failing to hold abusers accountable could hurt their careers.

Lawyers

The abuse of divorce clients by their attorneys has been well documented by the work of Mark Green in a report as New York City Commissioner of Consumer Affairs, by Monica Getz in her work with the National Coalition for Family Justice, by Karen Winner in her book *Divorced from Justice,* and by many others. I would like to believe that the women described in this book were treated well once they hired me, but several had had problems with prior attorneys. The lawyer I call Ted Johnson took advantage of Melanie Brewster and Emily Pollack and crippled their cases. Although the Bar Association issued a letter of caution as a result of Melanie's complaint, I doubt that it changed Johnson's tactics.

In fairness, there are many ethical and caring divorce attorneys who serve their clients well. Sometimes in the pressure and emotion of the moment, a divorce litigant fails to hear or understand what is said. Often, friends and family of clients tell them stories of better outcomes, but leave out crucial differences in the circumstances. I believe that the stories of abuses committed by attorneys are exaggerated, but what is true is more than enough to embarrass our profession.

The work of Mark Green, Monica Getz, and others resulted in New York State imposing reforms on the matrimonial bar. Divorce attorneys are now required to provide written retainer agreements at the start of the representation, and itemized bills. Clients must be advised of their rights and responsibilities. In case of a fee dispute, clients are entitled to mandatory arbitration of claims, and lawyers cannot place liens on a client's property without permission from the court. In addition, attorneys can no longer collect nonrefundable retainers. Divorce lawyers are prohibited from having sex with their clients. These are good reforms that have worked well in New York and should be adopted nationwide. The reforms correct obvious abuses that would be hard to justify. Less direct abuse and the failure to understand the problems faced by victims of domestic violence will be harder to overcome.

Clients often ask their attorneys at an initial meeting how much the divorce will cost. Lawyers are reluctant to respond with a dollar amount because of all the variables in how a divorce may proceed. Decisions the client and the other side make in the future will inevitably affect the final cost. The attorney can, however, provide rough estimates of the cost under likely scenarios. This will at least give the client an idea of what she is dealing with and prevent surprise when it is too late to alter the strategy. Some lawyers consider professionalism to include full use of discovery, motion practice, and other available tactics. Inevitably, this results in more legal fees and higher expenses. Particularly in cases involving clients with limited resources, lawyers should consider and discuss with their clients strategies that reduce the need for legal expenses.

"How come all your divorce cases have allegations that the husband sexually abused his wife?" This question came to me from an opposing attorney who was suggesting I was encouraging my clients to invent such complaints. We had three divorces pending, two in which he represented the husband and the third in which he was the law guardian. I might have dismissed his question as ignorant partisanship, but as I knew him to be an ethical attorney and a good person, I took the time to explain that a higher percentage of my cases involve abuse because many domestic violence agencies refer cases to me. More to the point, I take the time to gain my clients' confidence and ask them specific questions about how they have been treated.

Domestic relations lawyers must be trained to handle domestic violence cases. Knowing the law is not enough. We must know how to speak with women and children who have been traumatized by abuse. Recently, My Sisters' Place started a legal services clinic for their clients and offered to train attorneys who agreed to accept referrals from the clinic. This training was a tremendous opportunity for the attorneys in this area, because it will also improve the lawyers' handling of their own cases. Unfortunately, such training is rarely available. Law guardians in particular should be required to have effective training regarding domestic violence.

A battered wife coming to an attorney for a divorce is likely to be upset and nervous and have low self-esteem because of years of abuse. An attorney must understand the problem and go out of his or her way to help the client. The lawyer must show patience and give the client time to explain her situation. The husband has likely spent years telling his wife that no one will believe her, and that she has few or no rights. Inevitably, he makes these statements confidently, repetitively, and utterly wrongly. It is important that the woman be armed with knowledge of what her rights are and what is likely to happen.

Every opportunity should be taken to make the client feel better about herself. Often, she will say that she has no proof of the abuse because her husband always beat her in private. The client should be assured that her testimony is evidence, because what she says matters. The woman's description of the abuse will generally be understated. An attorney must ask specific questions and go over the incidents more than once to learn the full extent of the abuse.

Physical abuse should be defined as any nonconsensual touching. This need not result in broken bones, hospitalization, or even bruises to constitute abuse. What might be a friendly pat in good times can become a painful slap during fights, but women rarely volunteer such behavior as examples of abuse. In addition, a wife has the right to say "no" to sexual activity, and if her husband does not respect this, he has committed a crime. Many of my clients never considered sexual abuse as something illegal. "I thought it was part of my wifely obligations," many of my clients have told me.

Many of the suggestions here are time-consuming, and would lead to bigger bills if the attorney were to charge for all this time. Often the initial consultation is free and can provide an opportunity to answer all the client's questions. Attorneys can also take advantage of time waiting to be called into court to speak with their clients. I encourage clients to call me when they need to speak to me and generally do not charge extra for this. Most attorneys cannot be expected to adopt this practice, but they should at least be aware of the need.

The client should be actively involved in the decision-making process, both in order to strengthen her self-esteem and because she is entitled to participate. Victims of domestic violence should be encouraged to bring a friend, relative, or advocate to court to provide support. These methods benefit the client by discouraging her from going back to her abuser, providing the attorney with more information to fight the case, and making the client a better witness and participant by improving her self-esteem. They also make it easier to settle a case because the client has more faith in her attorney's opinions.

Our legal system is based upon the idea that if the attorneys do everything they can within the rules, the truth will prevail. Tactics such as the attorney for a rape defendant viciously attacking the victim, abusers seeking their own orders of protection, fathers with little interest in the children suddenly seeking custody, and the hiding of assets and income are harmful and highly offensive, leading some critics to suggest penalizing attorneys. As much as I would like to eliminate these tactics, this solution is impractical because it would interfere with attorney–client communication and undermine the basis of our jurisprudence. The attorney works for the client, and the client controls his lawyer's approach.

Instead, we must strive to make these tactics counterproductive. If an attorney were afraid that an overaggressive cross-examination of a rape victim would antagonize the jury, such tactics would rarely be employed. A court can penalize a bad-faith attempt to obtain custody, but this rarely happens. Abusive husbands are frequently given a free shot to play the custody card, and often are given economic concessions to induce them to drop the effort. Many times, women return to their batterers so as not to risk losing custody. In cases where there is little reason to take custody from the mother, the court should actively discourage the use of the "custody card" and penalize its use with a full award of legal fees, along with damage to the husband's credibility regarding other issues.

Courts will have to apply such sanctions carefully to avoid imposing crippling penalties on someone acting in good faith or based upon a misunderstanding, but it is up to the courts to make sure that offensive tactics will not be profitable. The client will have to pay for such strategy, but if the attorney fails to explain the possible consequences, the client can recover damages from the attorney. Lawyer self-interest will therefore start discouraging these tactics.

Mental Health Professionals

Albert Pauling was anti-women and a despicable excuse for a judge, but even Pauling would not have sent the Wong children for their molestation visitation without the cover provided by Dr. Schmidt. In the court battles over custody and visitation, the role of mental health professionals cannot be overemphasized. Courts generally require overwhelming evidence to negate the recommendation of a court-appointed evaluator. In treatment of victims or offenders, the ability of a therapist often determines success.

The fundamental issue for mental health professionals working in domestic violence court cases is their expertise in child abuse and spousal abuse. Whenever an evaluator or therapist is needed for a case involving abuse allegations, the professional selected should be required to have expertise in domestic violence issues. Such a requirement should not be controversial. Inevitably, the attorney representing the abuser claims there was no abuse and therefore no need for such expertise. In one case recently, both sides claimed abuse, but the real abuser's attorney did not want the therapist selected to have domestic violence expertise. Many judges believe that someone trained in psychiatry, psychology, or social work, particularly a professional frequently used by the courts, will automatically have the requisite understanding. As we saw in the Wong case, children can pay a high price for such assumptions.

Mental health professionals now being qualified receive more training in domestic violence issues than was provided just five or ten years ago, but established professionals do not always take advantage of available continuing education. Some states are starting to set standards and require certification for programs designed to treat batterers. I believe this requirement should be expanded to cover all providers working with abusers and their victims.

The professional associations for mental health professionals, preferably in cooperation with domestic violence organizations, should establish standards for expertise in domestic violence issues. The standards should include training, testing, and experience. In cases with allegations of spousal or child abuse, the courts should be limited to certified experts in domestic violence when selecting evaluators or therapists. Although an allegation does not necessarily mean the abuse occurred, an expert will be better able to determine the validity of the claims.

The court is the ultimate arbiter of the questions before it. Often, for technical evidentiary reasons or as a matter of pride, judges refuse to permit experts to testify about what the court deems "ultimate questions." We can play with legal technicalities in other areas, but if an expert in domestic violence has an opinion about whether or not abuse is taking place in the home, the courts have to find a way to hear the opinion. Too many judges have protected their own prerogatives, but failed to protect the children looking to the court for help.

Judges should be trained to recognize mental health professionals ignorant of basic domestic violence issues. Indications that the professional does not possess the knowledge or understanding necessary to participate in domestic violence cases include:

- seeking to treat or evaluate an abuser and his victim by bringing the parties together in the same room
- expecting young children to speak about abuse without taking time to develop a trusting relationship
- believing an abuser has overcome the problem without admission or treatment

- minimizing the extent of the abuse, or the effects of spousal abuse on children
- making statements to the effect that women often raise false allegations of sexual abuse in order to gain an advantage in court.

Many of my clients have had their self-esteem, if not their lives, saved by the hard work of caring therapists. Therapy and support groups can help women and children escape from an abuser and make a good life for themselves. Victims of domestic violence would be greatly assisted by a certification system in finding therapists to help them. Until such a system is available, women should seek recommendations from organizations fighting domestic violence to find the right therapist.

Child Protective Service

In New York, the agency established to investigate charges of abuse or neglect of children is the Child Protective Service (CPS). Other states have different names for these offices, but their purpose is basically the same. The job is difficult and subject to high pressure because the workers often have incomplete and contradictory evidence, and the wrong decision can have disastrous effects on the children. The need to err on the side of protecting children from serious injury or death might seem obvious, but removing children from parents who love them can have traumatic repercussions as well.

In my experience, there is a great disparity in the quality of CPS workers. I have seen caring professionals like Janet Robinson in the Wong case, but also workers who are burned out or who never really cared. The work is so important that salaries should be increased to attract competent professionals. They should be carefully trained and screened. Legal, mental health, and other resources should be made available to help with this difficult job. Therapy and support groups can be made readily available to minimize problems with burnout.

New York's CPS system for responding to reports of child abuse or neglect often forces bad decisions that are harmful to the children. The caseworkers are given only 90 days to make a determination regarding the validity of a complaint. The choices for the outcome are limited to "indicated" (that the abuse or neglect occurred) or "unfounded" (that there is insufficient credible evidence to support the charges). In practice, cases are routinely labeled unfounded unless there is strong evidence to prove abuse or neglect.

Abusers and their defenders are taking advantage of the flaws in this system to achieve scandalous results while protecting themselves from any consequences of their egregious behavior. The abuse generally occurs in the privacy of the home, where only the parent and child are present. Young children are often unwilling or unable to describe what happened to them. Even if the children bravely tell what was done, the adult is often believed. The CPS workers determine that the case must be unfounded and the abusers get away with mistreating their children. Although "unfounded" does not necessarily mean that the abuse did not occur, in recent years more and more abusers seek to use one or more determinations that reports against them are unfounded as a basis to remove the children from the custody of the parent deemed responsible for the reports.

An accusation of child abuse, and particularly sexual abuse, is a horrible experience to endure. This is true both for the person charged and for the child, who is repeatedly questioned about painful and embarrassing issues, and often subjected to unpleasant physical exams. Anyone deliberately making false or reckless accusations out of malice or to gain an edge in litigation should be severely punished. Not only do such actions hurt the child and the person accused, but they make it harder for genuine victims of abuse to be believed. The courts must remember, however, that a determination of "unfounded" does not mean that the abuse did not occur; also, a report concerning abuse can be made in good faith, despite subsequent proof that no abuse occurred.

Until recently, when domestic violence became an important public issue, there were no classes or other instructions about how to respond to indications of possible child abuse. Children can and do suffer marks, bruises, and other injuries in the normal course of childhood. Even trained professionals cannot always tell if a particular injury is related to abuse. Excessive masturbation, bedwetting, abuse of other children, inappropriate sexual language, tales of abuse, nightmares, aggression, social withdrawal, and other behaviors may be indications of sexual abuse, or there might be a more innocent explanation. Responding to such behaviors would be difficult under the best of circumstances, and impossible in the middle of a divorce or custody dispute.

Many of my clients have been in this situation. If they report possible abuse, their children will be subjected to unpleasant investigation, but if they do nothing, the children may blame them for failing to provide protection. If they don't make a report, the court will accuse them

SCARED TO LEAVE, AFRAID TO STAY

of neglect, but if the report is not confirmed, the court may accuse them of using the children to get even with the father. If they do nothing, the children could continue to be abused. This has to be the most important consideration. We cannot force mothers to choose between protecting their children and protecting their custody.

The false belief that mothers frequently make bad-faith allegations of sexual abuse in order to gain a litigation advantage has caused many judges to award custody to abusers or to pressure mothers to drop charges of sexual abuse. I get sick to my stomach when I have to advise clients who have good reason to believe their children are being sexually abused to drop allegations of sexual abuse in order to maintain custody. We must stop punishing a mother who makes a good-faith allegation, and stop rewarding the abuser who avoids detection.

CPS caseworkers must be given more options to make determinations regarding reports. If there is inadequate or conflicting evidence, the case should be categorized as undetermined. The agency could leave the case open and offer services to the family. If new information later becomes available, the caseworker could reevaluate the allegations. When the caseworker has good reason to believe that no abuse or neglect has occurred, a determination of bad faith on the part of the reporter can be made if supported by the evidence. When the report is undetermined or there is no proof of bad faith, the courts should not use the reports alone to punish the reporter.

CPS must guard against the potential conflict between dealing with child abuse and dealing with spousal abuse. Sometimes mothers are targeted for their failure to protect a child from a father's abuse. The child can be removed from the home because of the mother's mistake or because of the failure of CPS to recognize the spousal abuse component of the problem. With the abuser removed from the home, on the other hand, the child can be perfectly safe with the mother and the need for foster care can be avoided. Many communities have started successful programs where advocates fighting domestic violence work with CPS caseworkers to help identify and provide services for victims of spousal abuse. Families and taxpayers benefit by keeping mothers and their children together while providing services to help overcome the father's violence.

Mothers are often criticized for failing to stand up to their abusive partners, but CPS caseworkers are sometimes just as intimidated by the loud, aggressive, and threatening men they are sent to protect the children from. I have seen cooperative families harassed over minor matters by caseworkers who fail to confront serious abusers. It is easier and more comfortable for the workers to exercise their authority over a compliant parent than over someone who is intimidating. While more training would help, reduced caseloads and the support of supervisors in investigating the intimidators would make the system work better for the children.

Courts

A few years ago I represented a battered woman whose husband had been convicted of abusing her. After paying no child support and failing to visit the children for several months, the husband sought joint custody in the divorce action. He started taking his visitation and using the time with his children to berate my client. My client had taken care of the children throughout their lives and wanted sole custody. When we went for a conference, the judge's law assistant determined that a law guardian would be necessary if the parties could not agree on custody. The court ordered my client to pay $2500 for the law guardian if she wanted to seek sole custody. Having no way to come up with the money, she was forced to accept joint custody.

Courts often use the expense of litigation as a weapon to encourage parties to settle. Often people are emotionally involved in their cases and this pressure can benefit everyone, including the courts. This law assistant is a decent individual, but the tactic was inappropriate in this case. Financial pressures should not be used against victims of domestic violence for issues involving safety or the well-being of children. The courts must be reorganized so that monetary considerations do not force unsafe or unhealthy outcomes.

Civil courts working on domestic violence issues should be unified to avoid replication of services and judge-shopping. Such practices add unnecessary expense and delay to an already overworked system. In New York, the Supreme Court has jurisdiction over divorce, custody, visitation, support, division of marital property, orders of protection, and other incidental issues. The Family Court has concurrent jurisdiction for custody, visitation, support, and orders of protection, but cannot handle divorce or division of marital property. The Family Court generally has more support facilities and is faster and less expensive. For these reasons, victims of domestic violence often go first to Family Court when seeking support, custody, and protection. Abusers often obtain delays, and sometimes more sympathetic judges, by starting a divorce after Family Court petitions are pending. In order to consider all issues together, such cases are often removed to the divorce court. Sometimes, this is done after Family Court judges have made initial rulings favorable to the victim of abuse. Alternatively, if the abuser is lucky enough to get a judge like Albert Pauling, he can stay in Family Court.

Other states have unified court systems and reformers have taken up this cause. I believe there should be one court system to handle the cases now considered by Family or Juvenile Courts as well as divorce cases. A special part should be established to resolve disputes that include accusations of domestic violence. Such abuse would not have to be established, but merely alleged. Specialized courts should be better able to determine when allegations are false in addition to recognizing when abuse exists. The domestic violence parts should be staffed by judges and support staff with training and expertise in these subjects.

Mental health experts specially trained in domestic violence should be hired to work with the courts. Presently, courts appoint outside mental health professionals to perform evaluations or other services. When the parties have sufficient resources, or the court thinks they do, the professionals are paid by the parties; otherwise they are paid by the state or county. If the experts were hired by the court, the courts could require parties to pay for their evaluations in appropriate cases. I believe this arrangement would reduce the cost of evaluations to the parties while making evaluations more available for limited-income parties. In working full-time for the courts, these experts would also be more readily available. Too often, cases must be postponed because the report is not ready or the expert is not available for a few questions. Most importantly, I would expect that the experts would understand domestic violence issues better by concentrating on these cases.

I recommend a similar approach with financial experts. During divorces, there are commonly problems with respect to reporting income and evaluating businesses. Dishonest owners of cash businesses often fail to report significant parts of their earnings. As we saw in the case of Irene Horowitz, proving unreported income requires luck, hard work, ingenuity, and often significant assets. The income from a business is the primary factor in determining its value. Typically, the husband is hiding income and assets and the abused wife does not have the resources to discover the truth. Abuse is about control, and control of the family's financial assets and information is common in domestic violence cases. Victims of abuse often lose substantial monies they would otherwise be entitled to because they don't have the resources to hire an expert to evaluate their husband's business.

Presently, when the value of a business is at issue as part of the division of marital property, either the parties will hire their own expert or the court will appoint an expert. The parties have to pay the expert's fee, which is often several thousand dollars or more. I believe the courts should hire such experts as part of their staff. Parties who can afford the evaluations could pay the court, and other parties could pay on a sliding scale. I believe the efficiencies of scale and compensation by salary will reduce the cost for everyone, while providing evaluations for victims of abuse who might otherwise lose some of their property. The availability of such staff to answer questions during a court conference would allow everyone to work more efficiently and provide fairer outcomes.

The National Council of Juvenile and Family Court Judges recommends the employment of a family violence coordinator for the courts. The idea is to coordinate the responses of the various agencies responding to domestic violence, including other courts, probation officers, victims' advocates, drug and alcohol treatment providers, law enforcement, and social service providers. Victims of domestic violence often walk into a courtroom scared and emotional. As a result, they may not understand what is happening in court or why. Sometimes these misunderstandings can prevent the victim from obtaining help. The family violence coordinator can answer questions, help the victim understand the system, and provide information about the availability of other services.

I would expand the scope of this exciting idea. The family violence coordinator should be able to help the judges as well as the victims. In appropriate cases, where the judge has failed to understand the domestic violence component of the case, the coordinator should be able to intervene with the judge. If a judge wants to send children for unsupervised visitation (as in the Wong case, where the father admitted kissing the girls on their vagina), or to take custody from a mother because she failed to brave a snowstorm (as in the Morgan case), the coordinator can inform the judge that such decisions are inappropriate. If the judge refuses to correct such blatant mistakes, the coordinator should be able to help the aggrieved party appeal the decision.

Judges are presently given standards and goals in the form of time limits for finishing cases. They are evaluated, in part, based on their ability to adhere to the guidelines. While there are certainly horror stories about cases that never end, these goals give the judges an incentive to finish cases within time limits. I would like the judges to have goals with respect to protecting victims of domestic violence as well. Judges should be required to explain decisions in which they fail to protect people who claim to be victims of domestic violence. Statistics should be kept and evaluations made based upon this vital issue. The family violence coordinator should be in charge of keeping the statistics and speaking with judges who consistently fail to protect victims of domestic violence. I believe judges would make domestic violence a higher priority and would pay attention when the coordinator sought to intervene, if these reforms were adopted.

The Public

Throughout this book, I have tried to explain to the public why women stay with abusive men. I hear that question more than any other, but it is the wrong question. We should be asking how the abuser can do such a thing and how we can stop it. Blame must be placed where it belongs, one hundred percent on the abuser. The abuse is never right, never justified, and never acceptable.

In many ways, the stories described in this book are typical of the cases that occur every day in our family and divorce courts. One difference, however, concerns the support and encouragement provided by the victims' families. Most of the women in this book were helped by supportive families, but too often families minimize the abuse or even take the side of the abuser. Often, families in which men have abused women encourage their daughter to accept their husband's beatings and return to him. In this way, the cycle of violence continues. We must take charges of abuse seriously and help our children and grandchildren escape the violence. The public should know that women and children rarely invent claims of abuse, and frequently minimize the severity of the abuse they suffer.

There is a strong belief and tradition in this country that certain matters are private. The relationship between a husband and a wife and the disciplining of children are part of that privacy. Friends, family, and neighbors will often turn away from knowledge or suspicion of abuse, because they don't want to get involved in a "private matter." Society pays a high price for this restraint. Spousal abuse and child abuse are not private matters. The public must be involved in stopping this insidious crime.

Family and friends must provide support and encouragement for victims to leave their abusers. They should try to counteract the natural tendency of the victim to minimize the extent of the abuse. The average abused wife makes seven attempts to leave before she gets away from her abuser. If possible, friends and family should provide a place to stay, financial and other material assistance. They should obtain information about shelters, domestic violence programs, and community resources, and share the information. If the woman refuses to leave or decides to return to her abuser, people should understand this is not necessarily a permanent decision. Too often people think women who stay with abusers are stupid. In reality, they know the abusers best and know best how to protect their children and themselves. Family and friends should maintain contact and support, and encourage the woman to leave when she thinks it is safe.

Megan's Law—a law named after a murder victim which requires sex offenders to register and the public to be informed of their residence—has, at times, resulted in the public shunning and avoiding any contact with the sex abusers identified by the law. The public should apply similar social sanctions to people who engage in acts of domestic violence. The abusers often believe the violence is acceptable because it "only" involves their wife or child. When the public looks away while a friend or family member abuses innocent women and children, they are reinforcing the belief that society condones such actions. We can and should send a clear message to the abuser that such behavior is unacceptable. Telling a friend that his actions are wrong can be uncomfortable, but it sends an important message.

Everyone, even people living in loving, supportive homes, should learn about domestic violence. Abuse is so pervasive that inevitably most of us will encounter friends, family, business associates, or others affected by men's violence. Knowledge of domestic violence can be used to help and support victims of such abuse and discourage the perpetrators. Often, a victim will not reveal the abuse unless someone understands the signs and knows the right questions to ask. Surprisingly, women frequently are unaware that their husband's physical attacks or forced sexual activity are illegal. Very specific questions are often needed to determine whether domestic violence exists.

Finally, the public must use their votes and political activism to fight domestic violence. Electing judges for criminal or domestic relations cases should be about preventing domestic violence. The public should learn about the candidate's experience regarding domestic violence and the views of organizations and individuals working to fight abuse. In recent years, and particularly in the aftermath of the O. J. Simpson trial, a consensus has developed for greater government action to stop domestic violence. Candidates regularly seek votes by promising to support measures to fight abuse. The public needs to be careful about politicians who grandstand against judges who make unpopular decisions. There is a fine line between demanding that judges protect victims of domestic violence and interfering with judicial independence. The failure to protect Anne Scripps Douglas and the failure to protect Maria Delgado were equally wrong. The murder of Anne Douglas makes the mistake tragic, but the fact that Maria Delgado survived makes the decision no less wrong. Judges should be evaluated based on a pattern of protecting or failing to protect victims of abuse.

Working against domestic violence is a draining, gut-wrenching experience. The volunteers and staff fighting the battle every day deserve all the support and appreciation the public can muster. Repeatedly, I have seen domestic violence organizations cooperate with each other even while competing for limited funds. The first priority is helping the women and children facing men's abuse. The public and their leaders should support the educational and legislative goals advocated by the coalitions fighting domestic violence. Their caring and expertise can help society reduce this menace.

Books Available From Robert D. Reed Publishers

Please include payment with orders. Send indicated book/s to:

Name:_____

Address:_____

City:_____ State:_____ Zip:_____

Phone:(_____)_____ E-mail:_____

Titles and Authors	Unit Price
_____ *Scared To Leave, Afraid To Stay* by Barry Goldstein	$24.95
_____ *Gotta Minute? The ABC's of Successful Living* by Tom Massey, Ph.D., N.D.	9.95
_____ *Gotta Minute? Practical Tips for Abundant Living:* *The ABC's of Total Health* by Tom Massey, Ph.D., N.D.	9.95
_____ *Gotta Minute? How to Look & Feel Great!* by Marcia F. Kamph, M.S., D.C.	11.95
_____ *Gotta Minute? Yoga for Health, Relaxation & Well-being* by Nirvair Singh Khalsa	9.95
_____ *Gotta Minute? Ultimate Guide of One-Minute* *Workouts for Anyone, Anywhere, Anytime!* by Bonnie Nygard, M.Ed. & Bonnie Hopper, M.Ed.	9.95
_____ *A Kid's Herb Book for Children of All Ages* by Lesley Tierra, Acupuncturist and Herbalist	19.95
_____ *House Calls: How we can all heal the world one visit at a time* by Patch Adams, M.D.	11.95
_____ *500 Tips for Coping with Chronic Illness* by Pamela D. Jacobs, M.A.	11.95

Enclose a copy of this order form with payment for books. Send to the address below. Shipping & handling: $2.50 for first book plus $1.00 for each additional book. California residents add 8.5% sales tax. We offer discounts for large orders.

Please make checks payable to: **Robert D. Reed Publishers.**

Total enclosed: $_____. See our website for more books!

Robert D. Reed Publishers
750 La Playa, Suite 647, San Francisco, CA 94121
Phone: 650-994-6570 • Fax: 650-994-6579
Email: 4bobreed@msn.com • www.rdrpublishers.com